Illustrated **BUYER'S ★**

ALLIS-CHALMERS
TRACTORS AND CRAWLERS

TERRY DEAN

MBI Publishing Company

$7.50

CU00923401

First published in 2001 by MBI Publishing Company, Galtier Plaza, Suite 200, 380 Jackson Street, St. Paul, MN 55101-3885 USA

MBI Publishing Company books are also available at discounts in bulk quantity for industrial or sales-promotional use. For details write to Special Sales Manager at Motorbooks International Wholesalers & Distributors, Galtier Plaza, Suite 200, 380 Jackson Street, St. Paul, MN 55101-3885 USA.

Library of Congress Cataloging-in-Publication Data Available
ISBN 0-7603-0940-X

On the front cover: A collector's favorite, the Model IB is one of the smallest vintage Allis-Chalmers tractors. Although this model is slightly heavier than the regular Model B, it is much more compact with its shorter wheelbase and height. This beautifully restored Model IB belongs to Roger Culbert.

On the back cover: *Left:* The D-14 was a hit as soon as it arrived at the dealer showrooms. With a modern style and several new features, farmers could work their fields with utter pride as the bright orange tractor drew attention from passerbys. This new design came at an opportune time as competitor's tractors were surpassing the style of the Allis-Chalmers' line. Harley Veldhuizen of Elburn, Illinois, owns this sharp D-14. *Harley Veldhuizen*

Right: The impressive Model L crawler is a big 11-ton machine. The six-speed transmission was a welcomed improvement over the three-speeds of the Monarch 75 that the Model L replaced. *Andrew Morland*

Author Bio: Terry Dean lives in the countryside near Whitney Point, New York with his wife Lana and his three daughters, Kristy, Taron, and Maggie. Terry is employed by the local school and is a member of the town council. He has collected tractors for about 17 years and has authored several articles in *Engineers and Engines* magazine over the last decade. Terry has authored the book, *Allis-Chalmers Farm Tractors and Crawlers Data Book,* and co-authored *Antique American Tractor and Crawler Value Guide* with Larry Swenson.

Edited by Amy Glaser
Designed by Laura Henrichsen

Printed in the United States of America

Contents

Acknowledgments

Several individuals sacrificed precious time and effort to help make this book possible. I wish to especially thank Roger Culbert and his family from Fillmore, New York, for making many of the pictures in this book possible. Roger has an extensive collection of beautifully restored A-C tractors that put me in absolute awe. With cameras snapping away, my wife and I photographed numerous Allis-Chalmers tractors as Roger drove them out, one by one. The dedication this man has put into each tractor's restoration is immeasurable.

Another individual that was kind enough to pose several of his nicely restored A-C tractors is Martin Wilcox. When I arrived at his impressive farm, I walked to each barn until I found Martin and a friend in a building, working on one of his several D-21 tractors. The tractor was split at the transmission and both men were working to replace a bad bearing. The inside of the tractor was not foreign to either man. As busy as he was, trying to fix the tractor and run a farm, Martin made sure that we had a different tractor posed for the cameras every time we were ready. I met Martin at a tractor show that featured Allis-Chalmers machines. About 80 percent of the many A-C tractors at the show belonged to Martin.

Larry Swenson of Easton, Minnesota, is a man whom I must thank too. Larry has been supportive and informative. As a full-time dealer in Allis-Chalmers collectible tractors and parts, Larry has tremendous knowledge of the tractors and a long list of friends and customers that includes collectors of the rarest Allis-Chalmers models in existence. Rarely have I come across men with the high degree of integrity found in Larry Swenson. Larry worked diligently with me on a book recently, *The Antique American Tractor and Crawler Value Guide*. I thank him for his hard work on that book and the help he gave to this book. Larry's friends include collectors, Dave Pfouts, Al Schubert, Craig Detwiler, Charles Widlund, Lavern Greif, Mark Cade, and Bud Scmidt who were kind enough to supply certain pictures for this book.

I also am grateful to Bill Black, Harley Veldhuizen, Robert Lemmert Sr., and Dennis and Paul McNamara for photos sent in for the book. To find so many rare A-C tractors restored throughout the country is encouraging.

I wish to thank John Adams-Graf, Amy Glaser, Jane Mausser, and Roxanne Furlong, my editors, for always answering my questions and making sure that this effort is presented properly. The hard work that John puts into each project, surrounded by deadlines and multiple predicaments, can often pass by forgotten. I don't forget the pleasant answers to my questions when I could tell he was buried in some big projects.

The ones who helped me the most and deserve the biggest thanks are my wife and children. Lana and our three daughters, Kristy, Taron, and Maggie put up with me for many months as I sat with my face to a computer monitor, books, manuals, and magazines. On photography shoots, Lana helped take pictures while the kids patiently watched. One picture submitted in this book was taken by Maggie (age 9) with her 35mm SLR camera. This book was a family effort.

—*Terry Dean*

Introduction

The purpose of this book is to help the tractor enthusiasts, collectors, and potential collectors understand some history, facts, and rarity of models and versions of Allis-Chalmers tractors from the first model, the 10-18 in 1914, to the D-series of the 1960s. The chapters of this book are broken down into eras of Allis-Chalmers' tractor production and describe details, production history, and a star rating system. The star rating system is used in many Buyer's Guides from MBI Publishing Company. This book includes three rating systems; one for collectibility, one for reliability, and one for parts availability.

The Collectibility Rating System

This system is a general classification of collectibility based on rarity, demand, and historical importance. Condition is not a real factor with this system, but obviously an incomplete or poor-condition tractor does not accurately fit the following definitions. Here is a brief explanation of the star rating system:

★★★★★ When you see five stars, you can be assured that this tractor is rare and expensive. Extremely low production, poor survival rate, and high demand cause these tractors to be found mostly in the hands of advanced collectors. Finding these five-star machines in barnyards for $100 is pretty much only a dream. Investing in these tractors usually requires large sums of money and, they are most commonly sold through estate auctions or subtly arranged personal deals. Recent auction history has shown that the value of these machines has increased quite substantially in the past 10 years or so.

★★★★ The four-star tractors are usually rare because of their low-production totals. As an investment, these machines are an excellent choice. Many established collectors who spend hundreds of dollars plus hours and hours of their time restoring tractors tend to put their efforts in these machines rather than common models as the investment potential and collector desirability makes their efforts more rewarding than by renovating a two-star tractor. Prices are high on these four-star tractors, but as interest in Allis-Chalmers tractor collecting has been booming recently, these may prove to have the greatest potential for value increase in the next several years. The history of John Deere collecting, which currently has the largest following, has shown four-star tractors often have tripled in value over just a few years as tremendous demand overtakes limited supply. I do not encourage anyone to collect tractors for financial gain, but one would be imprudent not to consider the growth in the value of their collection as in any collecting hobby.

★★★ Three-star tractors are not common everyday machines. These tractors are usually a worthy investment and are on the verge of being rare. Most serious collectors are still attracted to these machines due to their limited numbers. Profitable investment potential is still probably excellent as the demand for three-star Allis-Chalmers tractors is still growing rapidly. These tractors are not extremely difficult to obtain and are the pride of many collectors.

★★ A two-star tractor is not rare. The value for these models is often based on the practical use of the tractor perhaps more than the collector's demand. Tractors produced in numbers of tens of thousands or having limited interest to the average collector fit this category. The future should bring more attention to these common model tractors as interest from collectors is on the rise. As far as investment, these tractors would be considered fair to good. A true Allis-Chalmers fan would not evade two-star machines, but would fill in his or her collection gladly when the buying price is attractive.

★ A one-star tractor does not really pertain to this book. Only tractors that are so very common and are viewed by collectors with apathy because they have almost no historical value would fit in this category. The tractors in this book all rate two stars or higher.

Collectors who love Allis-Chalmers tractors should not be disheartened by this rating system.I

own several two-star tractors and still treasure them. I hope other collectors as a whole don't tarnish the enthusiasm and joy of one buying a two-star tractor and putting their heart into the restoration without any attention to value increase. The sparkle in a collector's eyes as another enthusiast admires his restored tractor is a wonderful thing and should not be crushed by the ultra-perfectionists or the idea that the tractor is not special. The star rating is not meant to harm this wonderful hobby, but to guide the enthusiast in the exciting adventure of discovering and appreciating Allis-Chalmers tractors.

The Reliability Rating System

This star rating system is to measure the overall reliability of a tractor. Please keep in mind that the reputation of a tractor is a minor factor in the value of a rare machine. Many early tractors and crawlers had problems that caused a limited production life resulting in rare models. Although the collector value may be high on some of these models, the usefulness on a modern farm is often limited. This rating system may be more useful to collectors who plan to utilize their tractors for practical purposes. The following describes each rating:

★★★★★ A five-star tractor is an extremely dependable machine. This tractor has a reputation for having very few problems.

★★★★ A four-star tractor is quite reliable, but may be known for one or two minor problems.

★★★ A three-star tractor has an average reliability that will have certain minor problems that may irk its owner.

★★ A two-star tractor has certain problems that are substantial enough to give the tractor a rather poor reputation for reliability.

★ A one-star tractor is plagued with both minor and major problems. The reputation for reliability would tag it a "lemon."

The Parts Availability Rating System

To one restoring a tractor, this rating system may be helpful in determining the difficulty in obtaining replacement parts. The more rare models and versions of tractors are in higher demand by collectors as a whole, but the parts are obviously more difficult to acquire than high-production model parts. A tractor or crawler with extremely poor parts availability can discourage even the most dedicated restorers. The following describes each star rating:

★★★★★ A five-star rating is for models with parts that are relatively easy to acquire. New, used, or reproduction parts can be bought with little struggle.

★★★★ A four-star rating pertains to tractors with used parts that are fairly easy to find, but new or NOS (new, old stock) parts availability may be a bit more work to acquire.

★★★ A three-star rating is for a model that you can obtain used parts for in most cases, but new and NOS parts are a challenge to locate.

★★ A two-star rating denotes a tractor that is difficult to find parts for at all. Determination and a fat wallet are usually needed to get the parts needed.

★ A one-star rating is for extremely rare models that parts are seldom found without much hunting. Often parts for tractors with this rating need to be cast or fabricated as collectors find themselves at a dead end. A casual collector may give up on a restoration on one of these tractors because of the great challenge and expense of acquiring parts.

Buying an Allis-Chalmers Tractor

When you are contemplating the purchase of a collectible tractor, keep these facts in mind: All of the tractors featured in this book are at least 29 years old, some are over 86; most farmers used their tractors extremely hard to make a living; farmers often used welding and other cost-saving repairs on their tractors; sometime during its life, many tractor castings cracked due to internal water freezing; calcium chloride, an aggressive corrosive of metal was used in most of the rear tires for weight; and you are at the mercy of your wit and the seller's integrity.

Allis-Chalmers was a leader in the use of pneumatic tires on early tractors. By pumping water mixed with calcium chloride into the rear tires, hundreds of beneficial pounds of weight were added to the tractor. The added calcium chloride was an inexpensive type of antifreeze and was up to 28 percent heavier than water alone. The adverse quality is that the corrosiveness of this mixture eats away at metal like battery acid. The tire on this WC has no rim left and even the wheel center is perforated. Factory-built rear wheels are always in high demand on antique tractors and will often be quite costly. Rim damage is often more elusive than shown here and a tractor buyer should be alert to subtle signs of decomposition.

The grille on this Model CA is solid, but banged up. With a tremendous amount of time and patience, this grille can be made to look like new. A tractor with straight sheet metal and little rust will often bring much more money than a banged-up model in the same mechanical condition because the restoration process will be much less involved.

Even by taking the following advice when checking out a tractor, unforeseen problems can be found after a tractor purchase. This author has purchased dozens of tractors through the years and has always found more to repair than what was detected on careful prebuying inspections. The following information may help evaluate the overall condition of a tractor, but some risk and wonder is always involved and will cause an insecure individual to avoid buying a tractor. The excitement of collecting tractors overrides much of this fear in determined collectors; problems are expected and dealt with. Often tractors are acquired in a nonoperational state, and a good-sized gamble is made on the mechanical condition. By heeding the following steps, I hope you can at least determine a rough estimate on the amount of time and money needed to restore a tractor to your standards.

Identify and Confirm

A tractor model may not be what it appears. The serial numbers and facts from this book can identify a model even

though an unwitting seller or improper decals may create false assumptions. Some decal kits come with several different model designations and the wrong one can be applied to the tractor. I have a Model C tractor that came with a CA designation. The Model C never originally had a model designation decal. A Model CA tractor is worth quite a bit more than a Model C in the same condition. The lack of Power-Shift rear rims and four-speed transmission quickly let me know the tractor was mislabeled by the previous owner. Many of the serial numbers list the model designation as a prefix and can alleviate uncertainty. To most people, many Allis-Chalmers models look alike at first glance. By studying this book, you should be able to distinguish models easily. It pays to carefully check major components to make sure the tractor has the correct engine, transmission, differential, sheet metal, etc. Some WD and WD-45 models have been found to have engines switched. The engines are interchangeable, but are different. I came across a model RC with a WC rear end. The parts looked identical, but the differential gears were different as was the serial number stamped into the rear casting. This subtle difference greatly injured the value and potential of the tractor.

Tires, Wheels, and Rims

Steel wheels and hubs should be checked for rust damage, bends, and cracks. Check to be sure the wheels are the correct ones for that model and year. Steel wheels in nice condition are quite valuable, and a complete set can sometimes be worth more than the unrestored tractor it is mounted on. Many early tractors are found with steel wheels that were cut off at the rims then had new rims welded to the existing flat spokes to accommodate rubber tires. These cutdown wheels were often expertly welded and even though they may look presentable for restoration, they negatively affect the original appearance and value of the machine. The

This unbroken tractor lens is a welcome sight to a potential tractor buyer. These lenses as well as the dash gauges, wheel rim clamps, and air-cleaner caps are among many of the small items that are a nuisance to replace and could add up to a good-sized chunk of a restorer's wallet.

purchase of a pair of new rear tires on most tractors is a major expense. Tires should be checked for proper size and match, farmers often increased sizes or replaced only one rear tire, leaving the tractor with mismatched or oversized tires. Tires that ran too long with low air pressure developed weak sidewalls. Without close inspection for damage, these tires may tear out unexpectedly even though they appear to have a deep tread and shiny luster. Inspect the rear rims for damage from calcium chloride. Rust around the valve stem and blisters on the rim may indicate eroded rims. Minor damage is prevalent, but advanced rusting is hazardous if the tire detaches or the wheel clamps can't hold.

Castings and Steering Assemblies

Final-drive housings, steering boxes, and front-axle mountings are susceptible to cracking and should be inspected carefully for welds or hairlines. Try turning the steering wheel back and forth while watching the tie rods, drag links, and steering box. The shaft from the steering box should have only a slight thrust in and out before it rotates. Wide front axles should wag only slightly, and the socket joints in the steering linkages should be tight. It can be expected that a certain amount of wear in all the steering components will cause perhaps a quarter-turn or more of play in the steering wheel, but excessive play is not often properly remedied by a simple steering box or tie rod adjustment. It is common to spend money to make the steering acceptable on older tractors. Minor oil leaks around the steering box and axle housings are common because the seals often fail with age.

Engine Ailments

Check the fluids. The engine oil should be inspected to make sure no water or metal filings are present. Gray oil is a warning that water may be getting in the crankcase. An internal block or head crack can be the result of water in the oil, but can be as minor as rainwater in the exhaust pipe or head gasket failure. Inspect the engine block carefully, especially around the soft plugs and behind the manifolds. Flaws commonly found are hairline cracks or mends resulting from water freezing and expanding from forgetting to drain coolant water, just once, in the lengthy life of the tractor. A properly repaired crack can often save you from replacing the engine, but the value of the tractor will be diminished. Check for oil leakage from the crankshaft seals and all engine gaskets. Minor leaks are prevalent, but each leak adds labor to your restoration. Try to determine whether the generator, starter, ignition, and carburetor are original. A switched component can often be found by its improper fit to the engine. Inspect the manifolds carefully. Holes in the bottom or back side of the exhaust manifolds of Allis-Chalmers tractors are a common malady as are cracks around the exhaust outlet, broken mounting flanges, and warping. Intake manifolds are usually less troublesome, but still should be checked. Replacement manifolds for many of the old tractor models are becoming easier to find because of the tremendous demand.

Transmission and Differential

The transmission and differential are best checked while the tractor is operating. Feel each transmission shift position for signs of broken teeth or jumping, and listen for bearing squeals, clicking, or grinding. Look for cracks in the differential and transmission cases. Check the oil for water and filings. If the tractor sat outside for a long time, it is common to find water in the housings. If a good amount of water sat too long, it could ruin bearings or freeze and crack the gear case.

Sheet Metal

The sheet metal should be inspected for rusting, dents, and straightness. Fenders are often found rotting off at mountings and damaged grilles are a common problem; when available, replacement sheet metal parts are expensive. The overall appearance of the tractor depends heavily on the condition of the sheet metal. Black-bar grilles for some early D-series tractors for instance are difficult to locate and will likely cost a small fortune when you manage to find one. Consider the condition of the sheet metal seriously when negotiating the price of a tractor. Salvage yards tend to sell out of grilles, fenders, and hoods quickly if they are in an excellent state; you will sometimes be put on a waiting list on these parts.

Leaks

Check the radiator, hydraulic system, and power steering parts for leaking or repairs. Radiators often have patches of solder on some of the cores or even have cores sealed off with solder due to physical damage. Flaws in the hydraulic system and power steering components are usually only detected during operation.

Operation

If you are able to run and operate the tractor, don't be shy. After being sure of all the controls, start the tractor and listen to the engine as it warms up. With a warm engine and safe oil pressure, rev it up and idle it back down several times while listening for knocks or misses. See if the exhaust emits bluish smoke that could be a sign of worn cylinders or piston rings. Drive the tractor in each and every gear while checking the clutch for slippage or grabbing, and listen for any transmission problems. While going forward and reverse listen for free play, it will alert you to differential slack. Steer hard in each direction and observe any binding or power steering parts for leaking. Try out the hydraulic system. It should be tested for strength, draft regulation, and seal integrity.

Perspective

This advice should help tractor buyers determine the most expensive repairs needed. Expect to find some problems with any tractor you buy, even if it has been restored. Don't turn away from a tractor just because it seems to have a lot of flaws. If you are a perfectionist, tractor buying can be traumatic. A healthy perspective would be to visualize the potential of the machine to meet your standards, add the cost of parts, then add the hours of labor to determine whether the tractor is worth it all. Tractor collecting can be a rewarding hobby; fear can rob you of the joy this hobby has to offer.

Chapter 2

A Little History

Have you ever wondered what caused certain notable people to struggle against all odds to achieve monstrous goals? People, including Henry Ford and Cyrus McCormick, have struggled their way to success. As this author studies the history of several of these special individuals, one thing seems clear; most of them climbed to greatness even when they were set back over and over.

Edward Phelps Allis was one of these determined men. Achieving business success was a natural ability in this founder of a company that eventually became the great Allis-Chalmers Company. He was neither an inventor, machinist, nor designer; but a gifted businessman who knew how to orchestrate men and manufacturing equipment to create some of the foremost products ever marketed in America. Edward Allis' principles of quality and innovative technology carried on long after his death in 1889 into the fiber of the Allis-Chalmers Company that made the remarkable tractors in this book.

Born in Cazenovia, New York, on May 12, 1824, Edward was the son of Jere and Mary Allis. After receiving a B.A. degree in 1845, Edward joined a partnership with a good friend, William Allen. Allen had attended college with Allis and was from a family that was rather successful in the leather tanning business. With Allen's money and Allis' drive, their Empire Leather Store was opened in Milwaukee by 1846. Ten years later, after the business had expanded into one of the largest tanneries in the region, Edward Allis sold out his interest in the business.

During the next several years, Allis found positions on the boards of the local fire and railroad companies, and several other businesses. The Decker and Seville's Reliance Works was a producer of quality flour milling equipment and sawmills. An economic depression that began in 1857 caused this manufacturer to collapse financially. In 1861, Allis purchased the company through a foreclosure sale and operated it as his own. With Allis as the new owner, the new Reliance Works of E. P. Allis prospered.

In 1869, Allis bought out his largest local competitor, the Bay State Iron Manufacturing Company. With the combined capacity of these two companies, Allis had the capability to fill large orders. He expanded into new fields, and when the city of Milwaukee decided to build a new water system, Allis built a $100,000 pipe foundry and won a contract bid to cast the majority of the supply of piping. By 1872, the city needed huge pumping engines and Allis geared up to make these at the Reliance Works. The manufacture of pipe, and eventually steam engines, were fields in which the Reliance Works Company had no experience, but when he got a notion, Allis was unstoppable. Allis hired some of the finest experts in their field and manufactured pipe and engines of the highest quality. Profit seemed to be a minor motive for Allis: the pride from having his products used for the betterment of Milwaukee seemed to be the greater incentive.

Edward Allis married Margaret Watson in 1848. The oldest sons of their 12 children, William, Edward Jr., and Charles, eventually joined Edward Allis in operations of the Reliance Works. After Edward died in 1889, Charles and

"Old Number One," the first Oil-Pull, built in 1909, has worked ever since and isn't half through. Repairs cost less than 5c a day. Owned by Frank Schultz, Agar, S. Dak.

OilPull Number 174, built in 1909, 12 years ago. The owner, C. J. Chandler, Lincoln, Kan., says it will last another decade. The only renewed parts of motor are four piston rings.

OilPull Number 314, owned by F. Gasperich, Onida, S. Dak. Built in 1909, it has cropped from 600 to 900 acres a year. Pulls eight bottoms in soil so tough that eight horses can't pull a single bottom.

"The Swamp Angel," so named by proud admirers in Northern Indians for its ten years' work in the muck of the famed Kankakee. Has a record of marvelous performance and economy.

OilPull Number 437, bought in 1910, owned by James Moss, Blue Island, Ill. Is still "young" after 11 years of hard, faithful work on the farm, and moving buildings at odd times.

Buy a Tractor on Performance — not Promise

THAT'S the one right way to buy a tractor—not on promises of what it *may* do, but on the record of what it *actually has done* over a long period of years in the hands of thousands of owners.

The twelve year performance record of the Rumely OilPull tractor stands out as a safe guide post to the tractor buyer.

The first OilPull tractor, built over twelve years ago, is still on the job. And hundreds of other old OilPulls—still going strong—prove that unusually long life is the rule with the OilPull, not the exception.

And the OilPull you buy today has the same basic features of design and in addition is greatly improved and refined through twelve years of field service and constant factory tests. That is why the OilPull is, as it always has been, cheapest in cost per year of service.

The OilPull tractor has for years held all the world's official tractor fuel economy records. It is the only tractor with which is given a written guarantee to successfully burn kerosene at all loads and under all conditions.

Economy of upkeep is as marked. Less than $200 has been expended on "Old Number One" for repairs during its twelve years of work.

Truly, it is the part of wisdom to prefer a tractor with a record of performance such as this and in addition you have the assurance of such splendid features as 25% overload capacity, cooled with oil, double system of lubrication, Hyatt Bearings, and Rumely service including a factory trained expert for every ten tractors in use, scattered throughout the length and breadth of the land.

There are four sizes—one to fit your farm—3 to 10 plow. Talk with your Advance-Rumely dealer or write us direct.

ADVANCE-RUMELY THRESHER COMPANY, Inc.
LaPorte, Indiana
29 Branch Offices and Warehouses

ADVANCE-RUMELY

Rumely had a long and rich history of producing some of the finest tractors and threshing machines in the nation. Bad times hit several Canadian farmers who had financed expensive Rumely equipment at a time when the company was making costly acquisitions. Running low on cash, Rumely received no relief from bankers as it was struggling to stay afloat. In December of 1915, the Rumely family lost their business to investors and a reformed company was incorporated under the name of Advance-Rumely Thresher Company. This firm struggled to keep pace with the changing tractor industry that demanded smaller, less-expensive machines. The lighter Rumely tractors were still not selling well, and by 1931 a deal was made with Allis-Chalmers to take over the Rumely empire.

William continued to expand the business. Fraser & Chalmers, a producer of heavy commercial mining equipment was in a financial bind and merged with the brothers to form the Allis-Chalmers Manufacturing Company in 1901. Charles Allis was made president and his brother, William, became chairman of the board. Other companies were bought, including Gates Iron Works for its rock crushing machinery, Dickson Manufacturing Company for its air compressors and blowing engines, and by 1904, the Bullock Electric & Manufacturing Company for its electric-generating equipment. The Allis brothers were quick to enter the steam turbine business as Allis-Chalmers headed toward what could have become a great monopoly in the commercial energy business. However, by 1912, rapid expansion and some poor decision making by the board forced the giant Allis-Chalmers Company into receivership.

The president of the reformed Allis-Chalmers was Gen. Otto Falk. This powerful leader is a name to remember in the history of Allis-Chalmers tractors. As president, General Falk would not stand to be a puppet of the board and he ran the company with power, wisdom, determination, and respect. Falk closed some of the old factories and consolidated the entire line of equipment into two main plants. Production increased, employees were treated better, and confidence in the company grew strong. Almost as soon as his presidency began, the General worked diligently to diversify the company into the booming motorized agricultural market. Most of Falk's corporate decisions proved to be wise. However, his apparent obsession to enter the farm tractor business resulted in big profit losses during the first 10 years of manufacturing.

It is this author's belief that if it wasn't for Falk's stubborn attitude and the board's fear to stand up against his pet project, Allis-Chalmers would have stayed far away from the tractor industry, especially when it didn't have an agricultural dealer network set up. Regardless, his vision was confirmed; by the late 1930s, Allis-Chalmers turned its agricultural sideline into more than half of the company's total sales at about $50 million a year.

In 1928, Allis-Chalmers officially entered the crawler business. When the well-known crawler manufacturer, Monarch Tractor Company, fell upon tough times, Falk saw an opportunity to negotiate a good deal for Allis-Chalmers. A deal was made and the crawler firm was officially sold on April 2, 1927, for only $500,000. With the new facilities, Allis-Chalmers grew to an industry leader in crawlers by the 1940s.

In 1931, Advance-Rumely was bought by Allis-Chalmers. Once a giant in the tractor and thresher industry,

Aultman-Taylor had a long history of making superb threshing machines and large steam and gasoline tractors. These two letterheads reflect the grandeur of this company before the 1900s. The starved rooster was its mascot from at least the early 1880s; "fattened on an Aultman-Taylor straw stack," was its motto. Advance-Rumely was in less than ideal financial condition when it bought the ailing Aultman-Taylor Company in 1924. The optimism among the Rumely people was in vain and by 1931, the company succumbed to financial burdens and merged with Allis-Chalmers.

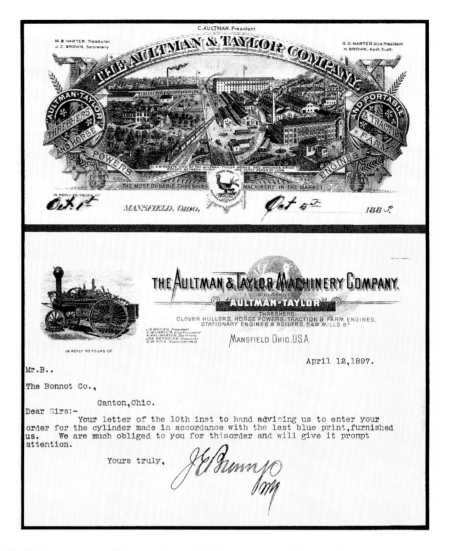

Advance-Rumely was brought to ruin by misfortune. Its threshers, combines, and tractors were introduced with only moderate-to-poor sales. Serious attempts to adjust to the small-tractor market only resulted in financial failure as its new DoAll and Rumely Six models made little impact on the tractor market. Advance-Rumely needed to be bailed out. Falk persuaded skeptical board members at Allis-Chalmers, and a deal was made. With the new purchase, Allis-Chalmers got an established and seasoned dealership network and an additional bonus of expanded manufacturing facilities. The buyout made them a major tractor producer.

On January 21, 1941, Allis-Chalmers was hit with a labor strike that lasted 76 days. Communist agitators were chiefly responsible for instigating it. The Local 248 workers were duped as they voted to strike: An investigation by a private firm, long after the vote, confirmed tampering by union leaders in 40 percent of the ballots. The United States had not entered World War II at this point, but were sending equipment and support to Allied forces. By shutting down Allis-Chalmers production for two and a half months, Britain, in particular, suffered. Eventually, production resumed as workers were compelled to help the war effort, but workers' negative attitudes toward management was pronounced as they blindly sided with their union leaders. It took several years for most workers to accept the fact that the Communist party had corrupted their leadership.

Allis-Chalmers had several successful tractor and crawler models on the market by the time the United States entered World War II. Government restrictions on farm machinery in 1942 dropped the industry total to about 80 percent of the previous year. The total for 1943 dropped to 62 percent. The following years of 1944 and 1945 saw increases in production for the agricultural industry as food shortages were felt from lack of manpower on farms. Even after the war, the Civilian Production Administration (CPA) dictated that no more than 15 percent of farm tractors and construction crawlers could be exported during 1946. The limited amount of exported machinery was desperately needed to relieve war-devastated areas in Europe and Asia. Rationing precious steel and tires during and right after the war by the CPA also dictated the amount of tractors and other farm machinery that each company could produce. In most cases, other government restrictions locked farm equipment companies out from introducing new models. Even with a strong patriotic attitude, tractor producers were often disgusted with limitations placed on their trade in the name of victory.

The determination of scientists and engineers to win World War II advanced technology in leaps and bounds. With the restrictions of war lifted, new tractor models were introduced with modern features. The demand for farm equipment was high throughout the world. Allis-Chalmers had weathered the storms of war quite well and had patriotically contributed much to the war effort. Damages to the relationship between A-C workers and management persisted for several years after the war. Even with sometimes-violent labor disputes, short-term strikes, and material shortages, the company maintained a strong position in the agricultural equipment industry. Chronic problems were dealt with methodologically.

As the fourth largest tractor maker in the United States, Allis-Chalmers continued to prosper in the tractor business until the 1980s. By around 1985, financial losses had broken up the giant company that had more than 70 plants at its peak that produced many, many different types of industrial products. By May of 1985, Deutz of West Germany, took over the ailing Allis-Chalmers and reformed it as Deutz-Allis. Deutz-Allis ended tractor production in the United States by December 1985. In 1990, the Allis-Gleaner Corporation (AGCO) was formed and it reinstated the "orange tractors." AGCO Corporation continues the legacy of the Allis-Chalmers tractors. AGCO Corporation has been receptive to farmers' and collectors' sentimental feelings toward Allis-Chalmers tractors. I hope that you can help keep the enchantment of the Allis-Chalmers tractors alive by handing down the history to future generations and by sharing your enthusiasm with others.

Chapter 3

The First Tractors

Before 1915, Allis-Chalmers produced a self-propelled rotary plow from a Swiss design and a tractor-truck—a half-track vehicle with an almost forgotten history. The company's president, Gen. Otto Falk yearned for a successful agricultural machine, but the financial injury from these early attempts made his desire seem even more distant.

The best seller of all tractors in 1914 was the Little Bull made by the Bull Tractor Company in Minneapolis, Minnesota. Competitors in the fledgling tractor industry clamored to devise just the right tractor for this booming market and in 1914, it appeared that the Bull Tractor was the one to match. Allis-Chalmers gave serious consideration to a joint venture with the Bull Tractor Company until General Falk decided that the company should build its own

This ad from 1920 shows the Model 6-12 and Model 18-30 as tractors for small farms as well as big operations. Allis-Chalmers relied heavily on advertising in its early years of tractors as it had a small and widely gapped dealership network.

Collectibility

Rating	Model	Comments
★★★★★	10-18	First production tractor built by Allis-Chalmers
★★★★★	6-12	Articulated front-wheel drive; 1,471 built
★★★★	"E" 15-30, 18-30	Four wheels; three-plow; 1,161 built
★★★★	"E" 25-35 (long fender)	Newer version of the 18-30; 1,909 built
★★★★	"E" 25-35 (short fender)	All green; modernized; 12,367 built
★★★★	"E" 25-40	Final version of the Model E; 1,426 built
★★★★★	Greyhound	Model E version sold through Banting Mfg. Co.
★★★★	"L" 12-20, 15-25	Small version of the E; 1,705 built

Reliability

Rating	Model
★★★	10-18
★★★	6-12
★★★★	"E" 15-30, 18-30
★★★★	"E" 25-35 (long fender)
★★★★	"E" 25-35 (short fender)
★★★★	"E" 25-40
★★★★	Greyhound
★★★★	"L" 12-20, 15-25

Parts Availability

Rating	Model
★	10-18
★★	6-12
★★★	"E" 15-30, 18-30
★★★	"E" 25-35 (long fender)
★★★	"E" 25-35 (short fender)
★★★	"E" 25-40
★★★	Greyhound
★★	"L" 12-20, 15-25

machine. Allis-Chalmers was trying to recover from an almost terminal financial difficulty just two years before this new tractor was introduced in 1914.

With a three-wheel design and transverse engine, the Model 10-18 had much in common with the already successful Little Bull Tractor. The 10-18 had a stronger frame and two drive wheels instead of the single drive wheel of the Bull. By all appearances, this new tractor was destined for greatness, but again, Allis-Chalmers gave birth to a financial flop. Not that the tractor was poorly built—by all means it was a marvelous machine. The fast-paced tractor industry left the 10-18 as well as the Little Bull in its wake as the demand for more modern tractors intensified. By 1919, the Bull Tractor was merging with another company to survive and the 10-18 production was down to only 71 units.

An Allis-Chalmers opposed two-cylinder engine with a 5.25-inch bore and 7-inch stroke powered the 10-18. The one-piece cast frame was constantly boasted to never sag by

Allis-Chalmers, a chronic phobia among the conservative farmers of the day derived from horror stories of tractors with faulty frames and drive trains. The company spent much effort to calm these fears based on their awareness that the farmer's trust was absolutely essential for any hope of success. It appeared that Allis-Chalmers had the right formula for a big moneymaker, but it seemed to be just one step behind the competition at every turn.

Allis-Chalmers introduced its Model 6-12 articulated tractor in 1918 with only a bit more success. Following the designs of already proven tractors like the Moline Universal and Indiana Tractor, the company hoped to have a winner. The quality, design, and trust were there, but again, bad luck loomed over them. Henry Ford, one of the most famous men of his day did to the tractor industry what he had already done to the automotive industry; he monopolized the market. His mass-produced little Fordson tractor was thrust into the market with a shocking result. Selling for only $395 through the world's largest automotive dealer organization, the Fordson gobbled up the tractor market with almost unbelievable fury. In 1916, all U.S manufacturers combined built only 29,670 tractors. Three years later, in 1919, about 175,000 tractors were built and more than 57,000 of them were Fordsons; only 529 were from Allis-Chalmers. Ford's dominance spelled out doom for the 10-18 and 6-12 tractor models.

With genuine determination, General Falk continued on with newer models. The Model E and Model L were aimed away from the small farms and targeted for the large and intermediate-sized farms as well as custom plow and threshing machine operators. Its future in tractors was beginning to look more promising.

Model 10-18 Tractor

Today, the 10-18 would be considered an odd-looking contraption. The fact is that Allis-Chalmers engineers studied the market and built a tractor that had a style in common with other major sellers of the day. The design offered both rear wheels as drivers and a solid backbone that, at the time,

The Allis-Chalmers Farm Tractor and the plant behind it—

The 10-18 was Allis-Chalmers' first farm tractor; it boasted excellent quality. The company was on a rebound from a painful reorganization that placed Otto Falk (retired brigadier general) as the president. This tractor and the next three models that Allis-Chalmers produced were financial failures for the company, mainly because of the unbearable competition of the time.

put many other tractors to shame. The Bull tractor stole the show in 1914 even though Allis-Chalmers had studied its design and marketing carefully. The 10-18 was superior in function and quality and offered farmers a small top-quality tractor. When entering the market in 1914, the Allis-Chalmers 10-18 sold for $1,950. The Little Bull 5-12 sold for only $335. Allis-Chalmers had a difficult time competing with such a huge difference in pricing.

The rear wheels of the 10-18 were driven by exposed roller pinions and bull gears. The one-piece cast frame was supported in the front by a single cast wheel. The steering was through a worm and sector gear, and the clutch was an expanding-shoe type. A Detroit lubricator, on external multi-station pump forced oil to critical engine

components of the two-cylinder transverse engine. The transmission was enclosed and ran in oil and it provided one speed of 2.3 miles per hour forward and reverse. The sturdy swivel drawbar had 14 inches of side-to-side adjustment.

Production of the 10-18 began in November of 1914. The first examples had engines designed to operate only on gasoline, but by about 1915, changes were made to operate with lower octane fuel. With a double-bowl Kingston carburetor, the tractor could be started on gasoline and when warmed enough to vaporize the less-expensive kerosene, the fuel would then be switched over.

Most restored examples of the 10-18 are painted dark green with red wheels. The "Allis-Chalmers" name is proudly displayed on both ends of the main fuel tank as well as on a plaque just below the radiator.

Collecting Notes: Very few 10-18 models exist and finding one for sale is an extremely rare occurrence. Expect to pay dearly if ever you happen to find a complete unit for sale. The waiting list is long and the 10-18 is for the collector with a fat wallet. Restoration on incomplete or deteriorated units is difficult, because missing parts may well have to be custom-made by casting and/or machining. The one thing to keep in mind is that a 10-18 in restored condition is the most valuable antique A-C tractor today.

Model 10-18 Tractor Specifications

Years built	1914–1923
Engine	Allis-Chalmers 303-cubic inch (720 rpm)
Cylinders	opposed, two: 5.25x7-inch bore and stroke
Horsepower (drawbar/belt)	10/18
Speeds (mph)	2.3 forward, 2.3 reverse
Weight (pounds)	4,800
Length (inches)	140
Width (inches)	70
Height (inches)	75
Rear wheels (inches, dia. x w.)	56x12 (steel)
Front wheel (cast, inches)	32 x 6
Belt pulley (inches, dia. x w.)	14.5 x 6.5; 720 rpm
Fuel capacity (gallons)	20 (kerosene)
Starting fuel tank (gallons)	5 (gasoline)
Cooling capacity (gallons)	6
Ignition (magneto)	KW or Kingston
Carburetor	Kingston dual
Suggested new retail price	$1,950 in 1914

Model 10-18 Tractor Production History

Serial number is found on the left side of the frame below the radiator.

Year	Units Produced
1914–1918	unknown
1919	71
1920	31
1921	45
1922	38
1923	4
Total Built	**unknown**

Model 6-12 Tractor

In 1918, most farmers were still farming with horses, and tractors were somewhat of a novelty to many of these conservative tillers of the soil. The only possible way to get many of these farmers to even consider a tractor would be to make it inexpensive and able to use existing horse-drawn implements. The 6-12 was among other similar tractors of its day that had these qualities. In 1920, one could buy a nifty little 6-12 for a mere $850. The big problem for Allis-Chalmers as well as scores of other tractor companies was that the fast-selling Fordson tractor was selling for less. The vast Ford dealership network and the notoriety of the Ford name left few buyers for the 6-12. By 1923, Allis-Chalmers was clearing out the 6-12 models for only $295 each and, for a time, concentrated more on higher-class tractors such as the Models E and L.

The 6-12 was an articulated tractor that had the capability to use wheeled implements in place of the rear sulky attachment that was supplied. A heavy vertical cast frame was hollowed to contain a fuel tank on top and a toolbox on the side. Pressed-in axles at each side of the yoke-shaped frame supported the steel drive wheels. A roller-type pinion gear and a segmented bull gear in turn drove the drive wheels. Although these gears were exposed, oil from holes in the pinion roller pins helped keep the wear tolerable. An option in sandy soil regions was a directed dual-exhaust aimed at the pinions to help blow them clean.

A little four-cylinder, 138-cubic inch LeRoi L-head engine propelled this tractor to a speed of 2 1/2 miles per hour. This engine required no water pump for its cooling system. The warmer water would naturally rise and flow into the top of the radiator where it was cooled and circulated back to the engine at the bottom of the block. This thermosiphon process was not used on larger models built by Allis-Chalmers.

By 1920, the Model 6-12 was offered in a "B" version as well as the General Purpose model. This Model B Orchard Tractor had the axles relocated to lower the engine and had shielded drive wheel centers. References are made of a Cane or High-crop version in production data, but no information has been located for this model other than the 45 built from

Allis-Chalmers had big hopes for its Model 6-12. Henry Ford's mass-produced Fordson was offered during the same time as the 6-12 and left little room for Allis-Chalmers' small tractor.

In 1919, the Model 6-12 had this single, 28-inch rear sulky wheel. By 1920, twin rear sulky wheels were standard. The tractor was submitted to Nebraska testing on August 17, 1920. The rated 1,000-rpm engine speed was boosted in the same year to 1,200 rpm.

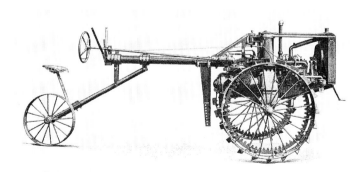

The LeRoi Model 2C engine used in the 6-12 General Purpose Tractor was a popular engine during its day. The Kingston Model L carburetor is shown in front of the magneto. At least three different magnetos were available for the Model 6-12 tractor.

This picture shows part of the Model 6-12 being assembled. The 347-pound vertical cast frame at the top has pressed-in axles and a built-in 9.5-gallon fuel tank. The second view shows the steering yoke and gears with the differential attached. The third view, with the transmission attached, shows the dome-shaped dust cover where the removable belt pulley attaches. The bottom view shows the LeRoi Model 2C engine bolted in.

1920–1923. An industrial version was offered for roadwork. This tractor had 20 massive flat spokes on each heavy-duty drive wheel to prevent hub and rim failures caused by the incessant jarring from the hard roadways. A Duplex model was a four-wheel-drive version that was made by attaching two 6-12 tractors together, back to back. The special adapter kit converted two 6-12 tractors into a single articulated machine with double the horsepower and traction. This version apparently received poor acceptance, with no examples known to exist at this time.

It is generally accepted that the Model 6-12 should be painted dark green with red wheels. Yellow accent stripes are used to highlight the sides of the radiator and fuel tank. This author has a sales bulletin from 1919 that shows a tan 6-12 with tan wheels. The tractor has yellow striping on the radiator and sides of the fuel tank and is shown against a field of green cornstalks. This, as well as another source, leans toward the theory that the pre-1920 Allis-Chalmers tractors were painted tan with a hint of green. Until stronger evidence emerges and proves otherwise, most pre-1920 A-C tractors will continue to be painted dark green.

Collecting Notes: The 6-12 is one of the more difficult Allis-Chalmers tractors to acquire. Expect to pay the greater share of $10,000 for an operating unit. Parts are difficult to obtain for nonrestored units. The LeRoi model 2C engine was used in several other brands of tractors in its day, including the Planet Jr., Indiana, Parrett, Toro, Bean Track Pull, Southern Motors Ranger, Emerson-Brantingham Cultivator, Heider Motor Cultivator, and Bailor two-row Motor Cultivator. Certain chassis and transmission parts may need to be custom-made for the Model 6-12. Often, cooperation with other owners may allow parts to be patterned.

Model 6-12 General Purpose Specifications

Years built	1919–1926
Engine	LeRoi model 2C: 1,000 rpm in 1919 (1,200 rpm after)
Cylinders	vertical, four: 3.125x4.5-inch bore and stroke
Horsepower (drawbar/belt)	6.27/12.37
Speeds (mph)	2.4 forward, 2.4 reverse
Weight (pounds)	2,500
Length (inches)	156
Drive-wheel tread (inches)	54
Height (inches)	72
Drive wheels (steel, inches)	48x6 (20 angle iron cleats each wheel)
Sulky wheel(s) (inches)	28x6
Belt pulley (inches, dia. x w.)	10x5.5 (1,000 rpm)
Fuel capacity (gallons)	9.5
Cooling capacity (gallons)	3.5
Ignition (magneto)	Eisemann, Dixie, or Splitdorf
Carburetor	Kingston Model L
Suggested new retail price	$850 in 1920

Model 6-12 Production History

Serial number is found on the brass plate on the vertical cast frame.

Year	Units Produced
1919	303
1920	467
1921	72
1922	249
1923	211
1924	99
1925	62
1926	8
Total Built	**1,471**

Model 6-12 Tractor Progression History

Year	Modification
1919	First 6-12 built
1920	Single sulky wheel changed to twin, engine rpm raised from 1,000 to 1,200
1926	Last 6-12 built, only eight for the whole year

Model E, 15-30, 18-30, and 25-40 Tractors

There was not one thing second-class about the Model 15-30 introduced in 1918. One could have purchased two new Fordson tractors for the 1920 selling price of $1,785. By 1922, the Fordson was selling for $395 and one could have bought four of them for every 18-30 sold that year. The massive 467-cubic inch four-cylinder engine had 4.75-inch pistons with a 6.5-inch stroke that came with removable cylinder sleeves and was outfitted with the foremost brand-name accessories.

The top view shows the first version of the Model 15-30 from 1918. By 1919, after only a few examples were built, the 15-30 took on the appearance of the bottom view. The rear wheels were beefed up and optional canvas curtains replaced the steel engine covers. A radiator with cast-iron tanks replaced the brass-tank radiator used on the early version.

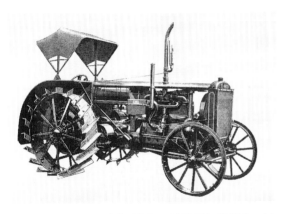

The 20-35 had a big-time change starting with serial number 8070 in 1927. In a successful effort to reduce the manufacturing costs of the tractor without forfeiting performance or durability, Allis-Chalmers reworked the Model E into the newer short-fender version. This newer version sold for $1,295 in 1927, almost $600 less than what the older Model E sold for in 1925.

The 18-30 was renamed the 20-35 in 1922. This 20-35 Special was sold to threshing machine operators. This version cost $200 over the standard version's price of $1,685 during 1925. The high-compression engine in the Special tractor had about 10 more horsepower than the standard model. With extra dash-mounted controls for the carburetor and governor plus a canopy and an exhaust whistle, this tractor was a viable replacement for the steam traction engines.

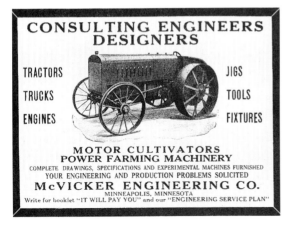

McVicker Engineering was perhaps the most well-known tractor designer in the early 1900s. Allis-Chalmers advertised in the 1920s that it had invested more than $3 million in its tractor venture. Perhaps some of this money was spent on outside resources. This ad from 1920 implies that McVicker Engineering was somehow involved with the design of the 15-30 Allis-Chalmers tractor. This author has found no other connections between the two companies. However, Walter McVicker, founder of the engineering firm, did help design the Twin City tractors sold by the Minneapolis Steel and Machinery Company.

The frameless construction had a massive cast oil pan and transmission case that made the 15-30 a rock-solid machine. The fin and tube radiator, centrifugal governor, and expanding-shoe clutch were all proudly proclaimed to have been built in Allis-Chalmers plants. A double-bowl, Kingston Model E carburetor with a vaporizing manifold made it possible to burn low-grade fuels such as kerosene or distillate. Besides fuel compartments for gasoline and kerosene, a water compartment was in the 18-30 tank. Water was mixed with the low-grade fuel to control engine knocking before the days of lead additives. The Allis-Chalmers-made engine featured removable gray iron cylinder sleeves and had a splash-lubricated crankcase. The rocker arms had oil cups for drip-lubrication. By 1927, the Model E engine was completely pressure-lubricated when the entire tractor was reengineered.

With early testing, the 15-30 tractor was renamed the Model 18-30 by the year 1919. The 830-rpm engine was boosted to 930, and by 1923 the tractor was renamed again, the Model 20-35. These model numbers represent conservative drawbar and belt horsepower ratings, respectively, based on the famous Nebraska tests that were started in April 1920.

Prior to 1920, numerous tractor companies sprouted up all over the country as the market for farm tractors boomed. Tractors with weak frames, poor traction, and overrated horsepower claims plagued the market. Wilmot Crozier had bought a Minneapolis Ford tractor (no association with Henry Ford) that performed so horribly that he demanded another, which again was no better. After a secondhand Bull tractor was tried with disappointing performance, Mr. Crozier bought a three-plow-rated Rumely tractor that could

The short-fender Model 20-35 was a handsome machine. In some cases, Allis-Chalmers found that parts from outside vendors were less expensive to use on its tractors than its own parts. With the wisdom of tractor manager Harry Merritt, the redesigned 20-35 sold well and saved the entire A-C tractor department from impending extinction caused by previous losses.

Durable pinion gears drove the one-piece bull gears in each rear wheel of the Model 20-35. In later Allis-Chalmers tractors, the final-drive gears would be enclosed within the differential case or final-drive housings.

pull five plows. Wilmont Crozier was elected to the Nebraska legislature in 1919 and proposed the bill that began the Nebraska tractor tests. No tractor could be sold in Nebraska without a permit. The permit would be granted only after the University of Nebraska Agricultural Engineering Department scientifically tested the tractor with results that substantiated the published performance claims of the manufacturer. These publicized Nebraska tests quickly became the standard for the whole country, exposing the tractor companies with low integrity, forcing most to leave the tractor market. The conservative horsepower ratings by reputable firms, including Allis-Chalmers helped promote the positive integrity of these companies. Nightmare stories of farmers betting their future on a tractor that became useless or the manufacturer disappearing with its service and parts support were all too common. Allis-Chalmers was keen to this apprehension of potential tractor customers, and its early advertising often emphasized the immensity and solidity of its manufacturing facilities.

On January 1, 1926, Allis-Chalmers appointed Harry Merritt as manager of the tractor department. The president, Gen. Otto Falk, was reluctantly convinced that the tractor division that only lost money for the company should be closed down. Harry Merritt was chosen for this disheartening deed. By dropping the price of the Model 20-35 to $1,295—down $700 from normal—the inventory moved so swiftly that the company took another look at the tractor venture. If it could sell the Model 20-35 for the lower price and still turn a profit, the tractor division might be rescued. Harry Merritt was allowed to work with the engineering

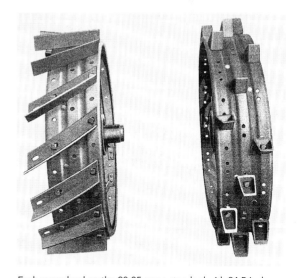

Each rear wheel on the 20-35 came standard with 24 5-inch spade lugs. Optional 6-inch lugs or angle iron cleats were available for special soil conditions. The well-known French and Hecht Company manufactured both the front and rear wheels.

department to redesign the tractor to see whether manufacturing costs could be reduced. J. F. Max Patitz, the proud chief consulting engineer, had another team do the same. Harry Merritt's project was selected for production. The new Model 20-35 was painted all green and had shortened rear-wheel fenders. Changes were made to the engine, transmission, clutch, and numerous other areas. The performance was not compromised, but by eliminating the frills and by purchasing some parts from outside vendors when prudent, the goal was met. The newly designed Model 20-35 sold fairly well at $1,295 and for a fair profit. Allis-Chalmers was still in the tractor business.

In 1930 the Model 20-35 was renamed for the third time. This time it was the Model 25-40 with the rated rpm raised from 930 to 1,000. A 5.5-inch engine bore became an option above the standard 5-inch bore. Rubber tires became available. The option of 12.75x28-inch rear and 7.5x18-inch front tires drove the 1934 price of the tractor to $1,425 from $1,000 for a standard steel-wheeled model. The Model E series continued until the 25-40 was replaced by the Model A in 1936.

Collecting Notes: The availability of the E-series tractor is fair. Expect to pay a steep price for a long-fender model. The later short-fender 20-35 and 25-40 models are more often found available and demand somewhat less money than long-fender models in the same condition. Restoration parts are a challenge to find but can usually be located with help of classified ads in tractor magazines or Internet chat rooms for Allis-Chalmers collectors.

A huge advertising campaign was launched in 1927 to promote the redesigned 20-35. This ad is from 1929. Now selling for $1,295, profits were beginning to improve for the tractor department. The small farm equipment sideline of the great Allis-Chalmers Company began to prosper into the major portion of the company's total sales within the next nine years.

Model E Tractor Specifications

	15-30/18-30	20-35 (long-fender)	20-35 (short-fender)	25-40
Years built	1918–1921	1923–1927	1927–1930	1930–1936
Serial numbers	5000–6160	6161–10000	12001–24185	24186–25611
Horsepower (drawbar/belt)	20.55/33.41	25.45/43.73	33.20/44.29	33.82/47.00
Cylinders	4	4	4	4
Engine bore and stroke (4-cyl.)	4.75x6.5	4.75x6.5	4.75x6.5	5.0x6.5
Engine rpm	830	930	930	1,000
Speeds (forward, mph)	2.31, 2.82	2.58, 3.16	2.5, 3.25	2.5, 3.25
Speed (reverse, mph)	2.30	3.16	3.25	3.25
Weight (pounds)	6,000	6,640	6,000	7,200
Length (inches)	146	152	140.5	140.5
Rear tread (inches)	66	66	70	70
Height (inches)	68	68	68	68
Rear wheel (steel, inches)	50x12	50x12	50x12	50x12
Front wheel (steel, inches)	36x6	36x6	36x6	36x6
Belt pulley (inches, dia. x w.)	15x7.5	15x7.5	13x8.5	13x8.5
Fuel capacity (gallons)	25	32	28	28
Cooling capacity (gallons)	10	10	10	10
Ignition (magneto)	Dixie, KW, Eisemann	Eisemann GS4	Eisemann GS4	Eisemann G4
Carburetor	Kingston	Kingston	Zenith C6EV	Zenith C6EV
Suggested new retail price	$1,785 in 1920	$1,685 in 1925	$1,205 in 1929	$1,000 in 1934

This rear view of the short-fender 20-35 gives a good look at the offset seat and steering wheel. It was built to give the operator a better view of the furrow wheel. The big lever on the left is the hand-operated clutch; the pedal next to it is the brake. The lever in front of the seat is the shifter. Pushing the shift lever forward and to the right is low gear; forward to the left is high gear; pulling the lever back and to the right is reverse; and neutral is the middle position.

Model E Tractor Production History

Serial number is found on the dash plate or on top of the transmission by the shifter.

Year	Serial Numbers
1918	5000–5005
1919	5006–5160
1920	5161–6014
1921	6015–6160
1922	none built
1923	6161–6396
1924	6397–6754
1925	6755–7368
1926	7369–8069
1927	8070–9869
1928	9870–10000, 12001–16761
1929	16762–20250, 22001–23251
1930	23252–24842
1931	24843–24971
1932	24972–25023
1933	25024–25061
1934	25062–25308
1935	25309–25581
1936	25582– 25611

Model E Tractor Progression History

Year	Serial Number	Modification
1918	Serial no. 5000	First 15-30 built
1919	not known (early)	Engine covers no longer used, cast radiator tanks replace brass, tractor renamed 18-30
1921	about 5929	Rpm raised from 830 to 930
1923	6161	Tractor renamed 20-35
1927	8070	Model 20-35 redesigned with shorter fenders, smaller operator's platform, wider hood, and shorter wheelbase; redesigned clutch assembly; wheels painted green instead of the earlier red
1928	9870	Steering assembly, dash, transmission case, and clutch redesigned; fan bearings improved
1928	16436	Transmission case and high-speed gears changed; oil pump is direct drive; tie rod, fuel filter, and differential changed
1930	24186	Tractor renamed 25-40; carburetor, water pump, and air cleaner changed
1936	25611	Last Model E 25-40 built

This ad for the 20-35 emphasizes the durability of the tractor with 94 forged parts, showing five views of its huge forging machines and heat-treating furnaces. On the left side of this ad near the bottom is a list of 11 radio stations that broadcast the Allis-Chalmers Radio Program. The radio was an effective modern advertising tool of the era that many other tractor companies were reluctant to use.

The Banting Manufacturing Company Tractors

The Banting brothers from Toledo, Ohio, sold a full line of threshing equipment from about 1912 until 1930. Originally marketing the Buffalo-Pitts steam traction engines, Banting Manufacturing Company began selling "Greyhound" steam engines about 1918. Allis-Chalmers tractors were advertised in Banting catalogs beginning about 1924 featuring the Model 6-12 and 15-25. In the following year, Banting sold the Allis-Chalmers Model 20-35 with the Greyhound name on a radiator screen and the Banting name on a casting at the rear of the fuel tank. About 1928, Allis-Chalmers Model E 20-35 tractors sold by Banting were called Greyhound tractors. With "Greyhound" embossed into the front of the top radiator tank and special accessories to suit threshing machine operators, these tractors were represented as Banting's own manufacturing. First introduced in 1928 as the "Special," by 1929 the Greyhound tractor was called the "Thresherman's Special." These Greyhound tractors all came with an operator canopy, extra-wide rear wheels, plus a generator and road lights. The last year for the Greyhound tractors was 1930. Banting was sold off and Carlos Banting continued on as a prosperous Allis-Chalmers equipment dealer until his death in 1954.

The Greyhound tractor had options available such as an exhaust whistle and road wheel weights that weighed 1,000 pounds apiece. Rear wheel cleats were either angle iron or square road cleats with countersunk bolts.

Threshing crews had much success with the Allis-Chalmers Model E tractors over the years with great reliability and a powerful engine. Threshing crews moved fast from farm to farm during harvest season and could not afford many equipment breakdowns. If a tractor or thresher failed, men would often work around the clock to have it ready the next day. A poorly designed tractor would put threshermen out of business in a big hurry. Banting and Allis-Chalmers both had a highly regarded reputation among threshing crews. Only the best tractors of the day, including such names as Hart-Parr, Advance-Rumely, Huber, McCormick-Deering, Nichols and Shepard, Twin-City, and Allis-Chalmers would suit the needs of these crews. Overheating, excessive fuel consumption, cracked rear-wheel hubs, and lack of power were only some of the problems caused by inferior tractors. Many miles of rough roads were traveled

Banting's "Greyhound" logo was displayed on the radiator of its tractor until 1930, when "Banting Machine Company" was used in its place. The tractor actually was an Allis-Chalmers Model E Thresherman Special sold under the Banting name. *Craig Detwiler*

Allis-Chalmers lacked a strong dealer network in the early years of tractors. Banting's connections in the retail farming business made it Allis-Chalmers' biggest retailer. The official mascot of the Banting Manufacturing Company was this greyhound. "Light, strong, and durable" are the small words inside the oval. By the second half of the 1920s, the Allis-Chalmers Model E tractors sold through Banting had the Greyhound name cast in the upper radiator tank.

The Banting Manufacturing Company was famous for its "Greyhound Line" of farm equipment; during the 1920s, it sold Allis-Chalmers Tractors, including this Model 6-12 with a mounted Oliver plow. Banting was a respected name in the threshing business as it offered almost any item a threshing crew could need, including steam traction engines and threshing machines along with a full line of accessories.

with threshing machines being towed by tractors to each farm. Hundreds of miles were often traveled during a single season. With the tractor working under full load with its belt power from the time the sun came up in the morning until it set at night, the engine would receive a workout like no other type of farming equipment. Threshermen often had tremendous loyalty toward certain brands of dependable tractors, including Allis-Chalmers and Greyhound.

In the early 1920s, Nichols and Shepard Company (N&S) sold the Allis-Chalmers Model E and L to enhance its own tractor line. N&S was among the most respected names in the threshing machine industry. Building massive gasoline tractors and steam traction engines, N&S was happy to offer the Allis-Chalmers tractors as first-class machines that would satisfy the needs of a thresherman who didn't need a heavy-weight model. About 1927, N&S dropped the Allis-Chalmers tractors from catalogs and were selling three tractor models built by the John Lauson Company of Wisconsin. Lauson tractors were well-built machines with a style similar to that of the A-C Model E.

Before Allis-Chalmers acquired Advance-Rumely in 1931, it only had five branch houses and a limited number of dealers. Selling its tractors through Banting as well as N&S helped sales at a time when Allis-Chalmers lacked retail outlets. With the Rumely acquisition came 24 additional branch houses plus well over 2,000 dealers. Before this time, Allis-Chalmers was an enormous company whose name was somewhat hidden from the public because the greater share of its products was built for commercial purposes. Generators, turbines, ship engines, pumping stations, rock crushers, and milling equipment were just some of the products that were the bread and butter of the Allis-Chalmers Company. With Rumely's dealership network, A-C finally had a successful way to sell its tractors without being at the mercy of other firms.

Collecting Notes: Few examples of the Greyhound tractor exist today. A complete Greyhound tractor that was in good condition sold for $12,800 in September 2000. The demand is high and the values will reflect this demand. Most Greyhound tractor parts are identical to the 20-35 Allis-Chalmers tractor parts, and are not impossible to acquire. The 20-inch-wide road wheels and the upper radiator tank are parts that may prove next to impossible to replace.

Model L, 12-20, and 15-25 Tractor

In 1921, the new Allis-Chalmers Model L was introduced to offer farmers a tractor that had all the major features of the Model E 18-30, but in a smaller package. Rated as a three-plow tractor, this Model 12-20 was targeted for farmers who found the big three- and four-plow Model 18-30 too expensive and too much wasted power. The Nebraska test number 82 in September 1921 was favorable enough for Allis-Chalmers to rename this tractor the Model L 15-25. It offered two forward speeds of 2.3 and 3.1 miles per hour. A Midwest-brand engine was selected to power the new Model L. This four-cylinder engine was a modern-designed, automotive-type with the crankshaft drilled for pressure lubrication.

In February 1924, an Orchard and a Road Maintenance version of the 15-25 were offered. The regular farm version came with 46x12-inch rear and 32x6-inch front steel wheels, while the Orchard had 42x12-inch rear wheels with full-orchard fenders and 27.625x6-inch front solid-disc wheels. The Road Maintenance model came with 46x15-inch rear wheels with 5/8-inch-thick rims and each with 20 spokes of 1.5-inch diameter. The front wheels were the same size as the farm version. The Orchard and Road Maintenance models each had individual foot-operated rear wheel brakes unlike the single hand brake on the farm model.

The little brother to the Model E was this 12-20 Model L that was introduced in 1920. After a favorable performance at Nebraska testing in September 1921, the tractor was re-rated Model 15-25. Allis-Chalmers was always conservative on its horsepower ratings, unlike tractor companies such as Avery that had to reduce its engine ratings after the Nebraska testing.

The carburetor, either a Kingston Model L or Wheeler-Schebler Model A, was used for gasoline-only models. A Kingston E Dual carburetor was optional with a special manifold for operators who wanted to use low-grade fuels. A Dixie Model 46C magneto supplied reliable spark for the ignition. An aluminum valve cover sporting the Allis-Chalmers name protected the rocker-arm assembly in the I-head engine. A Taco-brand water-type air washer filtered the air entering the carburetor. A Pomona Model 610 air cleaner (oil-type) was used on the Road Maintenance tractor because of its superior filtering qualities needed to deal with the dusty unpaved roads of the day. The Midwest engine was improved at engine number 11962. The water pump was flange-mounted instead of detached, and the rear camshaft bearing was increased from 1.25 inches to 2.187 inches. Despite its excellent products, the Midwest Engine Company ran into financial difficulty and discontinued operations in 1924. Allis-Chalmers continued on with the Midwest engine design, as did the Waukesha Motor Company and Huber Manufacturing Company. The cast-iron oil pans found on most Model L tractors up to 1924 were replaced by stamped-steel oil pans after Allis-Chalmers was compelled to make their own engines.

In 1921, the Model 15-25 sold for $1,495, and the price was reduced to $1,385 by 1925. This marvelous well-built tractor had sold sluggishly. In 1923, its best sales year, only 428 units were built; the industry total was 134,590 that same year. Production was stopped in 1927 at the time when Allis-Chalmers was seriously reevaluating the continuation of its tractor division. The Model L is perhaps this author's favorite Allis-Chalmers tractor model. Its total production of 1,705 was low, not because of its quality, but because of the unbearable competition of the day. This tractor reflects an era when Allis-Chalmers was building tractors with little else but quality on their mind. After 1927 when the Model L was dropped, the company was forced to compete with cost-saving manufacturing moves. With its cutting-edge engineering department, the durability and efficiency of the remaining post-1927 tractors was fine, but gone were the bold red wheels and fancy yellow pinstriping.

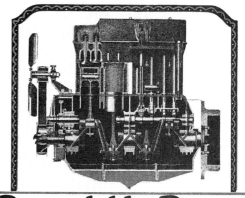

MIDWEST
TRUCK and TRACTOR ENGINE

Never Before Has There Been a Type of Dependable Power Like This

The first, and possibly the only, completely developed engine that can be safely operated under full load up to 1500 feet piston speed per minute —and an engine that is guaranteed under such conditions.

An engine that meets satisfactorily the present-day demand for increased average speed of heavy-duty trucks, rolling on pneumatic tires.

Dependable Power

The Midwest engine was a modern automotive type that powered the 15-25 Model L. Allis-Chalmers was one of at least four companies that built the engine design after Midwest of Indianapolis discontinued operations in 1924.

The right-side view of a 15-25 Model L shows a Wheeler-Schebler carburetor that was used on gasoline-only versions. Kingston carburetors with either a single float bowl for gasoline or a double for gasoline and kerosene were often used on this Midwest-engine. Notice the large hand-hole covers that allowed easy access to the crankshaft and bearings. Midwest made modern engines in its day with an I-head design and high-speed piston travel.

This ad for the 15-25 and 20-35 tractors shows the manufacturing capabilities of the Allis-Chalmers Company. No other manufacturer in the United States had the capabilities to produce these huge, triple-expansion-pumping engines. The advertising was used to help quell the phobia of the potential buyer of ending up with a tractor made by a fly-by-night outfit. Notice the size comparison between the man standing in the upper view and the pumping engine.

Collecting Notes: The Model 12-20 and 15-25 are rarely found for sale. With the low production of 1,705 units and a meager survival rate, this tractor is a true treasure to own. Parts for restoration are difficult to obtain. One can add a star to the collectibility rating for a complete Orchard or Road Maintenance version.

The Engineering Skill and Experience Back of Allis-Chalmers Tractors

THIS 25,000,000 gallon, Triple expansion Pumping Engine, for the city of Cleveland, was entirely designed and built by Allis-Chalmers in 1914. It is 56 feet 3 inches high, and 35 feet wide; weighs 1,750,000 lbs. Other similar Allis-Chalmers jobs have been in continuous service for forty years.

A big share of the world's largest power producing machinery is designed and built by Allis-Chalmers. For 69 years the Allis-Chalmers name has stood for dependable power machinery.

Allis-Chalmers tractors are the result of this ability and experience. The high quality of material used in their construction and the perfection of their design has been thoroughly demonstrated by over eight years successful practical use in the hands of farmers, and by the success of our dealers.

Will you ask us to send our dealer plan without obligation to you?

Allis-Chalmers Mfg. Co.

Tractor Division · · · Milwaukee, Wis.

BRANCHES: Wichita and Liberal, Kans., Enid, Okla., Amarillo, Texas, Lincoln, Nebraska, Fargo, N. D.

Back of the Dealer

You can join forces with Allis-Chalmers, assured of immediate profits as well as future success.

Our franchise gives you cash commission on time sales.

Farmer paper accepted without dealer endorsement.

Full cooperation in sales and service from our factory and branch organization.

A tractor you can be proud to sell.

20-35 Size · · · 15-25 Size

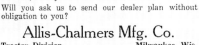 

Better Built By Better Builders.

Model L Tractor Specifications	
Years built	**1921–1927**
Engine	Midwest 280.6-cubic inch (1,100 rpm)
Cylinders	vertical, four
Engine bore and stroke (inches)	4.125x5.25
Horsepower (drawbar/belt)	21.42/33.18
Speeds (mph)	2.3, 3.1 forward; 3.1 reverse
Weight (pounds)	4,550
Length (inches)	130.5
Rear tread (inches)	54
Height (to top of radiator, inches)	63
Rear wheels (steel, inches)	46x12
Front wheels (steel, inches)	32x6
Belt pulley (inches, dia. x w.)	12.5x6.6 (817 rpm)
Fuel capacity (gallons)	20
Cooling capacity (gallons)	6
Ignition (magneto)	Dixie 46C
Carburetor	Kingston or Wheeler-Schebler
Suggested new retail price	$1,495 in 1921

Model L Tractor Production History

Serial number is found on a plate at the outside of the rear fuel tank support.

Year	Serial Numbers
1921	20001–20334
1922	20335–20497
1923	20498–20905
1924	20906–20995
1925	20996–21370
1926	21371–21681
1927	21682–21705

Model L Tractor Progression History

Year	Serial Number	Modification
1921	20001	First 12-20 built
1921	20134	Tractor tested at Nebraska, rerated 15-25
1922	20456	Steering box improved
1924	after engine no. 1196	Midwest engine design continued by A-C with steel oil pan to replace cast, flange-mounted water pump to replace floating type, and a larger rear camshaft bearing
1927	21705	Last Model L 15-25 built

Chapter 4

The First Orange Tractors and the Rumely

In the first half of the 1920s, Allis-Chalmers had already invested more than $3 million in tractor design and production. To their dismay, the company directors were met with financial losses in their tractor venture. Even with the redesigned 20-35 tractor selling for a profit, the entire farm equipment segment of the company was less than 7 percent of the total sales of the company during 1927. The following year was better with farm equipment total sales doubling. Part of the increase was due to the purchase of the Monarch Tractor Corporation, a prestigious builder of crawler tractors. Another factor in 1928 improved Allis-Chalmers' situation: Fordson tractor production ended in the United States.

Henry Ford unexpectedly pulled the plug on the American Fordson in January of 1928 using the excuse that factory space was needed for the new Model A Ford automobile. United Tractor and Equipment Corporation, was a cooperative of about 40 companies that had used the Fordson as the industrial tractor foundation for numerous pieces of mounted equipment. Allis-Chalmers started producing the United tractor by September 1929 as a larger replacement for the Fordson.

Adorned with Persian Orange paint, the United tractor took on a new look for Allis-Chalmers. This bold new orange now replaced the traditional dark green paint. At the same time, the 25-40 took on the color change as well as the succeeding Allis-Chalmers tractors for years to come.

As luck would have it, the United organization folded in 1930, leaving Allis-Chalmers with a new marketing predicament. Allis-Chalmers had a small dealership network compared to John Deere, International Harvester, and J. I. Case. Marketing the United tractor, which was swiftly renamed the Model U, was no longer being handled by the cooperative. Allis-Chalmers desperately needed a greater dealership network.

On June 1, 1931, the Advance-Rumely Company of LaPorte, Indiana, succumbed to financial crisis and merged with Allis-Chalmers. At the time it was represented as a merger, but actually, Allis-Chalmers bought the Rumely operations. In the early years of tractor production, Rumely had perhaps the highest reputation in the industry. It had built many models of the larger tractors that were usually only afforded by custom-plowing and threshing operators or farmers of huge acreage. With the market changing to small tractors, the DoAll and the Rumely Six were introduced to appeal to the average farmer. Financially, Rumely needed this merger and strategically, Allis-Chalmers needed Rumely's vast dealership network. An added bonus for A-C was now having a whole line of top-quality threshers to sell. The existing inventory of Rumely tractors was

Collectibility

Rating	Model	Comments
★★★	U (Continental engine)	Many carried the "United" name; 1,704 built
★★★	U (Allis-Chalmers engine)	About 13,000 built
★★★	UC (Continental engine)	Also called "All-Crop;" 1,268 built
★★★	UC (Allis-Chalmers engine)	Total production: 4,949 built
★★★	UC Cane (High-crop)	Also called "Thompson Cane;" 1,511 built
★★★	Rumely DoAll	Convertible or Non-convertible versions; 3,193 built
★★★★	Rumely 6A	Six-cylinder Waukesha engine; 802 built
★★★★★	WC (Waukesha engine)	About 27 were built
★★	WC (Non-streamlined)	Row-crop; full fenders; no full grille; 74,329 built
★★	WC (Streamlined)	Row-crop; clamshell fenders; grille; 103,873 built
★★★	WF (Non-streamlined)	Standard-tread; full fenders; no full grille; 1,900 built
★★★	WF (Streamlined)	Standard-tread; clamshell fenders; grille; 6,450 built
★★★★	TW (Speed Ace)	Industrial tractor for hauling dirt; 87 built
★★★★★	A	Standard-tread; replacement for the 25-40; 1,225 built

Reliability

Rating	Model
★★★★	U (Continental engine)
★★★★	U (Allis-Chalmers engine)
★★★★	UC (Continental engine)
★★★★	UC (Allis-Chalmers engine)
★★★★	UC Cane (High-crop)
★★★	Rumely DoAll
★★★★	Rumely 6A
★★★★	WC (Waukesha engine)
★★★★★	WC (Non-streamlined)
★★★★★	WC (Streamlined)
★★★★★	WF (Non-streamlined)
★★★★★	WF (Streamlined)
★★★★	TW (Speed Ace)
★★★★	A

Parts Availability

Rating	Model
★★★	U (Continental engine)
★★★★	U (Allis-Chalmers engine)
★★	UC (Continental engine)
★★★	UC (Allis-Chalmers engine)
★★★	UC Cane (High-crop)
★★	Rumely DoAll
★★	Rumely 6A
★★	WC (Waukesha engine)
★★★★★	WC (Non-streamlined)
★★★★★	WC (Streamlined)
★★★	WF (Non-streamlined)
★★★★	WF (Streamlined)
★★	TW (Speed Ace)
★★★	A

sold off over the next few years. In 1931, Allis-Chalmers workers assembled the last batch of DoAll and Rumely Six models from the remaining parts. They were the last of the great line of Rumely tractors. With the Rumely merger and the purchase of the Monarch facilities, Allis-Chalmers was now the fourth largest manufacturer of farm equipment in the United States.

In 1930, the Model UC became Allis-Chalmers' first true row-crop tractor. It was a modified version of the Model U with a narrow-front axle, adjustable rear tread, and higher

Meeting Every Farmer's Greatest Power Need » » »

The UNITED, Champion 3-Plow Tractor, Brings New Profit Possibilities to Every Farm . . . Sets New Standards for Dependable Low-Cost Power with Greatest Pulling Capacity per Dollar of Investment » » »

$895 CASH F.O.B. MILWAUKEE COMPLETE

COMBINED RESOURCES AND specialized abilities of over forty leading companies bring you the quality UNITED Tractor at an unrivaled low price.

The United tractor seemed to be a wonderful break for Allis-Chalmers. It lacked a strong tractor dealership network and this tractor would practically sell itself as an industrial base for many different brands of mounted equipment. Unfortunately, the United Association that started with about 40 companies fell apart, leaving Allis-Chalmers to market its own tractor.

crop clearance. Both the Model U and Model UC sold only moderately well, but in 1933, Allis-Chalmers changed tractor history: It was the first company to sell a row-crop tractor with rubber tires as standard equipment.

The Model W, later called the WC, hit the market strong and by 1935 sales of this model began to sweep the nation like a firestorm. Nebraska testing quickly proved the remarkable advantages of rubber tires over steel wheels: greater traction, greater efficiency, and a smoother ride. This lightweight tractor was rated at a full two-plow capacity and sold for only $825. By 1939, all of the major tractor builders were trying to catch up by selling rubber tires as standard equipment on their tractors. Allis-Chalmers was now flourishing in its agricultural line. Other tractors were built that met different needs. The Model WF was introduced in 1937 as a standard-tread version of the WC. The Model A replaced the slow-selling Model 25-40 in 1936. With the same engine as the 25-40 and the transmission and differential much in common with the Model U, the new Model A was a thresherman's dream, except the day of the thresher was fading fast. Only a total of 1,225 units were built before the model was dropped in 1942.

Model U Tractor

When introduced in 1929, the Allis-Chalmers United tractor, was predominantly aimed at the industrial market. A Continental S10 four-cylinder L-head engine with a 283.7-cubic inch displacement powered the United and early Model U tractors. In 1932 at serial number 7405, the engine was replaced by the Allis-Chalmers UM four-cylinder I-head with a 300.7-cubic inch displacement. This new engine was actually built by Waukesha, but because it was built to Allis-Chalmers specifications, this fact was not publicized. The rugged Model U came with a four-speed transmission, but on steel-wheeled models, the fourth gear was deactivated with the shifting fork disengaged from the sliding collar. The engine bore was increased from 4 3/8 inches to 4 1/2 inches in 1936 at serial number 12001.

On October 13, 1932, pneumatic tires officially became standard equipment on the Model U. Allis-Chalmers gained much publicity from breaking the tractor speed record on a specially geared Model U. It was driven by perhaps the most famous racecar driver in that era, Barney Oldfield, to a speed of 64.28 mph. Although Allis-Chalmers was offering rubber tires as standard equipment in 1932, the rest of the industry took six or seven more years to convert. The demand for faster-moving tractors and improved fuel economy ushered in the age of rubber-tired tractors, and the engineers at Allis-Chalmers were quick to foresee the outcome. The 24-inch rear tires on spoked wheels for farm models were increased to 28 inches on disc-style wheels at the same time the engine bore was increased.

Options such as higher gear ratios (3.8–16 mph and 4.3–18.5 mph) and PTO assemblies either on the side or rear of the tractor, made the Model U a versatile industrial machine. Other extras were the 1,800-rpm engine speed governor, foot accelerator, 18-inch drum-style hand brakes, heavy-duty spring-mounted front axle, and industrial seat.

This little Centaur tractor was marketed by the United Association as a smaller option to the Allis-Chalmers Model U (United).

Perfex was proud to use the United tractor in its ad to boast that the quality of its product was the reason Allis-Chalmers selected its radiators.

Hard-rubber tires (40x5-, 40x10-, and 40x12-inch rear plus 28x4- and 28x5-inch front) were offered for warehouse work and rear extension tires could be added. A 44-inch-wide Model UN was sold for narrow-aisle work. For the farm tractor one could add a muffler, belt pulley, road bands, rear wheel weights, and a number of rear steel wheel lug and cleat options. For the pampered farmer, electric starter and lights, spring seat, operator canopy, or fully enclosed cab could be purchased. An orchard version was sold with rear citrus fenders, front-wheel disc-type shielding, and lowered operator controls and stacks.

Fred E. Cooper Incorporated of Tulsa, Oklahoma, began to convert Allis-Chalmers tractors into special rigs to maintain oil wells. A limited number of Model U tractors with the larger Model A engines were built by Allis-Chalmers for the Cooper firm. The front frame on these special units was extended to mount a pair of winches, each with 5,000 feet of cable. You can add two stars to the collectibility rating for a Cooper conversion.

The Model U was a durable machine that was built for 24 years. With versions built into small railroad locomotives, dirt hauling trucks, cranes, crawlers, road rollers, etc., don't be too surprised at what other unusual configuration you might find for this tractor.

Collecting Notes: The Model U tractors are not usually difficult to find. Expect to pay more for a model with a Continental engine. Parts are not usually difficult to obtain except for certain industrial parts, such as special wheel or tire options. You can add a star to the collectibility rating system for a Model UN (narrow, 44-inch rear width).

This Continental S-10 L-head (flathead) engine was introduced with the first United tractors and was replaced by Allis-Chalmers' own engine in 1932 beginning with serial number 7405. Waukesha actually built the latter I-head engine designated the UM.

The Continental engine models of the Model U came with a Donaldson air cleaner. A better Vortox air cleaner was offered as an upgrade for this engine in later years when the newer UM engine was being used.

Model United and U Tractor Specifications

	With Continental S10 engine	With Allis-Chalmers UM engine
Years built	1929–1932	1932–1952
Serial numbers	1–7404	7405–not found
Horsepower (drawbar/belt)	25.63/35.04	30.07/34.02 (4 3/8-inch bore)
Cylinders	4	4
Engine bore and stroke (inches)	4.25x5.0	4.375x5.0 (4.5x5.0 in 1936)
Engine rpm	1,200	1,200
Speeds (forward, mph)	2.33, 3.33, 5.0, 10.75	2.66, 3.5, 4.75, 11.5
Speed (reverse, mph)	2.69	3.25
Weight (no added ballast, pounds)	4,821	5,140
Length (inches)	118.875	118.5
Rear tread (inches)	52 (steel wheels)	65–76 (rubber tires)
Height (to steering wheel, inches)	53.75	53.5
Rear wheel (steel, inches)	42x11.125	45x11
Rear rubber tire (inches)	11.25x24	11.25x28 (13x28 at serial number 22084)
Front wheel (steel, inches)	28x6	28x6
Front rubber tire (inches)	6.5x16	6.5x16
Belt pulley (inches, dia. x w.)	10x7.5 (option)	10x7.5 (option)
Fuel capacity (gallons)	23	23
Cooling capacity (gallons)	5	6
Ignition (magneto)	Eisemann, Bosch,	Eisemann, Bendix, or Bendix or Fairbanks-Morse
Carburetor	Schebler HD or Kingston	Zenith K5
Suggested new retail price	$895 in 1929 (steel wheels)	$840 in 1934 (steel wheels)

The UM engine had only a little horsepower advantage over the Continental engine it replaced. The earlier flathead engines were known for problems such as carbon deposits forming around valves, which in turn caused power loss.

The first production tractor with new pneumatic tires to be sold in the United States was the Model U. This model helped prove the advantage of rubber tires over steel wheels to many conservative critics who at first believed that tires would offer poor traction in wet conditions. The majority of the tractor industry offered rubber tires as standard equipment by 1939.

The New Model "U"
Air Tires

Model United and U Production History

Serial number is found stamped on the rear of the differential housing with prefix "U."

Year	Serial Numbers
1929	1–1974
1930	1975–6553
1931	6554–7261
1932	7262–7418
1933	7419–7684
1934	7685–8062
1935	8063–9470
1936	9471–12821
1937	12822–14854
1938	14855–15586
1939	15587–16077
1940	16078–16721
1941	16722–17136
1942	17137–17469
1943	17470–17801
1944	17802–17819
1945	not found
1946	not found
1947	20774*
1948	21022*
1949	22128*
1950	23029* not found

Information sources conflict as to these beginning serial numbers, which may not have been consecutive after 1946.

The Allis-Chalmers-built United Tractor was announced in September 1929. In October of the same year, the United Tractor and Equipment Corporation announced the involvement of 40 manufacturing companies. By the end of December, when this ad was released, 12 manufacturing companies were advertising their membership in the United organization. Apparently, certain member companies did not benefit as much as they hoped from this association, and the United organization collapsed in 1930. With the United name dissolved, the renamed Model U tractor and "Allied Equipment" were sold through the Allis-Chalmers Industrial Tractor Division.

Model United and U Tractor Progression History

Year	Serial Number	Modification
1929	1	First Model U "United" built
1929	946	Tractor tested at Nebraska (test no. 170), Continental engine
1930	5872	Stack-mounted Donaldson air precleaner replaces glass-jar type
1932	7405	Allis-Chalmers engine (built by Waukesha) replaces Continental engine
1935	8263	Tractor tested at Nebraska (test no. 237) A-C engine
1936	12001	Engine bore increased; rear spoke wheels for tires replaced by cast wheels, rear tire size changed from 11.25x24 to 11.25x28 inches; fenders modified and high-back seat used
1936	12401	Hannum-brand steering gear replaced by Levine's
1937	13501	Levine-brand steering gear replaced by Ross'
1937	14120	Front spoke wheels for tires replaced by steel disc type
1938	15314	Five-bolt front wheels replace six-bolt wheels
1948	22084	Rear tire size increased from 11.25x28 to 13x28 inches
1952	not found	Last year of production

Model All-Crop and UC Tractor

By using final-drive housings to raise the clearance of the Model U and mounting a narrow-front axle, the All-Crop tractor was introduced in 1930 as Allis-Chalmers' first true row-crop tractor. This machine was perhaps a little bit bulky compared to the John Deere and Farmall row-crop tractors. Sales were never astounding, but production lasted until 1953 as it finished its final 10 years in production as a cane version only. Sometime in 1932, the All-Crop was more commonly referred to as the Model UC. These tractors started out in production with the Continental S10 engine like the standard-tread Model U. In 1933, beginning with serial number 1269, the Allis-Chalmers UM engine with an I-head design replaced the Continental L-head (flat-head) engine. The bore was increased in 1936 at serial number 2282. The 4 3/8-inch bore was increased to 4 1/2 inches, which also raised the displacement from 300.7 cubic inches to 318.

With the same four-speed transmission as the Model U, the All-Crop had no fourth gear in the steel-wheel models with the Continental engine after serial number 31. The fourth gear had all of its parts in the Allis-Chalmers-powered UC models, but the shifting fork was not engaged into the fourth gear collar on models with steel wheels.

Several changes occurred in 1937 at serial number 2819. The tractor was restyled with smaller fenders, changes to the hood and dash, plus several other alterations to give a sleeker appearance. The original 42x2-inch rear steel wheels were the skeletal type and the size was increased to 45x2 inches at this time. Rear tire size was 11.25x24 inches and was increased to 11.25x28 inches.

Six-inch rear steel wheel extensions were available and by adding one to each existing 2-inch wheel, an 8-inch rim was built or by adding two, one would have a 14-inch rim. The tractor usually came standard with a standard-duty power lift and a clutch-type belt pulley. A special heavy-duty power lift and a 530-rpm PTO assembly were optional. Rear wheel weights or road bands could be purchased if needed. In 1939, an electric starter and lights became available

The cane versions were special models with a 25 1/2-inch crop clearance that were mainly sold by the Thompson Machinery Company in Thibodaux, Louisiana. From 1937 to 1941, about 361 cane units were made, but from 1944 to

The Model UC had a 30-inch crop clearance under the rear axle. The first 31 tractors (serial numbers 1–31) had several differences from later models such as a different rear-wheel style, operative fourth gear, and different steering gears. These tractors are of particular interest to serious collectors.

Allis-Chalmers offered the UC as a row-crop version of its popular Model U. Starting with production in 1930, the UC used the Continental S-10 engine until 1933, when it was replaced with the Allis-Chalmers UM engine.

When the UM engine replaced the Continental L-head in 1933, the Model UC tractor was considered a new model. The model shown is from 1935, but in 1937 more extreme changes occurred that effected the style for a third version.

1953, about 1,150 more cane models were built as the regular UC production had stopped. The later UC Cane models had 12x38-inch rear and 5.25x21-inch front tires. Speeds were increased about 22 percent over that of the regular Model UC.

Thompson continued to build its own cane tractors after 1953 and was still buying UC parts from Allis-Chalmers for production. Its UCG cane tractor was sold in an all-fuel version as well as a diesel or LPG version. Thompson's UCD, and the four-wheel-drive XTD models that replaced the UC Cane both used a General Motors two-cylinder diesel engine.

Collecting Notes: Model UC tractors are not extremely difficult to obtain for a moderate price. Most parts are the same as the more popular Model U and therefore are not difficult to obtain for restoration. Expect to pay about 40 percent more for a Continental engine version. Add a star to the collectibility rating for serial numbers 1 to 31; these tractors have several differences from later production models.

The streamlined version of the Model UC was introduced in 1937 beginning with serial number 2819. Note the shortened fenders and the arched hood panels forward of the gas tank. The rear tire size was increased from 11.25x24 inches to 11.25x28 inches. Rear steel wheels were increased from 42x2 inches to 45x2 inches. Five-bolt front wheels replaced six-bolt wheels at serial number 4337 in 1938.

Model UC Tractor Specifications

	With Continental Engine	With Allis-Chalmers Engine
Years built	1930–1933	1933–1953
Serial numbers	1–1268	1269–6217
Horsepower (drawbar/belt)	24.98/36.09	28.85/34.09
Cylinders	4	4
Engine bore and stroke (inches)	4.25x5	4.375x5.0 (4.5x5.0 in 1936 and up)
Engine rpm	1,200	1,200
Speeds (forward, mph)	2.33, 3.33, 5.0, 10.75	2.66, 3.50, 4.75, 11.50
Speed (reverse, mph)	2.7	3.0
Weight (no added ballast, pounds)	4,915 (steel)	6,115 (rubber)
Length (inches)	125.125	125.125
Rear tread (inches)	69–80	69–80
Height (inches)	67.625	66.375
Rear wheel (steel, inches)	42x2	42x2 (45x2 in 1937 and up)
Rear tire (optional, inches)	11.25x24	11.25x24 (11.25x28 in 1937 and up)
Front wheel (steel, inches)	24x5	24x5
Front tire (optional, inches)	6.5x16	6.5x16
Belt pulley (inches, dia. x w.)	10x7.5	10x7.5
Fuel capacity (gallons)	23	24
Cooling capacity (gallons)	5	6
Ignition (magneto)	Eisemann G4	Bendix C4 or Fairbanks Morse
Carburetor	Schebler HD	Zenith K5
Suggested new retail price	$925 in 1933 (steel)	$1,150 in 1934 (rubber tires)

Model All-Crop and UC Tractor Production History

Serial number is found on the rear of the differential housing with prefix "UC."

Year	Serial Numbers
1930	1–38
1931	39–1099
1932	1100–1231
1933	1232–1293
1934	1294–1551
1935	1552–2000
1936	2001–2770
1937	2771–3756
1938	3757–4546
1939	4547–4769
1940	4770–4971
1941	4972–5037
1942	none built
1943	none built
1944 (cane only)	5038–5067
1945	none built
1946	none built
1947 (cane only)	5068–5267
1948 (cane only)	5268–5525
1949 (cane only)	5526–5643
1950 (cane only)	5644–5805
1951 (cane only)	5806–5938
1952 (cane only)	5939–6142
1953 (cane only)	6143–6217

Model UC Tractor Progression History

Year	Serial Number	Modification
1930	1	First Model UC built
1930	32	Fourth gear disabled on steel-wheel models; rear steel wheel style changed; steering assembly changed
1931	217	Tractor tested at Nebraska (test no. 189), Continental engine
1933	1269	Allis-Chalmers UM engine replaces Continental engine
1935	1704	Tractor tested at Nebraska (test no. 238), A-C engine
1936	2282	Engine bore increased
1937	2819	Tractor restyled; rear wheel size increased (steel and rubber)
1938	4337	Five-bolt front wheels replace six-bolt wheels
1944	5038	All UC models after this point are cane type
1953	6217	Last UC tractor built

Model Allis-Chalmers Rumely DoAll Tractor

The DoAll was like no other machine on the market. The convertible version could be transformed from a four-wheel tractor to a front-wheel-drive cultivating tractor with high clearance and fantastic visibility. By removing the front axles, rotating the final-drive units downward, and adding a sulky wheel attachment, this cultivating version could ride between the crop rows handily with minimal crop damage. With a 32-inch crop clearance, this cultivating marvel could work in rows from 20 to 42 inches in width. A nonconvertible unit was also available with either a wide- or narrow-front axle. This version had a 46-inch rear tread and full-sized rear fenders. For cultivating, the narrow-front-axle version could use a pipe gang cultivator attachment without all the fussing as with the convertible unit.

J. S. Clapper, president of Toro Company, had been the sales manager for the Gas Traction Company in Minneapolis. After the Emerson-Brantingham Company bought the Gas Traction Company in 1912, Clapper founded the Toro Manufacturing Company two years later to build engines for the fast-selling Bull Tractors. The founders of the Gas Traction Company, D. M. Hartsough and Patrick Lyons also initiated the Bull Tractor Company. When the Bull Tractor venture began to crumble, Toro began to build tractors.

The Rumely DoAll was offered in three styles: convertible, narrow-front axle and standard (shown). The standard and narrow-front axle versions were sold with full rear fenders and with a fixed 46-inch rear tread.

Advance-Rumely was struggling with sales of the "dinosaur" tractors during the late 1920s. These huge tractors had sold well to custom operators in earlier years, but small tractors were now filling the market. Rumely knew it would have to adapt to the market to survive and clamored to offer two smaller tractors just before it was forced to merge operations with Allis-Chalmers in 1931.

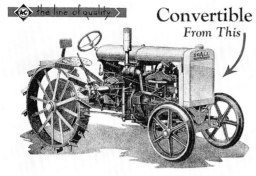

Convertible
From This

To This

A Tractor for Every Farm Power Job!

New!

Modern

Model GV-4

The DoAll used the Eisemann GV-4, one of the finest magnetos in the industry. An unreliable ignition would give a tractor a horrible reputation in a big hurry. Rumely and Allis-Chalmers were keen to this problem, and both companies always used top-of-the-line ignitions.

The convertible DoAll was changed from a standard four-wheeled tractor to the cultivator tractor by rotating the final-drive housings forward, removing the front wheel, bolting on the castor wheel assembly, and extending the operator controls. This clever invention was purchased from the Toro Manufacturing Company in 1927 by Rumely to offer farmers a versatile tractor for various applications. DoAll sales were never too outstanding; only 3,193 units were built, including the last batch assembled by Allis-Chalmers' employees in 1931.

The final-drive assemblies on the convertible version of the Rumely DoAll were rotated from the axle tube for the two different wheel configurations. With the center of the bull gear at about the eight o'clock position in relation to the drive pinion as shown, the tractor was set for the standard-tread jobs. By rotating the bull gear center directly below the pinion gear, the drive wheels were set for the cultivating version.

Toro's Combination tractor was selling fast in the early 1920s and caught the eye of Advance-Rumely, which desperately needed smaller tractors to keep up with the changing market. On October 10, 1927, Advance-Rumely bought the rights to the Combination tractor. With a few changes, the Rumely DoAll was introduced on April 13, 1928. Three years later on June 1, 1931, Advance-Rumely was taken over by Allis-Chalmers.

Allis-Chalmers apparently had no intentions to continue the production of the DoAll when it took over the Advance-Rumely Company operations. Remaining inventories of parts were used up as Allis-Chalmers employees built the last batch of DoAll and Rumely Six tractors. The remaining stock of DoAll tractors was advertised until at least 1933 even though production ended in 1931. Selling for only $543 in 1931, the DoAll still received a poor consumer's reception.

The Waukesha four-cylinder L-head engine powered the DoAll through only two forward speeds of 2.65 and 3.75 mph. A Twin Disc–brand hand-clutch could deftly feed power to the French and Hecht–brand 42x7-inch steel drive wheels. Independent differential brakes helped to make tight turns.

A 538-rpm PTO assembly and a 10-inch diameter belt pulley attachment were available as options. The 24 standard 2 1/2-inch spade lugs on each drive wheel could be replaced or mixed with optional angle-iron cleats.

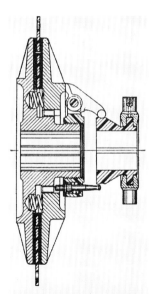

A popular Twin Disc clutch used in tractors and combines. A driving plate of tempered steel, true on both sides, bolts firmly to engine flywheel. The dark lines on both sides of driving plate show the large contact areas. Lock pin and threaded yoke for adjustment, and the simple method of applying clamping pressure are clearly shown.

The Twin Disc–brand clutch was perhaps the most durable and smoothest operating clutch available. The DoAll used this clutch with a hand-operated lever to shift among its one reverse and two forward gears.

The paint color of the DoAll was most likely Rumely Blue with red letters before Allis-Chalmers acquired the company and painted it dark green with red letters on later versions. Rumely used a dark green for many years, but used a blue paint with a gray tint on some of its final tractors, which probably included the DoAll.

Collecting Notes: The DoAll tractors have appeal to many dedicated Rumely tractor collectors as well as certain Allis-Chalmers tractor collectors. Complete units are usually fairly expensive. Parts for restorations are difficult to obtain, so expect to do a lot of investigating to locate them.

Model Allis-Chalmers Rumely DoAll Tractor Specifications

Years built	1928–1931
Serial numbers	501–3693
Horsepower (drawbar/belt)	16.32/21.61
Cylinders	4
Engine bore and stroke (inches)	3.5x4.5
Engine rpm	1,400
Speeds (forward, mph)	2.625, 3.75
Speed (reverse, mph)	2.875
Weight (pounds)	3,702
Length (inches)	108 (four-wheel version)
Rear tread (convertible, inches)	60, 66, or 75
Rear tread (nonconvertible, inches)	46
Height (to radiator top, inches)	59.25
Drive wheel (steel, inches)	42x7
Front wheel (steel, inches)	26x5
Belt pulley (inches, dia. x w.)	10x5.5
Fuel capacity (gallons)	15
Cooling capacity (gallons)	5.5
Ignition (magneto)	Eisemann GV4
Carburetor	Stromberg MI or Zenith
Suggested new retail price	$543 in 1931

Model Allis-Chalmers Rumely DoAll Tractor Production History

Serial number found on dash plate.

Year	Serial Numbers
1928	501–700
1929	701–2115
1930	2116–3513
1931	3514–3693

Model Allis-Chalmers Rumely 6A Tractor

The Rumely 6A and DoAll were advertised heavily by the Advance-Rumely Company with optimistic expectations that its financial woes would be relieved. Disappointing sales and $8 million in accounts receivable forced Rumely into a corner. Allis-Chalmers took over the company and was left to muster this last batch of tractors from the parts inventory of the two models and phase them out. The similar-sized Allis-Chalmers Model U and 25-40 left no real purpose to keep the Rumely 6A in production. The remaining 6A models were assembled by Allis-Chalmers in 1931 and were advertised until at least 1935 before the last one was sold.

A special six-cylinder L-head engine in the Model 6A was built by Waukesha to Advance-Rumely's specifications. Advertising boldly boasted that the tractor had six forward speeds. This model actually had only a three-speed sliding-gear transmission, but it had a governor with two rated engine speeds of 1,200 and 1,365 rpm. This gasoline-burning tractor was proudly rated at a four-plow capacity. Stopping the tractor was accomplished with a single transmission foot brake.

A removable belt pulley came as standard equipment and had a brake. Each 48x12-inch rear steel wheel came standard with 28 spade lugs that were 4.75 inches long. Front- and rear-wheel extensions plus rear-wheel scrapers were offered. Special heavy-duty rear wheels were optional using 32 lugs each. In 1934, one could purchase the tractor with 12.75x28-inch rear and 7.5x18-inch front tires all on special wheels with round spokes for the extra cost of $295 added to the base price of $1,100. Angle-iron cleats for the rear steel wheels and wheel weights for the models with tires were offered at extra cost. For industrial work, 50x10-inch rear and 29x5-inch front solid-rubber tires were available with or without rear extensions. A front hitch and road bands could be bought for threshing crews and the like. The front hitch could accurately position heavy threshing machines and the road bands would prevent one from being fined for mutilating the roads with the wheel lugs. Electric starting with a generator and lights were factory-installed features offered for an extra $100. A 785- and 892-rpm PTO assembly was an add-on feature.

Collectors usually paint the Model 6A a dark green with red letters. Double red pinstripes adorn each fender as well as a large pair of decals that are shaped like a diamond and have the model name on them.

Collecting Notes: Demand for the Rumely 6A is quite high because Rumely tractor collectors are attracted to this low-production tractor perhaps more than most Allis-Chalmers tractor collectors. Expect to pay a healthy price for a complete unit. Parts for restoration are a challenge to obtain.

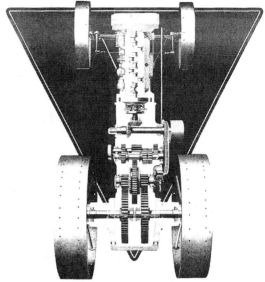

a 4·PLOW at the Weight of a 3

Sectional top view of new Rumely "Six," showing its rugged construction and extreme simplicity of design

The straight-cut gears of the transmission on the Rumely Six gave the tractor its three forward gears. With two governor settings, the tractor was touted as a six-speed. Massey-Harris used a similar sales strategy on its Twin-Power Pacemaker and Challenger models a few years after the Rumely Six production ended. It was perhaps a little less than honest for the Rumely Six to be called anything more than a three-speed.

The Rumely Model 6A, also referred to as the Model Six was advertised as having six forward speeds. The tractor actually had a three-speed transmission, but had two different governor settings that allowed engine-operating speeds of 1,200 and 1,365 rpm.

The Rumely Six had almost the same horsepower rating as Allis-Chalmers' 25-40 model, and the company had no need for this powerful tractor after the acquisition of Advance-Rumely in 1931. Allis-Chalmers advertised the Rumely Six until at least 1935 even though the last tractor was most likely assembled in 1931.

Allis-Chalmers Rumely 6A Tractor Specifications

Years built	**1930 and 1931**
Serial numbers	501–1302
Horsepower (drawbar/belt)	33.57/48.37
Cylinders	6
Engine bore and stroke (inches)	4.25x4.75
Engine rpm	1,200 and 1,365
Speeds (forward, mph)	2.82, 3.66, 4.72
Speed (reverse, mph)	3.44
Weight (no added ballast, pounds)	6,370
Length (inches)	163
Rear width (inches)	70
Height (overall, inches)	74
Rear wheel (steel, inches)	48x12
Front wheel (steel, inches)	30x6
Belt pulley (inches, dia. x w.)	13x8 (785 and 892 rpm)
Fuel capacity (gallons)	25
Cooling capacity (gallons)	9
Ignition (magneto)	American Bosch U6
Carburetor	Zenith 156
Suggested new retail price	$1,395 (rubber tires)

Allis-Chalmers Rumely 6A Tractor Production History

Serial number plate is found on the cowl.

Year	Serial Numbers
1930	501–502
1931	503–1302

An offset steering wheel and seat gave the farmer a better view as the WC straddled the rows of precious crops. The levers inside each fender are the individual hand brakes that were a hallmark of the WC during its entire production run of 16 years.

Model W All-Crop and WC Tractor

Allis-Chalmers' tractor department must have really done its homework when it came up with the Model WC. This two-plow tractor was produced with pneumatic tires as standard equipment and was powered by a short-stroke four-cylinder engine that would have seemed more fitting for an automobile at the time. Other major builders of tractors were using heavy long-stroke engines that the industry felt were needed to deliver great torque and durability. Rubber tires, before about 1939, were generally regarded as experimental or foolish by the industry; steel wheels were the rule. The new WC performed wonderfully at the Nebraska Testing Facility and with the selling price of only $825, this tractor sold faster than any other Allis-Chalmers tractor built before.

When first built, the models before serial number 29 had a Waukesha L-head engine with a 3.625x4.5-inch bore and stroke. Allis-Chalmers quickly outfitted the tractor with its own I-head engine with a 4x4-inch bore and stroke (called a square engine). First introduced as the Model W All-Crop, the tractor embraced the name WC in the first part of 1934 until production ended in 1948. The sliding-gear transmission had four forward speeds. The final-drive housings for the drive wheels boosted the rear axle up to a 26-inch crop clearance. Independent rear band hand brakes allowed a tight 8-foot turning radius. Two heavy-duty "C" channel frame rails supported the drive train components while rendering a flat mounting surface for the dozens of optional tillage tools.

In 1938, the WC took on a new look. Beginning with serial number 74330, the streamlined version sported smaller clamshell fenders, a rounded gas tank, sleek hood, and full-coverage grille. Mechanically, this newer tractor barely changed other than an electric starter, and lights became standard equipment. In 1939 at serial number 81757, the 11.25x24-inch rear tires were replaced by 11x28-inch tires.

A removable belt pulley came as standard equipment while the PTO assembly was an option. The PTO units prior to 1935 ran off the belt pulley access on the right side of the

The Model W All-Crop was introduced in 1933 and was renamed the Model WC in the first half of 1934. Sources indicate that more than 30,000 changes occurred during the production life of the WC. Allis-Chalmers had a cutting-edge engineering department that seemed averse to complacency.

The New Model "W" with Steel Wheels $675.00 f.o.b. Milwaukee

A shrewd farmer would save $150 by buying the 1933 Model W with steel wheels in place of the rubber tires. The starting crank was not removable on the dual-narrow-front version until serial number 68611 in 1938. The bold "A-C" diamond logo was not used on the radiator sides after 1935.

The wide-front axle was not a popular option on the Model WC. Besides not providing adequate crop clearance, the tread width was not adjustable to fit all crop rows. In the last two years of production, 1947 and 1948, an optional wide-front axle with adjustable tread was made available. A single, front-wheel version was available during the entire production run, but it also was unpopular in most regions of the country.

At serial number 74330, in 1938, the WC took on this new look. The streamlined design was the handiwork of Brooks Stevens, an industrial designer firm from Milwaukee. Brooks Stevens is still doing business today. An electric starter and lights were offered as a standard feature on this new version of the WC. The rear tire size was increased from 11.25x24 inches to 11x28 inches at serial number 81757 in 1939.

tractor and the later style mounted under the tractor and was powered by the transmission. International Harvester held patents on rear-mounted PTO assemblies that hampered Allis-Chalmers' capacity to use them on its early WCs. The PTO ran at a rated speed of 534 rpm. A power lift assembly could be bought for raising attached implements. For the conservative farmer, the WC could be purchased for less money with steel wheels in place of the standard rubber tires. Regular rear steel wheels were 40x6 inches, and the less-common skeleton-style tires were 40x2 inches. The front steel wheels were 24x4 inches. A wide-front axle and a single,

front-wheel configuration were both options that could be ordered for special needs. Starting in 1947, an adjustable wide-front axle became available; prior to this time, optional wide-front axles were nonadjustable. A limited number of cane or high-clearance WC tractors were built.

Model WCs were painted Persian Orange. The earliest examples apparently came without the "Allis-Chalmers" decals on the frame, but the nonstreamlined copies built in early 1934 and after used blue-letter decals that had a white rectangle border. The streamlined copies used blue-letter hood decals with no rectangle border. No "WC" decals were ever used by the factory on the sides of the grille.

Collecting Notes: The WC is one of the most collected and popular Allis-Chalmers models. Parts are easily obtained for restoration. The Waukesha engine models (serial numbers 1 to 28) are difficult to find and have several chassis parts that are not the same as later models. Add one star to the collectibility rating for a cane version and another star for WCs with all steel wheels.

Model W All-Crop and WC Tractors Specifications

	Nonstreamlined WC	Streamlined WC
Years built	1933–1938	1938–1948
Serial numbers	1–74329	74330–178202
Horsepower (drawbar/belt)	19.17/21.48	24.16/29.93
Cylinders	4	4
Engine bore and stroke (inches)	4x4 (non-Waukesha)	4x4
Engine rpm	1,300	1,300
Speeds (forward, mph)	2.5, 3.5, 4.75, 9.25	2.5, 3.5, 4.75, 9.0
Speed (reverse, mph)	2.0	2.0
Weight (no added ballast, pounds)	3,310 (rubber)	3,300 (rubber)
Length (inches)	136	136
Rear tread (inches)	65-76	65-76
Height (less stacks, inches)	63	68
Rear rubber tire (inches)	11.25x24	11x28 (after serial no. 81757)
Front rubber tire (inches)	5.25x17 or 5.5x16	5.5x16
Belt pulley (inches, dia. x w.)	9x6.5	9x6.5
Fuel capacity (gallons)	15	15
Cooling capacity (gallons)	4	4
Ignition (magneto)	Bendix or Fairbanks-Morse	Fairbanks-Morse
Carburetor	Kingston or Zenith 0-7078	Marvel-Schebler or Zenith
Suggested new retail price	$825 in 1934 (rubber tires)	$1,290 in 1947 (rubber tires)

Model W All-Crop and WC Tractors Production History

Serial number is found stamped into the rear of the differential housing with prefix "WC."

Year	Serial Numbers
1933	1–28
1934	29–3126
1935	3127–13869
1936	13870–31783
1937	31784–60789
1938	60790–75215
1939	75216–91533
1940	91534–103516
1941	103517–114533
1942	114534–123170
1943	123171–127641
1944	127642–134623
1945	134624–148090
1946	148091–152844
1947	152845–170173
1948	170174–178202*

* This is the last number on the records, but higher serial numbers exist.

Model W All-Crop and WC Tractors Progression History

Year	Serial Number	Modification
1933	1	First Model W All-Crop built
1934	29	Allis-Chalmers engine replaces Waukesha engine
1934	109	Tractor tested at Nebraska (test no. 223)
1934	not found	Model renamed WC
1934	511	Chained gas cap replaces hinged-type
1934	2045	Removable gas cap replaces chained-type
1935	not found	Optional PTO units mounted under the tractor instead of the earlier side-mount type
1935	3522	Flange-mount Fairbanks-Morse magneto replaces base-mount Bendix-Scintilla C4 magneto
1935	3665	Engine crank-pin diameter increased from 2-inch bearing size to 2 3/8-inch
1936	23529	16-inch front disc wheels replace 17-inch spoke wheels
1936	29845	Temperature gauge used in radiator top tank
1937	59628	Five-bolt front wheels for tires replace six-bolt wheels
1937	59636	Rear disc wheels for tires replace spoke wheels
1938	65623	Tractor tested at Nebraska (test no. 303)
1938	Not found	Cylinder head changed at engine no. 289000, uses different spark plug (Champion J8C replaces W10)
1938	68611	Removable starting crank used on dual-narrow-front-axle model
1938	74330	Tractor streamlined with electric starter and lights
1940	101353	Radiator shutters replace canvas radiator curtain
1944	approx. 132,000	Pressed-steel differential cover and bolt-on bull gear housing used during World War II years
1948	approx. 180,000	Last Model WC built

Seldom found with steel wheels, the nonstreamlined WF is a collector's treasure.

Model WF Tractor

When introduced in 1937, the Model WF looked like a little brother to the Model U. The fact was that the WF was a standard-tread version of the popular Model WC. John Deere, Case, International, and Allis-Chalmers, all the big names in tractors were producing a standard-tread version from its most popular row-crop tractors. It was generally understood that these standard-tread models would only sell in limited numbers, but because only a small number of special parts were needed to build these versions, profits could still be realized. With a lower stance than its row-crop counterpart, the standard-tread tractors were easily converted into orchard tractors, as were a limited number of WF models.

The final-drive bull gears for the rear wheels on the WF were placed forward of the drive pinions, unlike the WC, which had the bull gears mounted directly below the pinions. This forward placement of the bull gears lowered the height of the tractor, while at the same time shortened the wheelbase from that of the original row-crop WC. The nonadjustable wide-front axle of the WF was arched slightly for a modest 11-inch crop clearance. With the same engine and four-speed transmission as the WC, this brawny tractor was well adapted for the small-scale grain farmer.

The WF had full fenders and an exposed radiator until 1940, at serial number 1904, when the tractor was streamlined. This newer style sported clamshell rear fenders, a rounded fuel tank, sleek ribbed hood, electric starter, lights, and a full grille. The 11.25x24-inch rear tires were changed to 11x28-inch at this time. The rear wheels for the 24-inch tires were spoke-type until serial number 204, when the disc-style wheel became the replacement. The 5.5x16-inch front tires on all versions of the WF were mounted on wheels and rims manufactured by the French and Hecht Company.

As options, a 1,170-rpm belt pulley or a 534-rpm PTO could be added to the WF. Farmers who were not yet convinced of the benefits of the rubber tires were offered 40-inch rear steel wheels (regular or skeleton) and 24x4-inch front steel wheels. A low-grade fuel option would allow one to burn fuels that were less expensive than gasoline.

Model WF tractors were painted Persian Orange with blue-letter decals. The regular version of the nonstreamlined models had blue "Allis-Chalmers" decals on the frame with a white rectangle border. The orchard versions of the nonstreamlined versions had the same decals on the sides of the hood. Streamlined models used similar decals, but without the white rectangle border on the hood sides. No model designation decals were used on the grille sides.

Collecting Notes: Prices for the Model WF tractors are usually moderate. Considering the fairly low production numbers, the WF can be a great value today with prices bound to increase dramatically in a few years. Over 20 times as many row-crop WC tractors were built as the standard-tread WF. Most parts are shared by the popular Model WC and therefore are easily obtained. Add one star to the collectibility rating for a Model WF with all four steel wheels.

Model WF Tractor Specifications

	Nonstreamlined WF	Streamlined WF
Years built	1937–1940	1940–1951
Serial numbers	4–1903	1904–8353
Horsepower (drawbar/belt)	20.41/25.45	24.16/29.93
Cylinders	4	4
Engine bore and stroke (inches)	4x4	4x4
Engine rpm	1,300	1,300
Speeds (forward, mph)	2.67, 3.75, 5.0, 9.75	2.67, 3.75, 5.0, 9.75
Speed (reverse, mph)	2.25	2.25
Weight (rubber, pounds)	3,490	3,490
Length (inches)	122	122
Rear tread (inches)	46–57	46–57
Height (to top of hood, inches)	54.5	55
Rear rubber tire (inches)	11.25x24	11x28
Front rubber tire (inches)	5.5x16	5.5x16
Belt pulley (inches, dia. x w.)	9x6.5	9x6.5
Fuel capacity (gallons)	15	15
Cooling capacity (gallons)	4	4
Ignition (magneto)	Fairbanks-Morse FMJ4B3(A)	Fairbanks-Morse FM4B
Carburetor	Zenith 124.5	Zenith 161X7
Suggested new retail price	$1,340 in 1951	

Model WF Tractor Production History

Serial number is found stamped into the rear of the differential housing with the prefix "WF."

Year	Serial Numbers
1937	4–388
1938	389–1335
1939	1336–1891
1940	1892–2299
1941	2300–2703
1942	2704–3003
1943	none built
1944	3004–3194
1945	3195–3509
1946	3510–3747
1947	3748–4110
1948	4111–5499
1949	5500–7317
1950	7318–8315
1951	8316–8353

Model WF Tractor Progression History

Year	Serial Number	Modification
1937	4	First Model WF built
1937	204	Disc-style rear wheels for tires replace spoke wheels
1940	1904	Tractor streamlined, electric starter and lights added
1941	2304	Radiator shutters replace canvas curtain on models with manual temperature control
1951	8353	Last Model WF built

Speed Ace or Model TW Tractor

Only 87 of these big trailer-lugging tractors were made. Allis-Chalmers basically put wheels under its Model K crawler tractor and added a fifth-wheel trailer for hauling dirt. With its 7.5-yard bottom-dump trailer, this outfit weighed about 19,000 pounds.

The powerful 563-cubic inch engine was coupled to a four-speed transmission that allowed speeds from 4 to 16 mph. Steering clutches made a 24-foot turning radius possible; 18x24-inch rear and 9.0x24-inch front tires gave this tractor good clearance and traction.

Leveling land was accomplished efficiently by removing dirt from the hills and trucking it to the low areas. Bulldozers had to push the dirt and were slow in leveling vast areas. The Allis-Chalmers crawlers made in the late 1930s had top speeds just over 6 miles per hour. The Speed Ace trailer could be loaded with 7 1/2 yards of dirt and would move at speeds up to 16 miles per hour. The bottom of the trailer had two hydraulic doors that would open and dump the dirt at the desired location. Contractors could level a spot for a housing development, factory, or highway in much less time by toting the dirt rather than trying to push it with bulldozers. Self-loading scraper units did not have to rely on getting filled by a track loader like the Speed Ace. Saving the expense of an extra machine and operator on a site made the scrapers a favorite with contractors while the Speed Ace quietly disappeared from the market.

Allis-Chalmers sold towed scrapers that were built by Gar Wood and LaPlant-Choate for several years. In 1952, A-C bought out LaPlant-Choate, which put them into the motor scraper business in a big way. The Model TW Speed Ace was a large steppingstone in the Allis-Chalmers' earthmover line. The Speed Ace was not a commercial success, but rather a quality machine that did its intended job well. The idea of building a rubber-tired tractor with an extra-heavy-duty makeup to move soil faster than crawlers became the basis for the later motor scrapers. If the Speed Ace was equipped with a fifth-wheel-towed scraper instead of a wagon, it may have sold hundreds of copies instead of only 87.

Collecting Notes: This tractor is rare and seldom found for sale. Most surviving tractors no longer have the fifth-wheel trailer accompanying them. Expect to pay quite dearly for a TW if the seller understands what he or she has for sale. Many parts are shared with the Model K crawler and therefore are not difficult to obtain for restoration. Certain parts that are exclusive only to the Speed Ace may be nearly impossible to find and may need to be fabricated.

Speed Ace or Model TW Tractor Specifications

Years built	1935–1937
Serial numbers	1–87
Horsepower (engine, approx.)	70
Cylinders	4
Engine bore and stroke (inches)	5.25x6.5
Engine rpm	1,050
Speeds (forward, mph, approx.)	4, 6.75, 8.5, 16
Speed (reverse, mph)	5
Weight (includes trailer, pounds)	19,000
Rear rubber tire (inches)	18.00x24
Front rubber tire (inches)	9.0x24
Fuel capacity (gallons)	34
Cooling capacity (gallons)	10
Ignition (magneto)	Fairbanks-Morse
Carburetor	Zenith

With black wheel centers and Persian Orange rear rims, the Model A later featured Persian Orange wheel centers and black rims. The Model A is among the most valuable Allis-Chalmers tractor models. With its majestic size and low production of only 1,225 units, this model is a real standout at tractor shows.

The last 400 Model As manufactured had an improved transmission with a different shifting pattern and are even more in demand by collectors than the earlier version.

Speed Ace or Model TW Tractor Production History

Tractor serial number is found on the rib on the topside of the transmission case and on the dash. The wagon serial number is found on the right front side near the bottom.

Year	Serial Number
1935	1–10
1936	11–37
1937	38–87

Model A Tractor

Once upon a time, small children ran alongside the magnificent tractors and threshing machines as they traveled from farm to farm. The owners of the threshing rigs proudly belted the powerful tractor to the threshing machine as the farmer, family, and neighbors jubilantly labored to bring the harvest to the site. It was exhausting work, but a joyous time to finally realize a return from all their months of toil.

The powerful Model A was introduced in 1936 as a replacement for the aged 25-40. The 25-40 was the last of the grand E-series tractors that had reliably served farmers and threshing operators for 19 years. The Model A used the same basic engine as the 25-40, but offered a transmission with four speeds instead of the two on the Model E. With 51 belt horsepower and a road gear with a 9.5-mph top speed, this Model A was a dream come true for the thresherman. The predicament for Allis-Chalmers was that by 1936, the day of the thresherman was coming to a close. The combine, a machine that cut and then separated the grain while on the go, heralded the demise of threshing crews. Ironically, Allis-Chalmers was a leader in the tractor-

towed combines. Production of the Model A ended in 1942 with a total of only 1,225 copies built.

The Model A's gasoline engine had a 4.75-inch bore, but the distillate (low-grade fuel) engine had a larger 5.0-inch bore to bring about similar performance. The 13.50x28-inch rear tires could be replaced with 48x12-inch steel wheels with 5-inch spade lugs. An industrial version was offered with the steering column 9.3 inches shorter than the farm model.

The 13-inch belt pulley was standard, but the 531-rpm PTO was an added expense to the $1,495 selling price (1941). A six-volt starter and lights were offered as well as rear wheel weights.

In 1938, starting with serial number 26525, the transmission was changed to a design that used mostly Model U parts. The shifting pattern was different than before, but the speeds were not drastically effected. The front wheels were redesigned at the same time with a different wheel clamp style.

The Model A tractors were painted Persian Orange and had wheels (for tires) that were either black or orange, depending on what the company used at the time. Steel wheels were orange. Blue Allis-Chalmers hood decals were used that had a white rectangle border. An "A-C" diamond was used on the rear of the fuel tank.

Collecting Notes: The Model A is one of collectors' most desired Allis-Chalmers tractors. A determined collector should be able to find a Model A available every now and then. Prices run moderately high, but often reasonable when considering the limited production. Most parts for restoration are not too difficult to find. Many engine parts are the same as the short-fender Model E tractor, and the transmission and differential share many parts with the popular Model U tractor.

Model A Tractor Specifications

Years built	**1936–1942**
Serial numbers	25701–26925
Horsepower (drawbar/belt)	39.7/51.2
Cylinders	4
Engine bore and stroke (inches)	4.75x6.5 (gas), 5x6.5 (distillate)
Engine rpm	1,000
Speeds (forward, mph)	2.5, 3.5, 4.625, 9.5 (early)
Speed (reverse, mph)	3.0
Weight (no added ballast, pounds)	7,120
Length (inches)	138
Rear tread (inches)	62.625
Height (to top of hood, inches)	60
Rear rubber tire (inches)	13.50x28
Front rubber tire (inches)	7.50x18
Belt pulley (inches, dia. x w.)	13x8.5 (948 rpm)
Fuel capacity (gallons)	28
Cooling capacity (gallons)	11.5
Ignition (magneto)	Fairbanks-Morse or Splitdorf
Carburetor	Zenith
Suggested new retail price	$1,495 in 1941

Model A Tractor Production History

Serial number can be found on the top of the transmission near the shifting lever.

Year	Serial Numbers
1936	25701–25725
1937	25726–26304
1938	26305–26613
1939	26614–26781
1940	26782–26895
1941	26896–26914
1942	26915–26925

Model A Tractor Progression History

Year	Serial Number	Modification
1936	25701	First Model A built
1938	26525	14-inch clutch replaces 12-inch clutch
1938	26526	Transmission redesigned; front-wheel rim-clamp style change, 1.5-gallon auxiliary fuel tank replaces 1.0-gallon tank
1942	26925	Last Model A built

Chapter 5

The Streamlined Tractors

By building tractors that were affordable, durable, and practical, Allis-Chalmers sold tractors in large numbers during most of the 1930s. By introducing the Model B in 1937, A-C had a big seller for the small-farm operators. More versions based on the original Model B were offered in following years to widen the market into specialty-crop farming. The Model RC was offered in 1939 for two-row farming. This tractor used the chassis from the popular full-frame Model WC and a pepped-up engine from the little Model B. The RC was embraced by few farmers and only two years after its introduction in 1939, production ended. With a bit of ingenuity, A-C altered the wheel configuration of the Model B to handle two crop rows and called this version the Model C. This Model C introduced in 1940 soon replaced the slow-selling RC. The reception of this model was much better with more than 84,000 units sold during the 11 years of production.

A new tractor with its engine in the rear and the mounted implements in the front was offered in 1948. Now the truck or garden farmer had a tractor that was perfect for the job. This Model G filled a niche for which other tractor builders only put forward a half-hearted effort. The design of this tractor, introduced more

It was reported that Henry Ford had a couple of Allis-Chalmers Model B tractors at Fair Lane, Henry's country home. The Model B was carefully scrutinized by the entire industry as a tough little tractor that sold for less than $500 when introduced. As a mass producer of cars and tractors, it was the same kind of deal that Henry Ford loved to offer.

Collectibility

Rating	Model	Comments
★★	B (fixed wide front axle)	One-row tractor; non-adjustable wide front axle
★★½	B (adjustable wide front axle)	One-row tractor; adjustable wide front axle
★★★½	B Asparagus Special	High-clearance; 38-inch rear tires; about 500 built
★★★	B Potato Special	28-inch rear inset tires; adjustable wide front
★★★	IB	Industrial B; short and low; about 2,850 built
★★★	RC	125-cubic-inch engine on WC chassis; 5,501 built
★★	C (narrow front axle)	Two-row tractor; narrow front axle; 78,197 built
★★★★	C Cane	High-clearance version; 20 built
★★★	C (wide front axle)	Adjustable wide front axle; 5,149 built
★★★½	C (single front tire)	6x12-inch single front tire; 664 built
★★★	G	Rear engine; tube frame; 29,971 built
★★	WD	Narrow front (dual wheels); 112,358 built
★★	WD (wide front axle)	Adjustable wide front; 29,846 built
★★★	WD (single front tire)	9x10-inch single front tire; 1,074 built
★★★½	WD Cane	High-clearance version; 428 built
★★½	CA	Two-row tractor; narrow front axle; 21,410 built
★★	CA (wide front axle)	Adjustable wide front axle; 17,439 built
★★★½	CA (single front tire)	6x12-inch single front tire; 460 built
★★★½	CA Cane	High-clearance version; 190 built
★★	WD-45 (wide front axle)	Gasoline; adjustable wide front; 45,730 built
★★	WD-45 (narrow front)	Gasoline; narrow (dual) front; 36,896 built
★★★	WD-45 (single front tire)	Gasoline; 9x10-inch single front tire; 824 built
★★★★	WD-45 Cane	Gasoline; high-clearance version; only 86 built
★★★	WD-45 Diesel (wide front)	Diesel; adjustable wide front axle; 5,165 built
★★★	WD-45 Diesel (narrow front)	Diesel; narrow (dual) front axle; 1,240 built
★★★★	WD-45 Diesel (single front tire)	Diesel; 9x10-inch single front tire; 47 built
★★★★	WD-45 Diesel, Cane	Diesel; high-clearance version; only 57 built

Reliability

Rating	Model
★★★★★	B (all versions)
★★★★	RC
★★★★★	C (all versions)
★★★★½	G
★★★★½	WD (all versions)
★★★★	CA (all versions)
★★★★★	WD-45 (all versions)

Parts Availability

Rating	Model
★★★★★	B (fixed wide front axle)
★★★★½	B (adjustable wide front axle)
★★★½	B Asparagus Special
★★★½	B Potato Special
★★★½	IB
★★★	RC
★★★★★	C (narrow front axle)

Rating Model

Rating	Model
★★★½	C Cane
★★★★½	C (wide front axle)
★★★★½	C (single front tire)
★★★½	G
★★★★★	WD
★★★★½	WD (wide front axle)
★★★★	WD (single front tire)
★★★	WD Cane
★★★★	CA (dual narrow front)
★★★★	CA (wide front axle)
★★★½	CA (single front tire)
★★★	CA Cane
★★★★★	WD-45 (wide front axle)
★★★★★	WD-45 (narrow front)
★★★★½	WD-45 (single front tire)
★★★	WD-45 Cane
★★★★½	WD-45 Diesel (wide front)
★★★★½	WD-45 Diesel (narrow front)
★★★	WD-45 Diesel (single front tire)
★★★	WD-45 Diesel, Cane

The optional, adjustable wide-front axles on the Model B were offered before 1940 as these two arched styles. The axle on the left had tread adjustments of 38, 43, and 48 inches. The wider axle on the right allowed adjustments of 50, 55, and 60 inches. Each adjustment used a different length tie rod. After 1940, the optional adjustable wide front was a straight-type axle that used long spindle drops instead of an arched center to get the proper crop clearance.

Between 1947 and 1949, Allis-Chalmers shipped 2,000 Model B tractors to the United Kingdom. Tires were taxed heavily, so these units were shipped without tires and wheels to be fitted with British-made equipment. From 1950 to 1955, the Model B tractors sold in the United Kingdom were entirely British-built. As shown in this advertisement, an adjustable wide-front axle was a standard feature on the English B, also referred to as "EB."

than 50 years ago, has been imitated by other companies, even to today.

The Model WC was a huge success, but was beginning to show its age when it was replaced with the improved Model WD in 1948. This tractor looked much like the older WC, but with added horsepower, foot-operated brakes, and Power-Shift rear wheels, the WD was a welcomed improvement. The Model CA came out in 1950 to replace the Model C. Power-Shift rear wheels and a handclutch at the rear axle gave this more powerful tractor a big advantage over the Model C.

The WD-45 was the grandson of the time-tested WC. This tractor had features that farmers learned to love. With increased horsepower over that of the WD that this tractor replaced, farmers could accomplish more in a day than ever before. Other cost-saving fuel sources were utilized a short while after the WD-45's introduction, including LPG (propane) and diesel versions.

With great emphasis on a high horsepower-to-weight ratio on its tractors as well as innovative technology, Allis-Chalmers experienced high-volume sales and profits throughout the 1940s and 1950s. International Harvester, J. I. Case, and John Deere competed with Allis-Chalmers on tractor innovations that forced constant improvements on tractors.

The tractor before the 1930s, bought only to replace the horse, was now a versatile and efficient machine that farmers could no longer live without.

Model B, IB, and C Tractors

When Allis-Chalmers introduced the Model B in 1937, it seemed to be precisely what the small-acreage farmer was looking for. This smart-looking one-row tractor came standard with a three-speed transmission plus rubber tires and sold for less than $500. There most likely were some uneasy meetings in the competitors' boardrooms when the Model B began to steal the spotlight. The designers of this new Allis-Chalmers tractor changed the rules in marketing. To spend thousands of dollars on the aesthetics of an automobile was normal in 1937, but to do the same for a farm tractor was uncanny. And to believe that the conservative farmers would embrace rubber tires was unthinkable by the industry. Within two years, every major tractor producer was offering models with industrial-designed appearance and rubber tires as standard equipment. Word was that even Henry Ford himself was plowing furrows with a couple of Allis-Chalmers Bs before he introduced his famous 9N tractor in 1939. It seems that the marketing strategies of the tractor department at Allis-Chalmers were based on an exceptional feel for the market. Its boldness in straying away from the tractor industry's norm was rewarded with phenomenal success.

A Waukesha L-head engine was used to power the Model B tractors built before serial number 100. This four-cylinder engine had a 113-cubic inch displacement and was replaced by an Allis-Chalmers I-head engine with a 116-cubic inch displacement. In 1950, the bore and stroke was increased from 3.25x3.5 to 3.375x3.5 inches beginning with serial number 64501.

The IB was a compact version of the popular Model B that was sold through the construction equipment dealers. Many Allis-Chalmers collectors prize this model because only about 2,850 units were built. It's also one of the smallest farm tractors built by the company and are easy to tote around to shows.

The Model B came standard with a nonadjustable wide-front axle that was arched for added crop clearance. Before 1940, two adjustable, arched wide-front axles were optional; one with three width settings of 38, 43, and 48 inches and another with three settings of 50, 55, and 60 inches. In 1940 the optional wide-front axles were no longer arched, but straight and used a longer spindle drop to obtain similar crop clearance. The early Model B tractors had no electric starter or lights, but were offered within a few years of production on the "Deluxe" version. In 1941, at serial number 52718, foot-operated brakes replaced the hand brakes of earlier models. During World War II steel wheels were used on some of the Model Bs when rubber tires became unavailable. A 600-rpm PTO could be bought with or without a hydraulic pump assembly. This optional unit had a built-in belt pulley assembly.

An Asparagus Special, Potato Special, and industrial "IB" model were variations of the Model B that were made in limited numbers. The Asparagus Special was a high-crop tractor with a 28-inch clearance. This model had 8x38-inch rear tires and used an adjustable, arched-front axle with extended spindle drop. The Potato Special was a narrow version of the Model B with a rear tread adjustment of 36 to 56 inches. This tractor used 7x28-inch rear tires and had an adjustable, wide-front axle. The IB was a short version sold as an industrial tractor. This model had the rear wheel bull gears located forward of its drive pinion instead of below as on the farm version. The torque tube that connected the

The operator's view of the IB shows the fender-mounted battery box on the left. Just to the right of the amperage gauge is a disc-shaped foot throttle that overrides the standard quadrant setting when needed. This foot throttle was not offered on the regular B nor was the parking hand brake (not shown.)

engine to the transmission was almost 8 inches shorter than the one on the farm version. With a 2.5x1.75-inch solid steel nonadjustable wide-front axle, the IB was rugged enough to carry heavy front-mounted equipment. A rugged C-channel frame was used to mount mowers, sweepers, and other industrial implements and became a standard feature in 1946 and after. This 2x5-inch frame was bolted to the rear axle housings and surrounded the forward part of the tractor.

In 1940, Allis-Chalmers introduced the Model C. It was basically a two-row version of the single-row Model B tractor. The engine had a 3.375-inch bore instead of the 3.25-inch bore of the Model B in 1940. The Model B received the larger engine in 1943. With an adjustable 40.5- to 52.5-inch rear tread and a narrow-front axle with two front tires, the Model C was a fast-selling row-crop tractor. An optional adjustable, wide-front axle was offered as well as a single front tire and a cane version. More than 84,000 Model C tractors were built before production ended in 1950.

The IB was usually painted yellow or Persian Orange. Bernard Scott and Bill Black of Florida own this orange model as well as a yellow version.

To help in identifying the difference between the Model B and C, remember that the Model B was never made with a narrow-front axle and the Model C was never built with an arched wide-front axle. Both models were built with the adjustable wide-front axle.

All model B and C tractors were painted Persian Orange. The "C" decals sometimes found on the grille sides were never used from the factory. The "B" decal was used on models built about 1952 and after. The blue "Allis-Chalmers" decals on the hood sides were replaced by black letters apparently sometime during 1944. The book, *Original Allis-Chalmers 1933–1957* by Guy Fay and Andy Kraushaar from MBI Publishing Co. explains the original factory look of these and other models in great depth.

Collecting Notes: Regular Model B and C tractors are easy to find. Prices are often affordable when compared to other brands of the same size. Parts are easy to find. Expect to pay perhaps twice as much for special versions such as the Asparagus Special or Model C Cane. Add one star to the collectibility rating for models with all steel wheels. Add two stars for a Waukesha engine version of the Model B (serial numbers prior to 101).

Model B, IB, and C Tractor Specifications

	Model B (BE Engine)	Model B (CE Engine)	Model C
Years built	1938–1942	1943–1957	1940–1950
Serial numbers	101–61400	61504–127461	1–84030
Horsepower (drawbar/belt)	12.97/15.68	19.51/22.25	18.43/23.30
Cylinders	4	4	4
Engine bore and stroke (inches)	3.25x3.5	3.375x3.5	3.375x3.5
Engine rpm	1,400	1,500	1,500
Speeds (forward, mph)	2.5, 4.0, 7.75	2.75, 4.5, 8.0	2.5, 3.75, 7.5
Speed (reverse, mph)	2.875	3.0	2.75
Weight (no added ballast, pounds)	2,100	2,251	2,200
Length (inches)	111	110.25	110.25
Rear tread (inches)	40.5–52.5	40.5–52.5	52–80
Height (inches)	62	76.75	76.75
Rear tires (inches)	8x24	9x24	9x24
Front tires (inches)	5x15	4x15	4x15
Belt pulley (inches, dia. x w.)	8x5.5	8x5.5	8x5.5
Fuel capacity (gallons)	13	13	13
Cooling capacity (gallons)	2	2	2
Ignition (magneto)	Fairbanks-Morse	Fairbanks-Morse	Fairbanks-Morse
Carburetor	Zenith or Marvel-Schebler	Zenith or Marvel-Schebler	Zenith or Marvel-Schebler
Suggested new retail price	$518 in 1940	$1,130 in 1954	$1,180 in 1950

Model B, IB, and C Tractor Production History

Serial number is found stamped on top of the transmission by the shifter.

Year	Model B Serial Numbers	Model IB Serial Numbers	Model C Serial Numbers
1937	1–96 (Waukesha engine)		
1938	97–11799		
1939	11800–33501	31101–?	
1940	33502–49720	not found	1–111
1941	49721–56781	not found	112–12388
1942	56782–61400	not found	12389–18781
1943	64501–65501	not found	18782–23907
1944	65502–70209	not found	23908–30694
1945	70210–72264	not found	30695–36377
1946	72265–73369	1001–1002	36378–39167
1947	73370–74079 and 75080–80555	1003–1009	39168–51514
1948	80556–85833 and 87834–92294	1010–1281	51515–68280
1949	92295–102392	1282–1555	68281–80517
1950	102393–103578 and 106579–114526	1556–1878	80518–84030
1951	114527–118673	1879—2118	
1952	118674–122309	2219–2567	
1953	122310–124200	2570–2847	
1954	124201–124710	not found	
1955	124711–126496	not found	
1956	126497–127185	not found	
1957	126186–127461	not found	
1958		not found*	

With the production totals figured in, the last IB serial number should be somewhere around 3600.

Model B and IB Tractor Progression History

Year	Serial Number	Modification
1937	1	First Model B built
1938	101	Allis-Chalmers BE engine replaces Waukesha engine
1938	3712	Tractor tested at Nebraska (test no. 302)
1938	4381	Welded-steel clutch pedal replaced by a cast pedal
1939	31101	First IB built
1940	43301	Shutters replace canvas curtain on models with manual heat control
1940	not found	Optional arched adjustable wide-front axle replaced by a straight type
1941	52718	Foot-operated brakes replace hand brakes
1943	64501	CE engine replaces BE engine (bigger bore)
1946	IB1001	IB tractor starts its own serial number sequence
1947	73430	1947 tractor tested at Nebraska during 1950 (test no. 439)
1953	123996	Distributor ignition replaces magneto as standard equipment
1957	127461	Last Model B built

Highway mowers and street brooms were two of the more popular options on the Model IB. An optional gear-type hydraulic pump bolted to the front bumper frame and was driven by the front of the crankshaft. This high-capacity pump could operate hydraulic motors such as on the Anderson highway mower. Unlike the small pump available on the regular B, it was live hydraulics.

Model IB with Broom   Model IB with Mower

Model C Tractor Progression History

Year	Serial Number	Modification
1940	1	First Model C built
1940	78	Tractor tested at Nebraska (test no. 363)
1941	5756	Foot-operated brakes replace hand brakes
1950	84030	Last Model C built

For two crop rows, the Allis-Chalmers Model C had a wider rear tread than its predecessor, the one-row Model B. All Model Bs have a wide front with either an adjustable or nonadjustable front tread. Model C tractors usually came with this narrow-front version, but a single-front wheel design or an adjustable wide-front axle were optional. The Model C tractors were never made with the arched-front axle and it never had the model designation on the sides of the grille. Collectors often still use a model designation decal to help distinguish its tractor from other similar models. As authentic restorations are becoming more popular as the hobby advances, collectors will seldom use the after-market decals in the future.

Model RC Tractor

The RC was designed to fill a gap. This gap was the difference in size from the small one-plow B and the big two-plow WC. With little retooling, Allis-Chalmers installed the same engine that it was using in the little Model B, but with a little bigger bore in the WC chassis. The differential gear ratio of the RC was lowered from that of the WC to adapt to the lower horsepower and higher rpm. The large line of mounted implements for the popular WC would fit on this new RC without Allis-Chalmers having to manufacture a whole special line. This tractor was capable of pulling two 14-inch plows in average soil conditions. The RC was only built for three years and was replaced by the better-selling Model C.

The RC came with a 1,350-rpm belt pulley, rear fenders, and a platform. When bought with rubber tires, the tractor came with a nice seat cushion. Liquid ballast came in

the rear tires for added weight, and for extra cost 150-pound weights could be added to each of the wheel centers. The 10x28-inch rear tires could be replaced with optional 40x6-inch steel wheels and the 4.75x15-inch front tires could be replaced with 24x4-inch steel wheels. Skeleton rear steel wheels and offset rear steel wheels were offered for special conditions. The offset wheels would allow an expansive rear tread adjustment range of 57.125 to 83.375 inches. A 532-rpm PTO assembly could be added if needed. A buyer could have ordered a low-grade fuel engine to replace the standard gasoline-only engine. Apparently the RC was never offered with the wide-front axle.

The RC tractors were painted Persian Orange with orange wheel centers and black rims. No model identification decals were used on the grille sides. The "Allis-Chalmers" decals on the hood sides originally were blue.

Collecting Notes: Demand among collectors for the RC is quite high. Finding one of these models in nice shape is a real treat. Most parts for restoration are generally easy to find. Differentials have sometimes been robbed for WC tractor pulling competition and are difficult to obtain.

The RC was built from the popular Model WC chassis to fill a niche in the tractor market for an intermediate-sized two-row machine. The differential gear ratio was lowered from that of the WC to accommodate the smaller engine. The BE engine found in the pre-1943 Model B tractor was bored out a bit bigger and the governor altered to bring the rpm up to 1,500 to make this more powerful CE engine. This improved engine for the RC was placed in the Model C tractors that followed and the Model Bs built from 1943 and beyond.

Sales of the Model RC were not sensational. This two-row tractor was a bit less money than the popular WC, but was considered underpowered by most farmers. Only 5,501 RCs were built. Because this model had few setup costs, it is doubtful that Allis-Chalmers took a financial beating on this tractor.

Allis-Chalmers advertised the Model RC heavily. With less than exciting sales, this model was abandoned during 1941 in favor of a reworked version of the Model B called the Model C.

Model RC Tractor Specifications

Years built	1939–1941
Serial numbers	4–5504
Horsepower (drawbar/belt)	15.25/18.21 (distillate)
Engine	Allis-Chalmers 125.3-cubic inch
Cylinders	Four, vertical, I-head
Engine bore and stroke (inches)	3.375x3.50
Engine rpm	1,500
Speeds (forward, mph)	2.0, 2.8, 3.75, 7.5
Speed (reverse, mph)	1.75
Weight (no added ballast, pounds)	4,005
Length (inches)	136
Rear tread (inches)	65 and 76
Height (to top of steering wheel, inches)	68
Rear tire (inches)	10x28
Front tire (inches)	4.75x15
Belt pulley (inches, dia. x w.)	8x5.5 (1,350 rpm)
Fuel capacity (gallons)	12
Cooling capacity (gallons)	2
Ignition (magneto)	Fairbanks-Morse
Carburetor	Zenith 161J7
Suggested new retail price	$785 in 1940 (rubber tires)

Model RC Tractor Production History

Serial number is found stamped into the rear of the differential housing.

Year	Serial Numbers
1939	4–4391
1940	4392–5416
1941	5417–5504

Model G Tractor

What an unusual contraption the Model G appeared to be when it was introduced in 1948. The designers at Allis-Chalmers installed a pint-size 62-cubic inch Continental engine behind the seat. With just a dual tubular-steel front frame to support the adjustable wide-front axle, little obstructed the view of the operator as he deftly worked the crop rows. Many garden and truck farmers loved this little 10-horsepower sensation.

The Gadsden, Alabama, factory built the Model G; it typically built mowers and such. The West Allis factory built all the other wheeled farm tractors.

The 6x30-inch rear tires came as standard equipment, but dual-wheel extensions could be purchased for wet conditions. The $934 purchase price in 1953 included an electric starter and lighting equipment. An optional hand lift or hydraulic lift was usually purchased for mounted implement operation. A master tool carrier and a rear furrowing bar could be added for mounting the line of mounted implements offered. A 1,950-rpm belt pulley could be added, but no PTO was offered.

The unobstructed view of the operator makes this tractor a favorite among farmers even today. The hand-lift lever was used to raise belly-mounted implements; a hydraulic lift system was offered at extra cost.

The regular three-speed transmission could get an optional 1.6-mph "slow gear" that was an addition and not a replacement for the existing gears. This slow gear was valuable for cultivating tenderly between the crops with minimal loss of yield.

The attachments for the Model G were abundant. Besides the popular cultivators, Allis-Chalmers offered a 5-foot sickle-bar mower with a choice of five different guard styles. A one-row bedder, gear-type fertilizers, planters (one- or two-row), plows (moldboard or disc), and seeders (three- or five-row) were sold to farmers to fit their special needs. This tractor design introduced in 1948 was revolutionary and was imitated by other tractor builders in later years. John Blue Company, Hefty Tractor Company, and GBT Industries Incorporated were three companies during the 1970s that offered tractors that strongly resembled the Allis-Chalmers G. In 1982, Allis-Chalmers sold a Model GII in Canada through their Simplicity branch. The GII was powered by either a 16-horsepower Kohler engine, or one of two more Lombardini diesels. This tractor looks like the original Model G because of the round-tube frame. The attachment that the owners feel for these machines can be strong, because they are so handy and agile. At tractor shows, the Model G will get much attention, especially among people who haven't seen one before.

The Model Gs were painted Persian Orange with black "Allis-Chalmers" decals. The wheels were orange and most had silver rims. Apparently, the factory never used model designation decals on these tractors.

Collecting Notes: The Model G tractors are prized by their owners for their unique structure and small size. Ease of hauling these 3/4-ton tractors and the tremendous interest drawn to its unusual design, create a strong collector's demand. Expect to pay a premium when buying a Model G, especially when many modern-day truck farmers are reluctant to part with them. The demand for the hydraulic lift and the front weight is high, making these options somewhat hard to come by.

A 5-foot hay mower worked well on all but the thickest hay. The nimble Model G is great on fuel economy and a pleasure to drive.

Model G Tractor Specifications

Years built	**1948–1955**
Serial numbers	6–29976
Horsepower (drawbar/belt)	9.04/10.33
Engine bore and stroke (inches)	2.375x3.50 (four-cylinder)
Engine rpm	1,800
Speeds (forward, mph)	1.6, 2.25, 3.5, 7.0
Speed (reverse, mph)	2.0
Weight (no added ballast, pounds)	1,549
Length (inches)	114.50
Front and rear tread (inches)	36–64
Height (to top of steering wheel, inches)	55.69
Rear tire (inches)	6x30
Front tire (inches)	4.00x12
Belt pulley (inches, dia. x w.)	6x4 (1,950 rpm)
Fuel capacity (gallons)	5
Cooling capacity (gallons)	1.6
Ignition (magneto)	Fairbanks-Morse
Ignition (distributor)	Delco-Remy 1111708
Carburetor	Marvel-Schebler TSV-13
Suggested new retail price	$934 in 1953 (no hydraulics)

The planter was one of the nicer applications of the little G. To be able to keep a constant eye on the operation of the unit, one could feel much more confident about not missing rows with a clogged feeder or wasting precious seed by overfeeding.

Model G Tractor Production History

Serial number is found on top of the transmission by the shifter.

Year	Serial Numbers
1948	6–10960
1949	10961–23179
1950	23180–24005
1951	24006–25268
1952	25269–26496
1953	26497–28035
1954	28036–29035
1955	29036–29976

Big-time advertising exploited the new model WD when introduced in 1948. In six years of production, 146,525 units were built. A beefed-up version of the time-tested WC, this WD was destined for success.

Model WD Tractor

More than 146,000 Model WD tractors were built during its six years of production. One could hardly imagine how the improvements made to the aging WC tractor as it evolved into this new model would be so gladly received. Foot-operated brakes replaced the archaic hand brakes of the former WC. A new Traction Booster hydraulic system would allow optimum efficiency in plowing. The Power-Shift rear wheels allowed tread adjustment without jacking up the tractor or reversing the rims. The two-clutch power control would allow the PTO and hydraulics to continue running when the tractor was stopped. An rpm increase seized more horsepower from the old reliable WC engine. What a delight these features were to the farmer who was endeavoring to better himself.

The WD came standard with a 548-rpm PTO assembly and donned an electric starter and lights. The four-piston hydraulic pump delivered 3,500 pounds of pressure to the two rams on the lift system. The 10-inch dry master clutch was foot-operated, while the 7-inch transmission clutch, running in oil, was hand-operated. Ten different tread adjustments were possible within two different ranges with the Power-Shift rear wheels. A shock-absorber seat and improved steering efficiency showed that Allis-Chalmers was carefully considering the operator's comfort. The four-speed transmission was much sturdier than that of the WC that it replaced. This sliding-gear transmission was improved to a constant-mesh type in 1952 at serial number 127008.

Options such as larger 12x28-inch rear tires plus 142-pound rear or 93-pound front wheel weights were offered to increase traction. A 1,260-rpm belt pulley was offered. The narrow-front axle with dual wheels was standard, but an adjustable wide-front axle or single front tire was optional. Only 428 of the high-clearance (cane) versions were built. Special cotton picker units were mounted on 2,419 WD tractors that were run backwards with reversed operator controls.

The four-cylinder I-head engine of the WD transmitted power by means of a four-speed transmission. At serial number 127008 in 1952, the sliding-gear transmission was replaced by an improved constant-mesh design. The newer version has a curved shifting lever unlike the straight lever found on the earlier models.

The Model WD tractors were painted Persian Orange with orange wheels. The rear wheel rims were silver and the front rims were either silver or orange, depending on the year built. The hood decals were black with a long "A" and "S" until about 1950, when the decals were still black, but had letters that were all the same height. The model designation decals on the grille sides were first used about 1951.

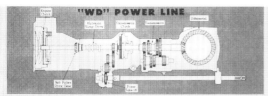

two-clutch power control system

The master clutch of the WD would interrupt power to the entire tractor, but this hand-operated clutch would stop power to the transmission while keeping the hydraulics and PTO active. This 7-inch transmission clutch had two plates and ran in oil for cooling and extended life.

The offset seat and steering gave the operator a better view of crops while cultivating. The seat has a double-acting shock absorber under it for a much smoother ride than earlier models. Fantastic sales proved the WD was a lot of tractor for the money; it sold for only $1,830 in 1953 in the dual, narrow-front version.

Collecting Notes: The availability of WD tractors is excellent. The value as a working farm unit rivals the collector value in common versions. Expect to pay a premium for a cane version or the single front wheel model. Parts for restoration of the Model WD are generally easy to acquire.

Model WD Tractor Specifications

Years built	1948–1953
Serial numbers	7–146606
Horsepower (drawbar/belt or PTO)	30.23/34.63 (gasoline)
Engine bore and stroke (inches)	4x4 (four-cylinder)
Engine rpm	1,400
Speeds (forward, mph)	2.5, 3.5, 4.75, 9.0
Speed (reverse, mph)	2.0
Weight (no added ballast, pounds)	3,388
Length (inches)	128
Rear tread (inches)	56–90
Height (to top of steering wheel, inches)	68
Rear tire (inches)	11x28
Front tire (inches)	5.5x16
Belt pulley (inches, dia. x w.)	9x6.5 (1,260 rpm)
Fuel capacity (gallons)	15
Cooling capacity (gallons)	3.5
Ignition (serial number 7–136317)	Fairbanks-Morse magneto
Ignition (serial number 136318–146606)	Delco-Remy 1111745 distributor
Carburetor	Zenith 161AX or Marvel-Schebler TSX159
Suggested new retail price	$1,830 in 1953 (narrow-front)

Model WD Tractor Production history

Serial number can be found stamped on the left rear of the axle housing or near the left brake cover.

Year	Serial Numbers
1948	7–9249
1949	9250–35444
1950	35445–72327
1951	72328–105181
1952	105182–131242
1953	131243–146606

Model WD Progression History

Year	Serial Number	Modification
1948	7	First production Model WD built
1949	10505	Convex belt pulley access cover replaces flat cover
1949	25129	Two-piece fork for single front wheel replaces one-piece
1950	48595	Tractor tested at Nebraska (test no. 440)
1952	127008	Constant-mesh transmission replaces sliding-gear type, seat mounting changed
1953	136318	Battery ignition replaces magneto
1953	146606	Last Model WD built

Model CA Tractor

It looked like the older Model C, but outstanding improvements on this new Model CA were significant. A four-speed constant-mesh transmission replaced the old three-speed sliding-gear type. Power-Shift rear wheels would allow tread adjustment within seconds using the tractor's own power. A small Lambert clutch was ingeniously placed on the right axle. With a simple pull of a lever, the tractor would stop while the PTO and hydraulics still functioned. This primitive form of a live PTO was a welcomed feature for a farmer who needed to control his harvesting equipment so that it wouldn't clog and stall. A governor change boosted the horsepower of the engine from that of the Model C with a higher rpm. The hydraulic system used a high-pressure 3,500-pound pump to raise implements with a pair of lift arms and rams. This reactive lift system could be used to constantly adjust the downward pressure on a mounted implement for ideal traction. Allis-Chalmers called this the Traction Booster. All these exciting improvements made the Model CA a popular tractor for the smaller farms. Allis-Chalmers engineers were responding quickly to the needs of the modern farmer. No longer was a tractor just a simple replacement for a horse, but an efficient precision machine aimed to allow the farmer greater earnings.

The optional adjustable, wide-front axle became almost as popular as the narrow-front with dual wheels that was a standard feature. The final-drive clutch was introduced as an option, but few CA tractors were sold without it. Allis-Chalmers was quick to learn that the conservative farming attitudes were changing. Luxuries such as electric starters, rubber tires, and spring-loaded seats had already became standard features on most tractors after World War II. Now,

The CA was a modernized version of the older Model C. The Model C was a big seller for Allis-Chalmers, but it had only three forward speeds, and without a live PTO, the C was less than ideal for operating choppers and balers. The CA had a little more power, a four-speed constant-mesh transmission, Power-Shift rear wheels, and a final-drive hand-operated clutch. This little tractor was meant for some serious farming.

The engine in this CA has evolved a great deal from its ancestor, the BE engine used in the Model B tractor of the pre–World War II days. This engine had the governor changed to spin the engine at 1,650 rpm. The BE engine ran at 1,400 rpm and with distillate fuel produced almost 10 horsepower less than this perkier gasoline engine. More horsepower was needed than ever before to operate the growing array of PTO-powered implements.

during the 1950s, many farmers would pay extra for even more added features.

Allis-Chalmers proudly offered its Snap-Coupler as an option on the CA. To be able to back up to an implement and have the hitch clasp to it, without the operator leaving the seat of the tractor was an attractive feature. A Traction Booster indicator could be added to show the operator how much hydraulic pressure was being applied to a mounted plow. For better traction, 90-pound side weights for the front and 145-pound rear wheel weights were offered. A single, front-wheel model and a high-clearance version were sold for specialized farming and were both made in low production numbers. (See star rating chart.)

The CA was painted Persian Orange and had black "Allis-Chalmers" decals on either side of the hood. The wheels were orange with silver power-adjustable rear rims. Model designation decals on the grille sides were apparently used starting in late 1951 and after.

Collecting Notes: The Model CA tractor is a wonderful tractor for the collector who is just starting out. Parts are readily available and the smaller size makes the tractor practical to use, easy to haul, and not too frustrating to restore. The versions with a wide-front axle are plentiful and resale is usually a bit easier than selling a narrow-front, dual wheel version. Be sure to test out the Lambert clutch on the right axle under load.

The four-speed constant-mesh transmission in the CA was a big improvement over the old sliding-gear units found on the Model B and C. The helical-cut gears offered more contact area on gear teeth and therefore, more strength. The lever on the right with the loop at the top will engage the belt pulley, PTO, and hydraulic pump.

These clutches are small and wear out quickly if abused. If the clutch slips, the tractor is rendered almost useless and new parts, although available, are quite costly.

Model CA Tractor Specifications

Years built	1950–1958
Serial numbers	14–39513
Horsepower (drawbar/belt or PTO)	22.97/25.96
Cylinders	4
Engine bore and stroke (inches)	3.375x3.5
Engine rpm	1,650
Speeds (forward, mph)	2.0, 3.5, 4.5, 11.25
Speed (reverse, mph)	3.5
Weight (no added ballast, pounds)	2,850
Length (inches)	124.625
Rear tread (inches)	52–80
Height (to top of muffler, inches)	76.275
Rear tire (inches)	10x24
Front tire (inches)	5.00x15
Belt pulley (inches, dia. x w.)	8x5.5
Fuel capacity (gallons)	13
Cooling capacity (gallons)	2
Ignition (prior to engine number CE149840)	Fairbanks-Morse magneto
Ignition (battery)	Delco-Remy 1111735 distributor
Carburetor	Zenith or Marvel-Schebler
Suggested new retail price	$1,540 in 1954 (wide-front)

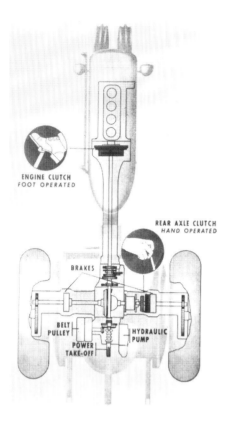

ENGINE CLUTCH
FOOT OPERATED

REAR AXLE CLUTCH
HAND OPERATED

BRAKES

BELT
PULLEY

HYDRAULIC
PUMP

POWER
TAKE-OFF

The two-clutch power was a wonderful feature on this CA tractor. The master clutch disconnected all power from the engine while the right rear axle had a dry clutch that interrupted power to the wheels while still powering the PTO and hydraulics. By allowing the differential to spin free as with a broken axle, the tractor could be slowed or stopped and still keep the PTO equipment running to catch up.

Model CA Tractor
Production History

Serial number can be found stamped on top of the transmission by the shifter.

Year	Serial Numbers
1950	14–321
1951	322–10538
1952	10539–22180
1953	22181–31423
1954	31424–32906
1955	32907–37202
1956	37203–38617
1957	38618–38976
1958	38977–39513

Model WD-45 Tractor

Most everyone who farmed in the early 1950s knew of someone who had owned a WD-45. "Overpowered," "too light," "snappy governor," and "just a good belt tractor" were some of the mumblings from critics. Whatever their opinions were, the WD-45 was a tremendous success as soon as it was introduced in 1953. Tested with more than 43 belt horsepower, this tractor sold more than 90,000 units in five years of sales. It was a major contender against the John Deere 60 and the International Super M. "More power" was what many farmers begged for in a tractor as the PTO-operated equipment was getting bigger and robbing precious horsepower. Allis-Chalmers was definitely in tune with the average farmer when it built this powerful WD-45. With basically the same frame as the older WD tractor, this new WD-45 had a new Power-Crater gas engine with a longer stroke and higher compression than the WD engine.

Besides the gasoline version, all-fuel and LPG versions were offered. The gasoline version was the most popular. All-fuel and LPG versions are quite uncommon and are of special interest to serious collectors. In 1954, a diesel model with a

The Power-Shift wheels used angled rails welded to the rims. A small clamp (shown) was set to the desired rim setting and with the rim locks loose, the tractor was driven forward or in reverse to screw the rims in or out until they stopped at the small clamp. The rim locks were then simply tightened to the rails. This design was a welcomed feature to the farmers who had to adjust wheels on splined axles with a lot of hammering resulting in banged-up rim locks and much frustration.

six-cylinder engine became available. Allis-Chalmers had purchased the Buda Company, a well-known diesel builder in 1953. It was quick to adapt a 230-cubic inch engine to the WD-45. The diesel version with a narrow-front axle cost $3,005 in 1955. The same configuration in a gasoline model cost $2,155. This option was extremely expensive and fewer than 8 percent of WD-45 buyers chose it for their farms.

Times were changing during the 1950s. More Allis-Chalmers tractor buyers chose the adjustable wide-front axle over the narrow-front. Increased horsepower was the strong demand from tractor buyers. No longer were the little one- and two-plow tractors dominating the market. John Deere replaced its Model A with the more powerful Model 60 in 1952 and International Harvester improved its popular Model M with the Super M. The WD-45 was the epitome of the WC and its descendants. Three- and four-plow tractors were in high demand and Allis-Chalmers was quick to adapt to the farmer's desires. As was historically true for Allis-Chalmers, the engineering department had some of the finest inventors and designers supported by a board that encouraged innovation. The two-clutch power control that was carried over from the model WD allowed the tractor to be stopped while the PTO and hydraulics were still enabled. The Snap-Coupler hitch that was optional on the WD became a standard feature on the WD-45 at serial number 151381 during the first year of production. The Traction Booster hydraulic draft system allowed optimum plowing performance. Power steering became available in 1956. A single, front-wheel option and high-clearance version was offered for specialty farming; even cotton-picking versions were built.

The WD-45s were painted Persian Orange with orange wheels and silver power-adjustable rear rims. The hood decals were black with letters of equal height.

Available in three fuel options, the WD-45 came with the "Big 4" conveniences shown. The engineering department at Allis-Chalmers came out with some of the most valuable features in tractor farming in its day.

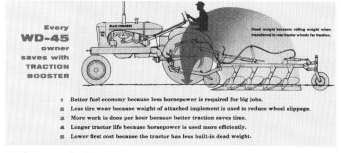

Fuel economy has been a major consideration for tractor farming from the beginning. The Traction Booster was touted to be a big fuel and time saver and with just cause. Unfavorable ground conditions could cause big problems with traction without this hydraulic system.

THE DYNAMIC NEW WD-45
POWER-CRATER ENGINE

The Power-Crater engine used in the nondiesel versions of the WD-45 tractor had pistons with a concave top. The turbulence created when the fuel mixture was drawn into this "crater" would give a more even combustion and greater power. The spark plugs were centered in the crater of the piston for optimum ignition.

Collecting Notes: The WD-45 seems to be one of the most respected Allis-Chalmers tractors built. Although the production numbers are high, the collector demand is still strong. The practical applications of the WD-45 make it a popular spare tractor on many working farms. Prices for a nice WD-45 are not usually inexpensive, but the reliability and usefulness of the tractor make it more than just a piece in a collection. The WD-45 is a wonderful tractor for a collector to own. Parts are not usually difficult to obtain, and a restored version is a handsome machine to take to shows. Be cautious of internal block cracks and secondary clutch problems that are not uncommon maladies.

The offset steering wheel and seat gave a better view of crop work under the WD-45 tractor.

Directions to adjust the Traction Booster system were printed on a transfer and placed on the right side of the battery box. The Traction Booster helped control the draft when plowing by adjusting hydraulic down-pressure as needed.

Model WD-45 Tractor Specifications

	Nondiesel	Diesel
Years built	1953–1957	1954–1957
Serial numbers	146607–236958	181341–236958
Horsepower (drawbar/belt or PTO	37.84/43.21 (gasoline)	39.50/43.29
Cylinders	4	6
Engine bore and stroke (inches)	4x4.5	3.4375x4.125
Engine rpm	1,400	1,625
Speeds (forward, mph)	2.4, 3.75, 5.0, 11.25	2.4, 3.75, 5.0, 11.25
Speed (reverse, mph)	3.25	3.25
Weight (shipping, pounds)	4,465	4,730
Length (inches)	127.1	128
Rear tread (inches)	56–90	56–90
Height (to top of muffler, inches)	81.5	88.25
Rear tire (inches)	12x28	12x28
Front tire (inches)	5.5x16	5.5x16
Belt pulley (inches, dia. x w.)	9x6.5	9x6.5
Fuel capacity (gallons)	15 (not LPG)	15
Cooling capacity (gallons)	3.5	4.25
Ignition (battery)/injector pump	Delco-Remy 1111745	Bosch PSB
Carburetor (gasoline or distillate)	Marvel-Schebler	
Carburetor (LPG)	Ensign Kg1 or Kgn1	
Suggested new retail price (narrow-front)	$2,155 in 1955	$3,005 in 1955

Model WD-45 Tractor Production History

Serial number can be found stamped on the rear face of the transmission on nondiesel models. On diesel models, the number can be found at the left brake cover or on the left rear side of the transmission housing.

Year	Serial Numbers
1953	146607–160385
1954	160386–190992
1955	190993–217991
1956	217992–230294
1957	230295–236958

Power steering became available for the WD-45 starting in 1956. The drive unit is seen here near the headlamp. For the farmer who worked all day on the tractor, it was a welcome feature. This tractor is part of Martin Wilcox's collection.

On October 1954, beginning with serial number 181341, the WD-45 diesel was introduced. The gasoline model cost $2,155 in 1955 compared to the diesel at $3,005. Only 6,509 diesel models were built compared to well over 80,000 nondiesel versions. Fuel economy was a big selling feature, but the huge initial cost frightened off many buyers.

Chapter 6

The D-Series

In 1957, Allis-Chalmers first introduced its new D-14 and soon after, the larger D-17. With a totally new look, these tractors antiquated the design of the WD-45 and CA. The tractor industry was advancing swiftly and Allis-Chalmers had a cutting-edge approach to change. No longer was the farmer expected to settle for just a plow-pulling machine. The tractor was now tailor-made to fit each type of farmer's needs. Much expense was now placed into the appearance of a tractor as the lifestyle of the farmer improved. Due to efficiency and highly improved reliability, diesel engines began to gain favor. All sorts of wheel configurations and options were offered by competent tractor manufacturers to meet the needs of the up-to-date farmer.

No longer was a three- and four-plow tractor great enough to satisfy the larger farms. Five-, six-, even seven-bottom plows were becoming more commonplace. The powerful D-19 and D-21 tractors were introduced in the early 1960s to meet this growing demand. Now, more than ever, was the time for tractor companies to expand or shut down; little room was left for the small enterprise.

From left to right are the D-10, D-12, and D-15. These models are in high demand, and collectors often pay high prices to own one. The D-10 and D-12 are similar but have different wheel spacing. The two-row D-12 had a bit wider tread range than the one-row D-10. Power-Shift rear wheels were standard equipment on the D-12 and came only as an option on the D-10. *Roger Culbert Collection*

Collectibility

Rating	Model	Comments
★★	D-14 Roll-Shift wide front	17,564 built
★★	D-14 tricycle, dual front wheels	4,662 built
★★★	D-14 single front wheel	54 built
★★★	D-14 LPG	About 750 built
★★★★	D-14 High-Clearance	6 built
★★★★	D-14 Grove	Orchard fenders and shielding

Rating	Model	Notes
★★	D-17 Series I, II, III, IV	Regular gasoline and diesel versions
★★★★	D-17 Orchard	Full citrus fenders
★★★★	D-17 Wheatland	Full width fenders; standard tread
★★★	D-10 Series I, II, III	One-row tractor
★★★★	D-10 High-Clearance	9x36-inch rear tires
★★★	D-12 Series I, II, III	Two-row tractor
★★★★	D-12 High-Clearance	9x36-inch rear tires
★★★	I-40 and I-400	Industrial versions of D-10
★★★	D-15 Series I and II	Replaced the D-14
★★★★	D-15 Series I Grove	Citrus fenders and special shielding
★★★★	D-15 Series II Grove (cage)	Cage-type orchard shielding, diesel
★★★★	D-15 High-Clearance	Roll-Shift or single front wheel
★★★	I-60 and I-600	Industrial versions of D-15
★★	D-19	Regular gasoline or diesel version
★★★★	D-19 High-Clearance	Over eight-feet tall overall; gas or diesel
★★★★	D-21 Series I	1,129 built
★★★★	D-21 Series II	2,409 built

Reliability

Rating	Model
★★★★	D-14 (all versions)
★★★★★	D-17 (all versions)
★★★★	D-10 (all versions)
★★★★	D-12 (all versions)
★★★★	I-40 and I-400
★★★★	D-15 (all versions)
★★★★	I-60 and I-600
★★★★	D-19 (all versions)
★★★★	D-21 Series I
★★★★	D-21 Series II

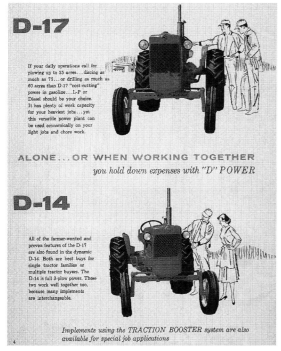

D-17

If your daily operations call for plowing up to 25 acres...discing as much as 75...or drilling as much as 60 acres then D-17 "cost-cutting" power in gasoline...L-P or Diesel should be your choice. It has plenty of work capacity for your heaviest jobs...yet this versatile power plant can be used economically on your light jobs and chore work.

ALONE...OR WHEN WORKING TOGETHER
you hold down expenses with "D" POWER

D-14

All of the farmer-wanted and proven features of the D-17 are also found in the dynamic D-14. Both are best buys for single tractor families or multiple tractor buyers. The D-14 is full 3-plow power. These two work well together too, because many implements are interchangeable.

Implements using the TRACTION BOOSTER system are also available for special job applications

Parts Availability

Rating	Model
★★★★	D-14 Roll-Shift wide front
★★★★	D-14 tricycle, dual front wheels
★★★★	D-14 single front wheel
★★★	D-14 LPG
★★★	D-14 High-Clearance
★★★	D-14 Grove
★★★★★	D-17 Series I, II, III, IV
★★★★	D-17 Orchard
★★★★	D-17 Wheatland
★★★★	D-10 Series I, II, III
★★★	D-10 High-Clearance
★★★★	D-12 Series I, II, III
★★★	D-12 High-Clearance
★★★★	I-40 and I-400
★★★★	D-15 Series I and II
★★★	D-15 Series I Grove
★★	D-15 Series II Grove (cage)
★★★	D-15 High-Clearance
★★★★	I-60 and I-600
★★★★	D-19
★★★	D-19 High-Clearance
★★★★	D-21 Series I
★★★	D-21 Series II

The new D-17 and D-14 were enthusiastically advertised through magazines and flyers. The Traction Booster system was the company's pride and joy. This hydraulic draft system eventually gave way to the more popular 3-point hitch by the 1970s.

The Power-Crater engine in the D-14 was a descendant of the engine from the older Model B. With more displacement and higher rpm, the new D-14 engine was quite a powerful unit. In less than four years, 22,286 D-14 tractors were built. Trust in the durability of the Allis-Chalmers engine and drive train was not earned without many years of proven quality and dealer support.

Model D-14 Tractor

What a sharp new tractor the D-14 was. With an entirely new look, this tractor was introduced in 1957 as a beginning step of the modernization of the entire A-C tractor line. With the advantageous Power-Director, the four-speed transmission now had two ranges for eight different forward speeds. Power-Shift rear wheels were now an Allis-Chalmers standard feature. The normal Snap-Coupler hitch could be adapted to a 3-point hitch system with an optional kit. The D-14 was a generous three-plow tractor in a tidy package.

The hood panels were easily removed to access the 149-cubic inch Power-Crater engine. Boasting more than 34 horse-power on the belt, this gasoline engine was a far cry ahead of the Allis-Chalmers' engines from the 1950s. The Power-Director could offer two speed ranges in every gear without using the master clutch. Instant change of speed was available with a simple throw to the Power-Director handle advertised as the "Big Stick." The popular Roll-Shift front axle was offered that allowed the front-axle width adjustments to be made by power from the steering assembly. Adjustments were quickly made in

the field without jacking the axle off the ground or pounding the axles into position with a sledgehammer.

Options galore were available on the new D-14. Power steering made life much easier for the farmer. With the three-point hitch, implements could be switched in a hurry without tools. It often took a couple of good men about an hour to trade certain mounted implements on the older WC and B models. Front-axle styles included the dual-narrow-front, single front wheel, and wide-front with either adjustable or fixed width settings. A high-clearance and an orchard version were offered as well as an industrial model that often had a shuttle clutch that replaced the Power-Director. The shuttle clutch would reverse the direction of all gears with a throw of a lever, a wonderful feature for the operation of a front loader. A belt pulley assembly that shifted was available as an option in the fading days of belt-operated equipment. Wheel weights helped give traction to this small three-plow tractor. Rear wheel weights were offered in 65-pound quarter sections that could be handled much easier and more safely than the traditional disc weights that often exceeded 100 pounds. To balance the tractor, 90-pound, front wheel weights could be added.

HIGH-CROP design

25" CROP CLEARANCE WITH LOW-SET DRIVE WHEELS

With Power-Shift rear wheels and a Roll-Shift front axle, the D-14 could swiftly be fitted to different row widths. This tractor had an excellent crop clearance for a machine that was less than 56 inches tall at the hood.

Coming standard with the Power-Director, the D-14 and D-17 had eight different forward speeds. The "Big Stick" would change between two different speed ranges in each of the four forward gears and the one reverse gear. The lever was used without the master clutch and by setting it in midposition, the tractor would stop as the PTO and hydraulics still functioned. International Harvester's Torque Amplifier was similar and was introduced a few years prior to the Allis-Chalmers D-14.

Exclusive power director...the "BIG STICK"

OIL TRACTION CLUTCH PROVIDES...
LIVE POWER TAKE-OFF
LIVE HYDRAULIC SYSTEM and Matched Traction
LIVE BELT PULLEY

8 SPEED CONSTANT MESH HELICAL GEAR TRANSMISSION
POWER DIRECTOR CLUTCHES
FULLY ENCLOSED HYDRAULIC SYSTEM

LIVE PTO
CLUTCH-TYPE BELT PULLEY
ENGINE CLUTCH

ENGINE CLUTCH CONTROLS ALL POWER OUTLETS

A LPG and low-octane fuel version were offered to farmers as cost-saving options that were popular in certain regions during the era. With so many versions and options, the D-14 was a big seller during its four-year life span with more than 22,000 copies sold.

The first models of the D-14 were painted Persian Orange as were the grille and wheel centers. Beginning with serial number 19001 in 1959, the appearance changed with the same Persian Orange chassis, but with a silver grille that had a black border and three horizontal black bars spaced evenly across. The early version had hood transfers that were silver and the later style had black letters on a white background. Only 5,050 units were built in the later style before the D-14 was replaced by the similar D-15 in 1960.

Collecting Notes: The D-14 is a handy tractor even on modern farms. Only in recent years has this model been considered collectible by most standards. The scarce high-clearance version is 4 1/2 inches taller than the common model and with only six factory units built, this version is destined for big dollars. The potential for value increase is great in certain later model tractors like the scarcer versions of the D-14. Most parts are not too difficult to find and the volatile market on 1950s and 1960s tractors often bring eye-opening auction results on previously ignored tractors.

Model D-14 Tractor Specifications

Years built	1957–1960
Serial numbers	1001–24050
Horsepower (drawbar/PTO, gasoline)	30.91/34.08
Horsepower (drawbar/PTO, LPG)	28.67/31.86
Cylinders	4
Engine bore and stroke (inches)	3.50x3.875
Engine rpm	1,650
Speeds (high-range, forward, mph)	2.2, 3.75, 4.75, 12.0
Speeds (low-range, forward, mph)	1.5, 2.6, 3.4, 8.5
Speeds (reverse, mph)	2.6, 3.75
Weight (shipping, pounds)	4,100
Length (inches)	129
Rear tread (inches)	54–80
Height (to top of hood, inches)	55.875
Rear tires (inches)	11x26
Front tires (inches)	5.5x16
Belt pulley (inches, dia. x w.)	9x6.5
Fuel capacity (gallons)	14.5
Cooling capacity (gallons)	2.25
Ignition (distributor)	Delco-Remy
Carburetor (gasoline or distillate)	Marvel-Schebler TSX670 or TSX701
Suggested new retail price	$2,875 in 1960 (gasoline, narrow-front)

Model D-14 Tractor Production History

Serial number is found stamped on the left front side of the torque housing.

Year	Serial Numbers
1957	1001–9399
1958	9400–14899
1959	14900–21799
1960	21800–24050

Model D-17 Tractor

Following the 1957 introduction of its nifty D-14, Allis-Chalmers introduced the bigger D-17 by the fall of the same year. The D-17 became the best-selling version of the entire D-series with 62,867 built during its 11 years of production. This total is less than 3,000 units shy of matching the totals of all of the other D-series tractors combined. As a heartier replacement for the venerable WD-45 tractor, this

The narrow hood gave the operator of the D-17 a clear view of the work ahead, while the pedals and controls were placed for operator convenience. The gauge cluster indicated engine and hydraulic functions. Notice the "Big Stick" that is partially hidden by the right side of the steering wheel. *Martin Wilcox Collection*

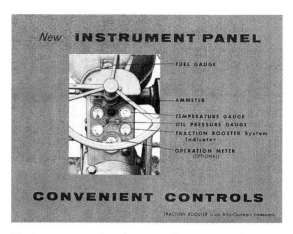

The instrument panel on the D-14 and D-17 came with up to six gauges. The convenience of having the gauges together gave the potential buyer a little more security about protecting his investment by keeping watch over many functions. Certain older Allis-Chalmers tractors often placed gauges at the front of the hood or at the base of the oil filter assembly.

This D-17 shows the large black muffler and full-length side decals that distinguish the Series III and IV from earlier versions. The Series IV shown here looks almost identical to the Series III. If you look carefully on the white transfer on the side of the fuel tank, "Series IV" is labeled.

D-17 put out in excess of 10 more drawbar horsepower than its gasoline-fueled predecessor did. Numerous versions and options became available to fill the needs of almost every phase of farming. Diesel, all-fuel, and LPG models were available as well as the more popular gasoline examples. Adjustable, wide-front axle, single-front wheel, and dual-narrow-front axle were available for the row crop tractors with the luxurious option of power steering offered. Eventually, orchard, industrial, cane, and Wheatland versions were offered. Four series of the D-17 were made. Only Series III and IV had the series designation displayed on the tractor.

The Power-Director (Big Stick) was a standard feature on agricultural models that allowed an instant speed change with a quick throw of the lever without using the clutch. The Power-Shift rear wheels and Roll-Shift front axle were standard equipment that made wheel adjustments an expeditious operation. A live PTO assembly made a farmer's life much easier for operating choppers and balers. Live hydraulics came with the introduction of the Series IV.

The Industrial D-17 came without the Snap-Coupler hitch that was a standard feature on the agricultural models. This version had a fixed-tread heavy-duty front axle and came standard with a shuttle clutch that changed the direction of the tractor in every gear. The shuttle clutch was installed in lieu of the Power-Director and could be substituted on farm versions on special order. With heavy-duty clutch and solid rear rims, the Industrial D-17 was a fine candidate to carry a front-end loader or street sweeper.

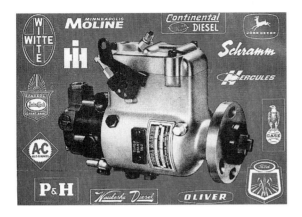

Vernon Roosa had been servicing and installing large diesel generators in New York City. The early injector pumps were "gang" types that used a separate pump for each cylinder. In 1947 Vernon introduced a single pump with a distributor head that decreased initial cost and increased reliability while simplifying servicing. Roosa-Master pumps were used extensively by Allis-Chalmers as well as most other tractor manufacturers. Diesel versions of the D-series tractors came with the Roosa-Master as standard equipment. Roosa went on to develop the pencil injector in 1963 that had similar advantages in reliability and costs as this revolutionary pump.

The orchard version was dressed in full citrus fenders and had downward exhaust. Rear tires were 16.9x26-inch instead of the 28-inch tires on the row-crop tractor. Rear rims were not Power-Shift as on most other farm versions. A grove version of the D-17 was similar, but with 18.4x26-inch rear tires and no citrus fenders.

The high-clearance (also called cane) version came with either a single-front wheel or the Roll-Shift adjustable wide-front axle. The single-front tire was 16.5x16 inches and the tires on the Roll-Shift version were 7.5x20 inches on these cane tractors. The final-drive units had an extended drop and transmitted power to the 13.6x38-inch rear tires. The rear tread was adjustable from 60 to 96 inches. The overall height of this cane tractor was 85 inches, and with the Roll-Shift axle there was a 26-inch crop clearance.

The Wheatland version was apparently built for only a brief period around 1960 to satisfy the demands of certain Midwest farmers. With huge full fenders protecting the farmer from debris being thrown by the fat 18.4x28-inch rear tires, the Wheatland was ideal for large acreage tilling. The rear rims were the standard type, and the tractor came with a heavy-duty swinging drawbar to hold up against the rigors of ceaseless plowing.

Rear wheel weights were available on the regular D-17 that were quarter sections weighing 75 pounds apiece and fit like pieces of a pie within the wheel rims. Single 90-pound weights could be added to the front wheels. The six-cylinder diesel engine cost about 20 percent more than the more popular four-cylinder gasoline version. In 1962, it cost an extra $319.50 to have a LPG fuel version over the $4,053 selling price of a gasoline version of the D-17 with a dual-narrow-front axle. A Power-Director release was available that would kick the Big Stick into neutral if one hit a large obstruction when plowing. A 1,384-rpm belt pulley could be added if needed. Power steering was an option that was becoming quite popular during the production life of the D-17.

The diesel version of the D-17 had six cylinders, unlike the four cylinders of other fuel versions. Allis-Chalmers bought out Buda Manufacturing Company of Harvey, Illinois, in November 1953. Buda was a well-known builder of engines that specialized in diesels. Allis-Chalmers quickly adapted its newly acquired diesels into its tractors and crawlers including the D-17. The WD-45 was Allis-Chalmers' first tractor to use the Buda diesel. *Martin Wilcox Collection*

Collecting Notes: As one of Allis-Chalmers most popular models, the D-17's parts are not hard to obtain. The common versions of the D-17 have a fairly high value already due to their usefulness for today's farms. The collectible values are beginning to pass the utility value on these common versions only in the last few years. Collector interest in the uncommon Wheatland, orchard, and high-clearance versions is growing in leaps and bounds. If these rare versions follow trends as in the John Deere realm, one may expect the values to multiply many times over the next several years

Model D-17 Tractor Specifications

Years built	1957–1967
Serial numbers	1001–89213
Horsepower (drawbar/PTO, gasoline)	48.64/52.70
Horsepower (drawbar/PTO, LPG)	46.23/50.79
Horsepower ratings (diesel)	46.20/51.14
Engine bore and stroke (gasoline and LPG, inches)	3.50x3.875 (four-cylinder)
Engine bore and stroke (diesel, inches)	3.563x4.375 (six-cylinder)
Engine rpm	1,650
Speeds (high-range, forward, mph)	2.6, 4.0, 5.4, 11.9
Speeds (low-range, forward, mph)	1.8, 2.9, 3.8, 8.3
Speeds (reverse, mph)	2.4, 3.4
Weight (gasoline, shipping)	5,300
Length (inches)	140
Rear tread (inches)	58–92
Height (to top of muffler, inches)	81
Rear tires (inches)	13x28 (14.9x28 after serial no. 42001)
Front tires (inches)	6.00x16
Belt pulley (optional, inches, dia. x w.)	9x6.56 (1,384 rpm)
Fuel capacity (gallons)	20.8
Cooling capacity (quarts)	14.5
Ignition (distributor)	Delco-Remy
Carburetor	Marvel-Schebler (LPG-Ensign Mg 1)
Diesel injector pump	Roosa-Master
Suggested new retail price	$4,053 in 1962 (gasoline/narrow-front)

Model D-17 Tractor Production History

Serial number is found stamped on the left front side of the torque housing.

Year	Serial Numbers
1957	1001–4299
1958	4300–16499
1959	16500–28199
1960	28200–32099
1961	32100–38069
1962	38070–43358
1963	65001–70610
1964	70611–77089
1965	77090–80532
1966	80533–86060
1967	86061–89213

Model D-17 Tractor Progression History

D-17 Series	Years	Serial Numbers	Description
Series I, first style	1957–1959	1001–23363	Persian Orange tractor, grille, and wheel centers; silver hood transfers; silver cylinder-type muffler; headlights on grille sides 22,362 built
Series I, second style	1959–1960	24001–31625	Persian Orange tractor and wheel centers; silver grille with a black border; hood transfers are white with a black border; silver cylinder-type muffler; headlights on grille sides 7,625 built
Series II	1960–1962	32001–41540	Persian Orange No. 2 tractor with cream grille and wheel centers; metal hood plate with black letters and cream background; silver cylinder-type muffler; headlights on grille sides 9,540 built
Series III	1962–1964	42001–72768	Persian Orange No. 2 tractor with cream grille and wheel centers; black oval muffler; fender-mounted headlights; Series III transfer on fuel tank sides 9,126 built
Series IV	1964–1967	75001–89213	Persian Orange No. 2 tractor with cream grille and wheel centers; black oval muffler; fender-mounted headlights; Series IV transfer on fuel tank sides 14,213 built

Model D-10, D-12, I-40, and I-400 Tractor

The day of the little tractors as primary units on the farm was coming to a close when Allis-Chalmers introduced its one-row Model D-10 and two-row Model D-12 in 1959. Farmers who had once been satisfied with a one- or two-row tractor were now looking to three- and four-row models, or even bigger. Sales of the D-10 and D-12 were never sensational.

Offered only with an adjustable wide-front axle, the regular and high-clearance tractors could be custom fit to the width of most any crop row.

The D-10 was built to replace the aging Model B while the D-12 replaced the Model CA. With many parts shared with the older Model CA, these two new models were offered without excessive retooling at the factory. The engine in the D-10s and D-12s were similar to the Model CA's 125-cubic inch version except that the stroke was increased slightly to raise the displacement to 138 cubic inches. Improvements on the two D-models came in 1961, giving an increased displacement of 149 cubic inches, the same as the earlier D-14 engine. The D-10 and D-12 each were made in three different series. The engine size increase occurred partway into the Series II production.

Options available on the D-10 and D-12 include a belt pulley assembly and a deluxe seat as well as wheel weights and even the popular Snap-Coupler or three-point hitch. The

This D-10 has the standard rear wheels. By reversing the wheel centers and also reversing the wheel rims as needed, eight different tread adjustments of 42, 46, 52, 56, 58, 62, 68, and 72 inches were possible. The Power-Shift wheels were optional and a welcomed feature for farmers who had to change tread adjustments frequently. *Roger Culbert Collection*

Fewer than 1,000 D-12 tractors were made with the early black-bar grilles. Although this style was more rare than later versions, collectors don't usually value it much higher than later versions in the same condition. As collecting expands and the production numbers are scrutinized more closely, one might expect this version to increase in value more than later models in the next several years.

The Power-Crater engine had recessed pistons as shown on the decal of this D-10 engine. The piston design increased turbulence inside the engine cylinders for a more complete combustion. More power and efficiency were derived from this innovative concept. *Roger Culbert Collection*

LIFT SHAFT for lifting and lowering mounted implements hydraulically. Available on all styles.

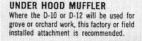

TRACTION BOOSTER System matches traction to the load hydraulically . . . automatically. For D-10 or D-12 regular tractors only.

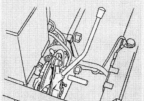

UNDER HOOD MUFFLER Where the D-10 or D-12 will be used for grove or orchard work, this factory or field installed attachment is recommended.

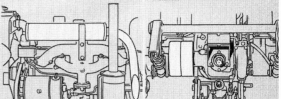

PTO AND BELT PULLEY Provides handy spray rig or similar power for all tractor styles. PTO is factory installed attachment — Belt Pulley is field installed.

Options for the D-10 and D-12 allowed farmers the convenience of belt power, PTO power, hydraulic lift, and many other features. Of course Allis-Chalmers' famous Traction Booster system could be added for automatic draft control. Provisions for use of three-point hitch implements were first offered with a special Snap-Coupler adapter, but later versions could be bought with a true three-point hitch.

The three-point hitch was offered on the D-12 as well as this D-10. This option became more popular on the Series III versions and is not as often found on a Series II tractor. Small tractors with a three-point hitch are still in demand. These days, the popularity of the D-10 and D-12 as a farm tractor is second to that of landowners with large lawns or gardens. Harry Ferguson installed his three-point hitch on thousands of Ford tractors since 1939; it still is standard on farm tractors directly. *Roger Culbert Collection*

This D-10 has the silver grille with a black border and three bands. It was the first style, built only in 1959 and 1960. Later versions had grilles and wheels that were painted a cream color. This early-style tractor was painted Persian Orange while the later versions had the redder Persian Orange No. 2 paint.

Series III version could be purchased with a two-range transmission. The D-12 came standard with Power-Shift rear wheels, but came at extra cost on the D-10. The Traction Booster hydraulic system was available on only the regular versions, but lift and lower hydraulics was a high-clearance option to power either the lift shaft or three-point hitch arms.

A high-clearance version of the D-10 and D-12 sported either 9x36- or 11.2x36-inch rear tires and 5.5x16-inch front tires. The 24.5-inch crop clearance on the D-12 was about 4 inches more than that of the regular version and the 26.25-inch clearance on the D-10 was 5.25 inches higher than the regular version. The Snap-Coupler hitch was offered for all versions of the D-10 and D-12.

Industrial versions of the D-10 and D-12 were offered through construction equipment dealers. These versions had a heavy-duty fixed-tread front axle, standard rear wheel rims, and a heavy-duty clutch. Power steering was a standard feature

as was three-point hitch and padded seat. These versions were most often painted yellow. By 1964, the grille was changed to a heavy-duty box style and the model was renamed I-40. By 1966, the model was redesignated the I-400 with little change. A shuttle clutch was a common option on the Series III industrial model and the following I-40 and I-400. A two-range transmission was offered on these models in place of the shuttle clutch, if preferred.

Collecting Notes: The D-10 and D-12 tractors are popular models among Allis-Chalmers collectors. With options such as the two-range transmission and three-point hitch, these tractors will demand some hefty prices when sold. Interest in the industrial versions, the I-40, and the I-400 tractors is limited. this author expects the values of the high-clearance versions to jump up rapidly in the ext several years. Most parts are not difficult to obtain, but finding a nice black-bar grille can be a challenge.

The D-12 High-Clearance came with 36-inch rear tires and a higher front axle design. The tractor was about 5 inches higher than the standard model for improved crop clearance. A similar version was built for the D-10. These High-Clearance models are in high demand by collectors today. Although production totals are not known, the scarcity and novelty are accepted to make these versions very, very special. Following the trend of John Deere tractors, this author expects the values of the High-Clearance models to soar in the next few years.

If stretched out, the front tread on the D-12 High-Clearance would reach more than 7 feet. Notice how the rear wheel centers are dished outward to widen the rear tread. Power-Shift rear wheels were not available on High-Clearance D-10 and D-12 tractors, but its special arrangement allowed similar rear tread adjustments as on the regular versions.

Model D-10 and D-12 Tractor Specifications

	D-10	D-12
Years built	1959–1968	1959–1968
Serial numbers	1001–10100	1001–10172
Horsepower ratings (drawbar/PTO, G138 engine)	25.73/28.51	23.56/28.56
Horsepower ratings (drawbar/PTO, G149 engine)	28.78/33.46	29.43/33.32
Cylinders	4	4
Engine bore and stroke (G138 engine, inches)	3.375x3.875	3.375x3.875
Engine bore and stroke (G149 engine, inches)	3.50x3.875	3.50x3.875
Engine rpm	1,650	1,650
Speeds (forward, mph)	2.0, 3.5, 4.5, 11.4	2.0, 3.5, 4.5, 11.4
Speed (reverse, mph)	3.5	3.5
Weight (no added ballast)	3,001	3,051
Length (inches)	121	121
Rear tread (regular version, inches)	42–72	52–79
Rear tread (high-clearance version, inches)	43–71	51.5–79.5
Height (to top of hood, inches)	52.5	52.5
Rear tires (inches)	11x24	11x24
Front tires (inches)	5.00x15	5.00x15
Belt pulley (optional, inches, dia. x w.)	8x5.5 (1,220 rpm)	8x5.5 (1,220 rpm)
Fuel capacity (gallons)	12	12
Cooling capacity (gallons)	2	2
Ignition (distributor)	Delco-Remy	Delco-Remy
Carburetor	Zenith	Zenith
Suggested new retail price	$2,659 in 1962	$2,766 in 1962

Model D-10 and D12 Tractor Production History

Serial number is found stamped on the left front side of the torque housing.

Year	D-10 Beginning Serial Number	D-12 Beginning Serial Number
1959	1001	1001
1960	1950	1950
1961	2801	3001
1962	4522	3638
1963	6801	5501
1964	7675	6012
1965	9204	9192
1966	9486	9508
1967	9795	9830
1968	9979	9979
Ending serial number	10100	10172

Model I-40 and I-400 Tractor Production History

Serial number is found stamped on the left front side of the torque housing.

Year	I-40 Beginning Serial Number	I-400 Beginning Serial Number
1964	1055	
1965	unknown	
1966	unknown	1003
1967		1281
1968		1495
Ending serial number	1608	1750

Model D-10 and D-12 Tractor Progression History

D-10 and D-12 Series	Years	Serial Numbers	Description
Series I, first type	1959–1960	D-10 1001–1950 / D-12 1001–1730	Persian Orange tractor and wheel centers; silver grille with a black borde and three horizontal stripes; cylinder-type silver muffler; headlights on grille sides; G-138 engine
Series I, second type	1960–1961	D-10 1951–3262 / D-12 1950–2800	Persian Orange No. 2 tractor; cream-colored grille and wheel centers; cylinder-type silver muffler; headlights on grille sides; G-138 engine
Series I, third type	1961–1962	D-10 3501–4500 / D-12 3001–3638	Persian Orange No. 2 tractor; cream-colored grille and wheel centers, cylinder-type silver muffler; headlights on grille sides; G-149 engine
Series II	1963–1964	D-10 6801–7850 / D-12 5501–6144	Persian Orange No. 2 tractor with cream-colored grille and wheel centers; cylinder-type silver muffler; headlights on grille sides, G-149 engine
Series III	1964–1968	D-10 9001–10100 / D-12 9001–10172	Persian Orange No. 2 tractor with cream-colored grille and wheel centers; black oval muffler; fender-mounted headlights; Series III transfer on both sides of the fuel tank support, G-149 engine

Models D-15, I-60, and I-600 Tractors

The D-15 replaced the popular D-14 in 1960. Three-plow tractors were in great demand on smaller farms. The D-15 came with the new Persian Orange No. 2 paint from the start. With a higher compression ratio and increased rpm, the 149-cubic inch engine put out more power than the same-sized engine of the older D-14. The novelty of the diesel had developed into a reliable fuel-efficient engine in high demand among most farmers. Allis-Chalmers offered a 175-cubic inch diesel engine as an alternate to the gasoline and LPG versions of the D-15. With numerous options available, a D-15 could be ordered to meet the need of most any type of farming.

Two series of the D-15 were made. A bore increase gave the Series II gasoline and LPG engines a welcomed boost of horsepower while the diesel version was left unchanged. A few improvements to the appearance of the tractor were made on the Series II. The small cylindrical silver muffler was replaced with a black oval style and the headlights that were on the grille sides were relocated to the fender tops. These aesthetic changes were similar on all the D-series of this time.

The Roll-Shift adjustable wide-front axle was the most popular type on the D-15, but a dual-narrow-front axle or single-front wheel were available. The standard-feature four-speed transmission could be bought with the Power-Director to give two speed ranges in every gear. For extra cost, one could add power steering or a belt pulley as well as front and rear wheel weights. The Traction Booster system came on the regular D-15 and a Snap-Coupler or three-point hitch were popular options, finding favor among most farmers. Power-Shift rear wheels came standard on this tractor, which gave farmers a break from having to spend so much effort on adjusting the rear tread.

For special needs, high-clearance, grove, and industrial versions were offered. The high-clearance D-15 had 28.5

This D-15 Series II gasoline engine has a displacement of 160 cubic inches. Notice the semi-frame that doesn't rely on the engine block to carry the entire front weight of the tractor. The use of hood latches made it much easier to access the engine. *Roger Culbert Collection*

The D-15 was simply a newer version of the older D-14. All D-15 farm tractors were painted Persian Orange No. 2. This D-15 is a Series I and has the smaller silver cylindrical muffler plus headlights mounted near the front of the tractor. Later Series II versions have the bigger black oval muffler and fender-mounted headlights.

inches of crop clearance riding high on 11.2x38-inch rear tires and extended chassis. The grove version came with full orchard fenders and shielding. Later versions of the grove (Series II) had full citrus fenders and a tilt-up mesh-type shield to protect the engine and operator. An industrial model was offered through construction equipment dealers with a fixed-tread wide-front axle, power steering, and a shuttle clutch (reverse direction). In 1965, the D-15 industrial was changed with a box-shaped heavy-duty grille and renamed the I-60. During 1966, the tractor was renamed again, the I-600. These I-models came with a front-mounted 15.5-

gallons-per minute hydraulic pump. The industrial 12.4x24- or 16.9x24-inch rear tires were mounted on standard-type rims.

Collecting Notes: The D-15 is an attractive tractor for a collector as well as a valuable machine for today's farming. Most parts are not difficult to obtain, but the sheet metal can be costly if in need of replacement. The cage-type grove version of the Series II is extremely rare and may likely become one of the most valuable Allis-Chalmers collectible tractors in the next few years.

The cutaway view of the D-15 shows all the wonderful features of this powerful tractor. The three-position hand-operated clutch would give 54 percent more power when thrown into low range. This secondary clutch ran in oil and gave a smooth shift from high and low ranges while allowing the operator to use the midposition to disengage the clutch for reducing speed. The hydraulic pump is seen behind the master clutch and was not interrupted when the operator used the hand-operated clutch to slow down or stop.

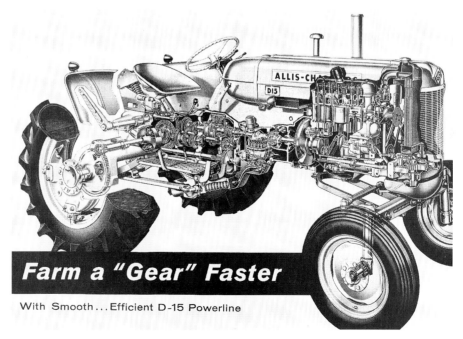

Farm a "Gear" Faster

With Smooth...Efficient D-15 Powerline

Model D-15 Tractor Specifications

	D-15 Series I	D-15 Series II
Years built	1960–1962	1963–1968
Serial numbers	1001–8169	13001–25419
Horsepower (drawbar/PTO, gasoline)	35.33/40.00	38.33/46.18
Horsepower (drawbar/PTO, diesel)	33.32/36.51	33.32/36.51
Horsepower (drawbar/PTO, LPG)	33.22/37.44	36.02/43.55
Cylinders (all engines)	4	4
Engine bore and stroke (nondiesel, inches)	3.5x3.875	3.625x3.875
Engine bore and stroke (diesel, inches)	3.5625x4.375	3.5625x4.375
Engine rpm (all engines)	2,000	2,000
Speeds (forward, high range, mph)	2.7, 4.7, 6.1, 15.3	2.7, 4.7, 6.1, 15.3
Speeds (forward, low range, mph)	1.9, 3.3, 4.3, 10.9	1.9, 3.3, 4.3, 10.9
Speeds (reverse, mph)	3.3, 4.7	3.3, 4.7
Weight (gasoline, pounds)	3,985	4,025
Length (inches)	130.19	130.19
Rear tread (inches)	54–80	54–80
Height (inches)	80.19	80.19
Rear tires (inches)	12.4x26	12.4x26
Front tires (inches)	6.00x16	6.00x16
Belt pulley (optional, inches, dia. x w.)	9x6.56 (1,384 rpm)	9x6.56 (1,384 rpm)
Fuel capacity (gasoline and diesel, gallons)	14	14
Fuel capacity (LPG, gallons, 80 percent usable volume)	15.8	15.8
Cooling capacity (quarts)	9	9
Ignition (distributor)	Delco-Remy	Delco-Remy
Carburetor (gasoline)	Marvel-Schebler	Marvel-Schebler
Carburetor (LPG)	Ensign MG 1	Ensign MG1
Diesel injector pump	Roosa-Master	Roosa-Master
Suggested new retail price (gasoline/Roll-Shift)	$3,315 in 1962	$4,180 in 1967

Model D-15 Tractor Production History

Serial number is found stamped on left front side of the torque housing.

Year	Serial Numbers
1960	1001–1899
1961	1900–6469
1962	6470—8169
1963	13001–16927
1964	16928–19680
1965	19681–21374
1966	21375–23733
1967	23734–25126
1968	25127–25419

The Power-Shift rear wheels on this D-15 worked like a giant screw. When the four small square clamp nuts were loosened, the operator would place a stop on the rail with the holes (near the valve stem) and use the tractor's power to screw the wheel in or out as needed. The operator needed to hold the brake on the opposite wheel, then place the tractor in first or reverse gear, jerk the clutch a bit, and have the clamps slide on the rails until the stop was reached. The clamps would be retightened and the tractor was ready to work. *Roger Culbert Collection*

Model D-19 Tractor

In 1961, Allis-Chalmers introduced the D-19, an all-new tractor that would meet the demands for more horse-power. The farmers of the 1960s were tilling more soil and with less manpower than ever before. The bigger farms often needed a tractor that could comfortably manage a five-bottom plow, and the new D-19 could fill that bill. This Allis-Chalmers machine was built to work and work it did. The regular model had live axles that eliminated the need for final-drive housings and gears that could fail under tremendous loads. The large cooling system held more than 4 gallons. The powerful gasoline engine would crank out more than 71 horsepower on the belt with the LPG and diesel engines not far behind. A Power-Director would give the tractor's four-speed transmission two-range control for eight different forward speeds. Power steering, lights, and a live PTO assembly were all standard features.

A turbocharger was a standard feature on the diesel-engine versions of the D-19. This turbocharger was an industry first, reinforcing Allis-Chalmers' engineering supremacy of this era. This Thompson-brand turbocharger would spin at around 80,000 rpm from the passing exhaust as it forced compressed air into the engine cylinders. The power increase was tremendous. It wouldn't be long before most tractor manufacturers would put turbochargers on their models. One could get a lot more power out of a diesel without increasing mass.

The dual-narrow-front axle could be replaced with the Roll-Shift wide-front axle with tread adjustment made using force from the power steering. A single front-wheel version was optional. Along with the regular D-19, a high-clearance model was built that used special final-drive housings and extended spindle drops on the front axle along with 20-inch front tires to give a vaulted 37-inch ground clearance. A total of 1,385 high-clearance models were built in the diesel version alone. The diesel version had an overall height of more than 8 1/2 feet. The speeds for the high-clearance D-19 were rated the same as the regular model and were available with any of the front axle styles. For wet areas, a D-19 Rice Tractor was available that was much the same as the regular model, but with 23.1x26-inch R20 (rice) rear tires and mud-shielding extensions under the fenders. The Rice Tractor was often a dealer conversion that was usually used on a D-19 with the Roll-Shift front axle with the larger 7.50x16-inch front tires. The Rice conversion kit including tires cost $583.50 in 1964; that was in addition to the $5,443 price for the wide-front regular gas tractor in the same year. A high-clearance diesel model with the wide-front cost $7,292. A kit to convert a gasoline model over to an LPG-fuel tractor would have cost $360.50.

An optional belt pulley was offered as well as Power-Shift rear wheel rims. The Snap-Coupler and three-point hitch were popular add-ons that made modern farming a reality. Rear 38-inch tires were available as were both front and rear wheel weights.

The D-19s were painted Persian Orange No. 2 with cream-colored wheels and grille. The rear wheel rims were silver.

Collecting Notes: The D-19 has not been extremely popular as a collectible. The value of the usefulness of this tractor rivals the collector value at the present. Expect to pay much more for a nice model with the three-point hitch. The Rice model is likely to become a little more valuable than the regular version; most were dealer kits with the total number of conversions unknown. I suspect that although the high-clearance versions are not extremely rare, the values for these tractors may soar in the next few years. On the more-established John Deere collectible tractors, the high-clearance models are among the most sought-after versions with some bringing more than $30,000. Don't expect the Allis-Chalmers models to get that valuable, but wait and see what happens.

Most parts are not overly difficult to obtain on any of the D-19 tractors. Check out the turbocharger and injector pump for problems on the diesel models as the rebuilds on these components can get rather costly.

The visibility due to the sleek design and the handy operator's station makes the D-19 a comfortable tractor to operate. The standard feature of power steering was a welcomed treat.

The D-19 came standard with power steering and two-range transmission. The big six-cylinder engine was available in gasoline and LPG as well as a diesel that came standard with a Thompson turbocharger. The Roll-Shift front axle was overwhelmingly more popular than the dual narrow front that probably sold at a ratio of about 10:1. Collector interest in the D-19 is perhaps the weakest of all the D-series tractors, but increased interest over the next several years can be expected.

The rugged final-drive units on the D-19 High-Clearance allowed an extended height without using specially built rear wheels or spacers. Notice that Power-Shift wheels are still used. Front tires were 20 inches instead of the 16-inch tires used on regular versions.

This diesel version of the D-19 High-Clearance is 8 1/2 feet tall. This version also came standard with the "Big Stick" and had eight forward and two reverse speeds. The speeds of this high-clearance model were the same as the regular version.

The first production tractor to have a turbocharger as a standard feature was the D-19 Diesel. The Thompson-brand turbocharger would spin at terrific speeds from the escaping exhaust as it pumped huge volumes of fresh air into the engine cylinders for increased horsepower. The power advantage of the turbocharger gave a 20 percent boost of engine power over a normal engine.

Model D-19 Tractor Specifications

Years built	1961–1964
Serial numbers	1001–16266
Horsepower (drawbar/PTO, gasoline)	63.91/71.54
Horsepower (drawbar/PTO, diesel)	62.05/66.92
Horsepower (drawbar/PTO, LPG)	58.29/66.19
Engine bore and stroke (all engines, inches)	3.625x4.375 (six-cylinder)
Engine rpm (all engines)	2,000
Speeds (forward, high range, mph)	3.0, 4.1, 6.3, 13.9
Speeds (forward, low range, mph)	1.9, 3.1, 4.7, 9.0
Speeds (reverse, mph)	2.6, 4.0
Weight (gasoline, pounds)	6,645
Wheelbase (inches)	102.375
Rear tread (Power-Shift wheels, inches)	60–88
Height (gasoline, wide-front, inches)	84.375
Rear tires (inches)	18.4x34 or 15.5x38
Front tires (inches)	6.50x16 or 7.50x16
Belt pulley (optional, inches, dia. x w.)	9x6.56 (1,678 rpm)
Fuel capacity (gasoline and diesel, gallons)	23
Cooling capacity (nondiesel, quarts)	16
Cooling capacity (diesel, quarts)	17
Ignition (distributor)	Delco-Remy
Carburetor (gasoline)	Marvel-Schebler
Carburetor (LPG)	Ensign XG
Diesel injector pump	Roosa-Master
Suggested new retail price	$5,305 in 1964 (gasoline, narrow-front)

Model D-19 Tractor Production History

Serial number is found stamped on top of the primary cast housing under the seat.

Year	Serial Numbers
1961	1001–1249
1962	1250–7331
1963	12001–14944
1964	14945–16266

Model D-21 Tractor

On July 6, 1963, the most powerful Allis-Chalmers tractor ever built up to that day came off the assembly lines of the Allis-Chalmers' West Allis plant. With a big six-cylinder diesel engine producing more than 103 PTO horsepower, the new D-21 was a magnificent seven-plow tractor. This tractor was built from scratch by the engineering department as a totally new model. By creating a heavy-duty four-speed transmission with a rugged Power-Director two-range speed control, the drive train was rugged enough to handle the most burdensome loads. Allis-Chalmers' own industrial designers developed the modern look mated with user-friendly controls and service features. An adjustable wide-front axle was the only wheel configuration offered and it was blessed with full-hydrostatic power steering. The farmer sat proudly atop the seat with all the controls within easy reach. The impressive white steering wheel could be tilted into four different positions along with the dash to suit farmers of different stature. A live PTO assembly was designed into the D-21 from the beginning.

In 1965, Allis-Chalmers added a Thompson-brand turbocharger to the already powerful D-21 tractor and added the designation Series II on the rear of the hood decals. This turbocharger added more than 24 PTO horsepower and 23 drawbar horsepower. With this improvement, the D-21 Series II was tested to have a maximum pull of 15,261 pounds. Never before had an Allis-Chalmers tractor been built to handle such big jobs and with more than a $10,000 price tag, never had an Allis-Chalmers tractor cost so much. Farmers were losing their conservative attitudes about tractors as new generations took to the fields. Big tractors were in demand, and Allis-Chalmers was there to deliver.

The regular model of the D-21 came either as a drawbar tractor (flat-back) with no lift system or as a three-point-hitch version with either category-two or category-three sway blocks. Construction equipment dealers sold an industrial version. The industrial model often came without any hydraulic lift system and was usually painted yellow. An upholstered seat and swinging drawbar were standard features.

Rear tires with sizes of 24.5x32 inches were common, but 18.4x38- and 15.5x38-inch tires could be substituted; 28.1x32-inch diamond-tread and 18.4x34-inch rice-tread tires were offered for special applications. Dual rear wheels were available in the 34- and 38-inch tire sizes. Either 450-pound rear wheel weight discs (280-pound on 32-inch wheels) or sectional six-piece weights that weighed 77 pounds each were optional. A 367-pound set of three weights was offered that bolted to the front of the tractor.

To appease the cold-weather farmers, an ether dispenser was offered. The regular D-21 came with two 12-volt batteries, but two more could be added for hard starting on cold days. A Traction Booster system and a special Traction Booster drawbar could be added at extra cost. An optional hydraulic system came with either a one- or three-spool control valve. A Deluxe upholstered seat or Super Deluxe seat with armrests were extra options to replace the contoured metal seat found on farm versions of the D-21. For dusty conditions, an extended intake for the air cleaner was offered as well as an air filter service indicator.

Collecting Notes: Parts for the D-21 are not usually a big problem to find. Finding nice chrome pieces for the grille can be an effort.

In 1963, Allis-Chalmers introduced its biggest tractor yet, the mighty D-21. With more than 100 PTO horsepower, this tractor could handle up to a seven-bottom plow! Designed new from the bottom-up, this tractor had an all-new chassis. The modern styling is evident as this tractor stands majestically in front of Martin Wilcox's barn. Martin owns seven D-21 models.

The 3500 engine in the D-21 Series II is a turbocharged version of the 3400 engine that was used in the first series. It produced almost 128 PTO horsepower. Efficiency was also improved on this engine over the 3400 engine; power increased greatly while the fuel consumption went up only slightly. Allis-Chalmers revealed the advantages of the turbocharger to the entire tractor industry. In a short period of time, most other tractor companies were installing it on their primary diesel models. *Martin Wilcox Collection*

The steering wheel with the dash tilted to four different positions. Operator comfort was a priority to the designers of the D-21 as farmers were looking for bigger machines without the worry of bigger backaches. With the power steering and easily accessible controls, an operator could plow all day in comfort and undoubtedly with a hint of pride. *Martin Wilcox Collection*

The new BIG D . . . newly designed from the tire tracks up for the man who farms big, thinks big. Top of the long leadership line.

We rewrote the "big tractor book" with the new D21...

AND OUR DEALERS ARE REWRITING THE SALES BOOK THANKS TO WHAT OUR ENGINEERS AND DESIGNERS HAVE DONE

We feel fortunate to be teamed with the greatest group of farm equipment dealers you can find.
  They're all tractor folks, like us.
  We're proud that our factory people work so hard to design and manufacture high quality products. And that our retail tractor folks believe in high quality service.
  What does it all mean?
  Careers in farm machinery.
  Dealers with get up and go. Men who think like we do . . . who are proud to handle the leadership line.
  Community leaders.

ALLIS-CHALMERS
MILWAUKEE, WISCONSIN

THE COMPANY WITH
GET UP AND GO

Big tractors are impressive, therefore many collectors tend to favor the large models. Most variations of the D-21 are insignificant and will add little interest to most collectors. An exception to this generalization would be a single example of a front-wheel assist D-21 that may still lurk somewhere. According to Norm Swinford's research, 10 were built with front-wheel assist and 9 were converted back to regular two-wheel drive. The man who ends up with the one remaining tractor will be the envy of hundreds of Allis-Chalmers enthusiasts.

Allis-Chalmers' advertising of the D-21 stressed the word "big" as it boldly entered the 100-horsepower class. A big D-21 stands mighty proud at a show as smaller tractors are lost in its shadow.

Model D-21 Tractor Specifications

Years built (D-21 Series I models)	1963–1965
Years built (D-21 Series II models)	1965–1969
Serial numbers (D-21 Series I)	1001–2200
Serial numbers (D-21 Series II)	2201–4609
Horsepower (drawbar/PTO, Series I)	93.09/ 103.06
Horsepower (drawbar/PTO, Series II)	116.41/127.75
Engine bore and stroke (inches)	4.25x5.0 (six-cylinder)
Engine rpm (both series)	2,200
Speeds (forward, high range, mph)	2.4, 4.4, 8.7, 16.2
Speeds (forward, low range, mph)	1.6, 3.4, 5.8, 12.5
Speeds (reverse, mph)	1.8, 6.8
Weight (pounds)	10,675
Length (inches)	160.625
Rear tread (inches)	68–88
Height (to top of hood, inches)	71.75
Rear tires (inches)	18.4x34 or 24.5x32
Front tires (inches)	11.00x16
Fuel capacity (gallons)	52
Cooling capacity (quarts)	21
Diesel injector pump	Roosa-Master
Suggested new retail price	$10,295 in 1965

Model D-21 Tractor Production History

Serial number is found stamped on the left side of the torque housing on the front flange.

Year	Serial Numbers
1963	1001–1416
1964	1417–2078
1965	2079–2407
(Series II begins with no. 2201)	
1966	2408–2862
1967	2863–3776
1968	3777–4497
1969	4498–4609

Chapter 7

Other A-C Tractors Sought by Collectors

By the 1960s, diesel tractors had proven themselves as cost saving and reliable. More and more farmers were looking for diesel tractors and Allis-Chalmers was quick to fill the need. An Allis-Chalmers factory in Essendine, England, began producing a nifty diesel tractor called the ED-40 beginning in 1960. Imports to Canada sold fairly well, but the 450 units that arrived in Baltimore developed a less than enthusiastic following. Soon after it was sold, problems with the lift assembly gave farmers and dealers fits. The reputation was marred at a time when many farmers considered foreign tractors inferior already. A D-272 had been introduced in 1957, three years before the ED-40, but the United States was not targeted for sales of this tractor. Canada imported a fair number of the D-272s and several found their way south into the United States over the years. Models were made in gasoline, kerosene, or diesel versions. A high-clearance version followed. These tractors are a true novelty to Allis-Chalmers collectors today, but searching for some of the parts needed for restoration can be traumatic. Tractors built in Europe have a limited collector appeal in the United States. As conversation pieces at shows, the ED-40 and D-272 create some genuine interest. As the history of these tractors becomes more prevalent and the exotic stereotype fades away, This author expects the demand and values to increase dearly over the next 10 years

By 1969, the D-21 evolved into the Two-Twenty. With some improvements, the tractor became a farming Goliath with almost 136 PTO horsepower. A slightly smaller tractor emerged a year later in 1970 called the Two-Ten. With a little less power and a favorable price advantage, the Two-Ten began to outsell the Two-Twenty. Collectors seem to be attracted to these big models with low production numbers. Although these models were built during the 1970s, a decade that has not yet appealed to most tractor collectors, these Allis-Chalmers tractors are definitely in great demand. A true prize is possessing one of the only 100 front-wheel-assist Two-Twenty tractors built.

Model D-272 Tractor

In Great Britain, the Allis-Chalmers Model B was a cherished tractor by many owners. To abandon this tractor for a completely different machine might have caused rejection by conservative farmers in the United Kingdom. In September 1955 a tractor that had much in common with the Model B, but with more features, was introduced. This tractor was called the D-270 and was a steppingstone to the newer D-272. With gasoline, kerosene, or a diesel engine, this D-270 evolved into the D-272 within two years. The D-272 was announced in

Collectibility

Rating	Model	Comments
★★★	D-272	British
★★★★	D-272 high clearance	British; rare version with 36-inch rear tires
★★★	ED-40	British; 450 were imported to the USA
★★★	Two-Twenty; two-wheel drive	1,765 built
★★★★	Two-Twenty; front-wheel assist	100 built
★★★	Two-Ten	1,471 built

Reliability

Rating	Model
★★★	D-272
★★★	D-272 high clearance
★★★✦	ED-40
★★★★★	Two-Twenty; two-wheel drive
★★★★✦	Two-Twenty; front-wheel assist
★★★★★	Two-Ten

Parts Availability

Rating	Model
★★	D-272
★✦	D-272 high clearance
★★	ED-40
★★★✦	Two-Twenty; two-wheel drive
★★★✦	Two-Twenty; front-wheel assist
★★★★	Two-Ten

The D-272 was built in the Allis-Chalmers factory at Essendine, England, as a replacement for the earlier D-270 model. Offered in gasoline, kerosene, or diesel versions, a limited number have found their way into the hands of collectors in the United States. Unknown numbers were sold in Canada, and some D-272s slowly migrated south into the States. Certain collectors are fond of this model even though certain parts can be a real challenge to locate. Charles Widlund of Palmer, Iowa, owns this nicely restored copy.
Charles Widlund

1957. The model looked like no other Allis-Chalmers tractor built before (or after). A three-cylinder Perkins engine with a 12-volt starter powered the diesel version. Allis-Chalmers-built four-cylinder engines powered the gasoline and kerosene models with 12-volt starting as an option. Allis-Chalmers Great Britain Ltd. put its heart and soul into this tractor. A four-speed transmission gave the tractor speeds up to almost 12 miles per hour. In the gasoline version, the tractor was much like the Allis-Chalmers Model CA that had a fine seven-year sales record when the D-272 was introduced. The diesel was one thing that you couldn't get with a CA or even its successors, the D-10 and D-12. Precious gasoline in Europe was expensive and the United Kingdom was eager to adapt its small tractors to the economical diesel engines. The gasoline version used an 8-inch clutch while the diesel used a 9-inch clutch. Both tractors used 6-inch enclosed contracting brakes. With a 29-inch ground clearance, the D-272 tractors could cultivate most crops with little damage. A high-clearance version with added height was made in limited numbers for taller crops.

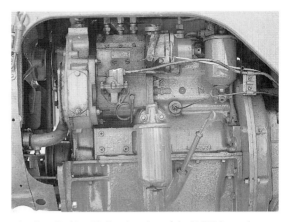

The short Perkins P3 diesel engine of the D-272 has only three cylinders. Fortunately the same engine was used in other tractors such as the Fordson Dexta, therefore, parts for it are not impossible to locate.

The grille of the D-272 has this tapered bottom and is topped with a metal plaque that boldly states its model number.

Options were available such as a three-point hitch that was adaptable to the Snap-Coupler hitch. A hand-operated clutch was offered that interrupted power to the right axle and made the D-272 perform like a live-PTO tractor. This clutch was much like the one used in the Model CA that was built in the United States. Power-Shift rear wheels could be added for the farmer who needed to change tread adjustment often. The popular PTO and belt pulley assemblies were not standard features and were added only at extra cost. Both low-clearance and high-clearance versions of the D-272 were built for special farming conditions.

The D-272 had a good reception in its home country and several models were sent to Canada. The United States apparently did not import any D-272 tractors for marketing, but some models have migrated from Canada. A-C enthusiasts across the United States are finding these wayfarers and giving them a second life as collector tractors. The diesel versions seem to be the most commonly found in the United States.

Collecting Notes: The D-272 is seldom found in the United States, but more and more models are popping up. Collector interest is lukewarm among most American collectors. Engine parts can be found and an added plus is that the Perkins diesel was used in other brand tractors such as Ford. Many other parts on the tractor can cause a collector much frustration when searching leads to dead ends or extremely costly parts. My advice to a collector in the United States for finding parts is to befriend a collector who has found the proper contacts or to look north, into Canada. A restored D-272 commands much attention at shows and one can almost count on the fact that the value of the tractor will increase substantially in the next several years.

Model D-272 Tractor Specifications

Years built	1957–1963
Serial numbers	not found
Horsepower (gasoline)	30 brake
Horsepower (kerosene)	26 brake
Horsepower (diesel)	31 brake
Engine bore and stroke (nondiesel, inches)	3.375x3.5, four-cylinder
Engine bore and stroke (diesel, inches)	3.5x5, three-cylinder
Engine rpm (all engines)	1,900
Speeds (forward, mph)	2, 3.5, 4.75, 11.75
Speed (reverse, mph)	3.5
Weight (gasoline, pounds)	3,200
Weight (diesel, pounds)	3,500
Length (inches)	122
Width (inches)	58
Ignition (distributor)	magneto
Carburetor (gasoline)	Zenith
Diesel injector pump	C.A.V. BPE3A60S

Model ED-40 Tractor

In the first half of 1964, Allis-Chalmers had 450 ED-40 tractors shipped from its Essendine plant in England, to Baltimore, Maryland. This model was first introduced in November 1960. It was a small diesel and the demand for such a tractor seemed strong in the United States; it was logical that it should be sent overseas. The D-10 and D-12 were not ever produced in a diesel version and sales were lagging. The similar-sized ED-40 came with a Standard-Ricardo diesel engine that boasted excellent fuel economy. The lift arms on the rear of the ED-40s had problems from overextending. The resulting broken lift-arm housings created a great inconvenience and expense for both farmers and dealers. Foreign-built machines already suffered from the negative attitude of many American farmers who had heard horror stories about expensive parts that one could have to wait for weeks to get from overseas. Often a farmer would carefully choose a foreign tractor after satisfying any doubts, only to be the joke among other farmers for owning such an exotic "bomb." This negative attitude feasted on the lift-arm problem. Limiting chains were installed to prevent further casting breaks, but the stigma remained. The ED-40 was an excellent machine that perhaps never had a fair chance in the United States.

Weighing 3,584 pounds and rated at 41 horsepower, these ED-40s could handily pull a two-bottom plow in most soils. ED-40 tractors were usually painted Persian Orange No. 2 and had features similar to the D-10 and D-12 tractors. Three different versions of the ED-40 were sold in the United States: the Standard, the Deluxe, and the Super Deluxe. All three came with the same diesel engine and an adjustable, wide-front axle. The Standard came with the Depthomatic hydraulic lift system, PTO, 12-volt starter, three-point hitch, and a high- and low-range four-speed transmission that allowed eight different speeds forward and two in reverse. The Deluxe version came with the added features of a differential lock, live PTO, Tractormeter, mechanical fuel gauge, and wider front tires. The Super Deluxe had even more features of lights, horn, swinging drawbar, and wider rear tires. Options that could be added to any of these versions were Power-Shift rear wheels, belt pulley, radiator shutters, hand brake, wheel weights, and a combined oil pressure and temperature gauge.

The Standard-Ricardo engine of the ED-40 was pepped up in 1963, about halfway through the production life of the tractor. Nebraska testing wasn't considered—only about 450 units were sold in the United States. Acceptance of this model in the United States was poor, partly because it was foreign (exotic) and partly due to some problems resulting in broken lift housings. Even after the company installed a fix on the design, American farmers still didn't want to take a chance. The model was built until 1968 in Essendine, England.

The operator's view on a Model ED-40 is much like the D-14. The ED-40 came only as a diesel version and only with an adjustable wide-front axle. Options were usually offered in packages. One could buy a Regular, Deluxe, or Super Deluxe model, each with progressively more features.

The four-cylinder diesel in the ED-40 eventually put out 41 brake horsepower. Without the Nebraska testing, factory brake testing would be close to the PTO horsepower rating of a tractor. The CAV injector pump was used throughout production. Small diesels were becoming popular in the United States at the time the ED-40 was offered, but this tractor scared off potential buyers even though it was built well.

Canada received an unknown number of ED-40s, and many of the machines found their way down into the United States, raising the chance of a collector finding one there. No serial number lists have been found to determine the exact year of manufacturing, but with the known changes in production, the total of all ED-40s built appears to be about 4,000 or 5,000 units.

Collecting Notes: The ED-40 is a handsome tractor, with growing collector interest. Obtaining parts can be a nightmare for a collector with no prior resources. Some parts machines are out there, and Canada is a good place to start looking. Finding a former Allis-Chalmers dealer who will go the long mile for you would be a blessing. If you want a rare Allis-Chalmers tractor that draws some special attention at shows, don't give up on the ED-40. The rewards of a difficult restoration are much more than monetary.

Model ED-40 Tractor Specifications

Years built	1960–1968
Serial numbers	1001–not known
Horsepower (prior to July 1963)	37 brake
Horsepower (July 1963 and after)	41 brake
Engine bore and stroke	3.3125x4.0 (four-cylinder)
Engine rpm (prior to July 1963)	2,000
Engine rpm (July 1963 and after)	2,250
Speeds (forward, high range, mph)	2.47, 3.94, 6.52, 16.4
Speeds (forward, low range, mph)	1.22, 1.94, 3.23, 8.14
Speeds (reverse, mph)	2.52, 5.1
Weight (shipping, pounds)	3,584
Length (inches)	114
Rear tread (inches)	48–72
Height (inches)	68
Rear tires (Standard and Deluxe, inches)	10x28
Rear tires (Super Deluxe, inches)	11x28
Front tires (Standard, inches)	4.00x19
Front tires (Deluxe and Super Deluxe, inches)	6.00x16
Fuel capacity (gallons)	11.75
Cooling capacity (gallons)	2.128
Diesel injector pump	C.A.V.
Suggested new retail price	£636 in 1963

Only 100 Two-Twenty tractors were built with the front-wheel assist. Seldom will you find such an example in the field today as A-C enthusiasts quickly add them to their collections. *Dennis McNamara*

Model Two-Twenty Tractor

The success of the Model D-21 led engineers to make a newer version with a stronger rear axle and a new sprung countenance that kept with the times. The rear axles on this new Model Two-Twenty were beefed up from that of the D-21 and dual rear wheels could be used with much less chance of axle failure. The straddle-mounted final-drive gears were supported on both sides by bearing assemblies. This feature was also used at the Springfield factory at this time on the A-C crawlers. The pinion gear that drives the bull gear would have a certain amount of deflection under big loads on earlier D-21 models with the gear at the end of a shaft. A straddle-mount gear worked like a rolling pin with pressure being pressed evenly downward. Straddle-mounted gears would wear longer and would rarely break.

The diesel engine was basically the same as was used in the D-21 Series II. With only about an 8 horsepower advantage on the PTO, the Two-Twenty performed almost the same on the drawbar tests at Nebraska with less than a 1-horsepower advantage. Similar features were handed down from the D-21 such as the four-position tilting steering wheel and dash. The four-speed transmission with high and low ranges offered a selection of eight different forward speeds. Large rear fenders were each fitted with two lights within a shelter on the fender crown. The new title, "Landhandler" was placed on a decal just under the Allis-Chalmers name on the hood sides. The Two-Twenty was a product of many, many years of tractor refinements. The contrast between this tractor and the Model 10-18 from the year 1914 is like a Ferrari compared to a Ford Model T. Allis-Chalmers not only kept up with the competition through the years, but it often led the way. Innovations such as rubber tires, Power-Shift rear rims, and turbochargers were a few features that A-C was first to offer as standard equipment on farm tractors. Although it is only this author's opinion, it is doubtful whether there was a better tractor in its day than the Model Two-Twenty.

Options for the Two-Twenty were plentiful. Rear tire sizes of 30, 32, and 38 inches were offered. Power-Shift rear wheels could be added for the 38-inch tire sizes. The 18.4x38-inch rear tires could also be put on dual rear wheels in either the standard or Power-Shift styles. Inner and outer rear-wheel weights could be countered with nose weights on the front frame. A three-point hitch and a fully enclosed cab were helpful options that add much to the value of this tractor today.

The most valuable option today on the Two-Twenty would be, by far, the front-wheel-assist (FWA) version. This expensive option did not sell well. Introduced in June 1970, only 100 copies were built. This version rates high in demand by A-C tractor collectors.

Collecting Notes: The Two-Twenty is considered collectible even though it is a fairly modern tractor. Most parts are not difficult to obtain for restoration, but big tractors can create some big expenses. A Two-Twenty is still a wonderful tractor for modern farming and collectors must compete with this demand. A restored Two-Twenty is valuable and will only increase in demand as the years roll by. The front-wheel-assist versions are hard to come by because only 100 units were ever built. Anyone owning one of these precious tractors should see the value increase substantially over the next several years as A-C enthusiasts strive to complete their collections. Restored, this version rates among the top five antique A-C tractors in value.

Model Two-Twenty Tractor Specifications

Years built	1969–1972
Serial numbers	1004–2866
Horsepower (drawbar/PTO)	117.21/135.95
Engine bore and stroke (inches)	4.25x5.0 (six-cylinder)
Engine rpm	2,200
Speeds (forward, high range, mph)	2.5, 4.7, 9.4, 17.4
Speeds (forward, low range, mph)	1.7, 3.7, 6.3, 13.5
Speeds (reverse, mph)	2.0, 7.3
Weight (shipping, pounds)	15,116
Length (inches)	164
Rear tread (inches)	68–88
Height (to top of hood, inches)	71.75
Rear tires (inches)	18.4x34
Front tires (inches)	7.50x20
Fuel capacity (gallons)	51
Cooling capacity (quarts)	21
Diesel injector pump	Roosa-Master
Suggested new retail price	$13,435 in 1972 (two-wheel-drive)

Model Two-Twenty Tractor Production History

Serial number is found stamped on the left front side of the torque housing.

Year	Serial Numbers
1969	1004–1937
1970	1938–2450
1971	2451–2625
1972	2626–2866

Model Two-Ten Tractor

Although the model numbers seem to be out of sequence, the introduction of the Model Two-Ten followed the Model Two-Twenty by one year. As a slightly smaller brother to the Two-Twenty, this Two-Ten became a popular diesel tractor during its three years of production.

The turbocharged 426-cubic inch, six-cylinder engine put out 122 PTO horsepower, more than enough for many farmers. The big crowned fenders each came with dual 12-volt headlights. Power steering, a 12-position seat, and a fully adjustable steering wheel made almost any operator comfortable on this impressive machine. The uncluttered platform offered 9 square feet of legroom. Allis-Chalmers worked diligently toward operator comfort, which the company was quick to realize is where sales often hinged.

Optional rear tires were offered in several different sizes, 15.5x38, 16.9x38, 18.4x38, 20.8x38, 24.5x32, and 23.1x30. Power-Shift wheels were available on the popular 38-inch rear tires. Dual rear wheels were offered in the 18.4x38-inch size with either regular or Power-Shift rims. Inner and outer rear-wheel weights were available on all tire sizes and special weights were offered on dual-wheel versions. Up to 15 68-pound suitcase weights could be added to the front of the tractor to keep the wheels of the adjustable wide-front axle from coming off the ground.

The three-point hitch (Cat. III) was a popular option that included a 1,000-rpm PTO operated by a hydraulic clutch. The farmer could add a Hi-Back Deluxe Seat for comfort and a cab was offered to keep out the elements. A heater and windshield wipers were available on this cab if needed.

Collecting Notes: The Model Two-Ten is a fairly modern tractor that would normally not be considered collectible if it were not for the limited numbers produced. Most parts are readily available and the engine is a popular model used in other tractors such as the D-21 and Two-Twenty. Collectors covet options such as dual rear wheels and a full set of weights. The cab was offered in the last year of production, and a Two-Ten with one would be a rare find and would also deserve an additional star for its collectibility rating.

With a full set of 15 suitcase weights, an additional 1,020 pounds was added to the front of the Two-Ten. With both the front and rear weights and no calcium in the tires, the tractor weighed over 7 tons! With all that weight and 120 PTO horsepower, this tractor could do some big jobs in a big hurry.

The big 426-cubic inch engine in the Two-Ten was turbocharged and tuned to deliver 120-PTO horsepower. It featured the same basic Model 3500 engine that was used in the D-21 Series II. The Two-Ten was much like the D-21 Series II, but with the transmission and differential beefed-up for added strength.

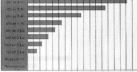

Geared to work wide!

"Keep the transmission big . . . tough, with an extra margin of strength in every shaft, tooth and key. Give it wide working capability." Farmers asked for it.

So we did.

And we delivered a bonus. More engine power on the ground. How? We kept the gear train simple. Made it a compact transmission. But big. With shafts that easily resist flexing and distortion under shock loads . . . the strain of continuous heavy going with wide-working tools.

Constant mesh design. Eight speeds — five in the heavy-duty range.

You could forget what downshifting is.

With a nicely restored Two-Ten in the foreground and the very rare Two-Twenty FWA just beyond it, you can see the similarities in the two models. The Two-Ten was built to cost a little less money and have a bit less power than the regular version of the Two-Twenty. Dennis McNamara

Model Two-Ten Tractor Specifications (with 18.4x34-inch rear tires)

Years built	1970–1972
Serial numbers	1004–2469
Horsepower rating (drawbar/PTO)	104.95/122.40
Engine bore and stroke (inches)	4.25x5.0 (six-cylinder)
Engine rpm	2,200
Speeds (forward, high range, mph)	5.5, 8.7, 12.6, 16.2
Speeds (forward, low range, mph)	1.5, 2.4, 3.4, 4.4
Speed (reverse, mph)	1.8, 6.8
Weight (shipping, pounds)	14,400
Length (inches)	164
Rear tread (inches)	69–92
Height (overall, inches)	107
Height (to top of hood, inches)	70 (at the front)
Rear tires (inches)	18.4x34
Front tires (inches)	10.00x16
Fuel capacity (gallons)	51
Cooling capacity (quarts)	21
Diesel injector pump	Roosa-Master
Suggested new retail price	$11,640 in 1972

Model Two-Ten Tractor Production History

Serial number is found stamped on the front left side of the torque housing.

Year	Serial Numbers
1970	1004–1106
1971	1107–2081
1972	2082–2469

Chapter 8

The First Allis-Chalmers Crawlers

On April 2, 1928, Allis-Chalmers bought the Monarch Tractor Company for a mere half-million dollars. Monarch was a renowned builder of crawler tractors with a history that went all the way back to 1913. As one of the finest lines of crawlers on the market, the Monarchs were well respected in the road-building and lumber industries. A financial bind forced Monarch to sell. This company became one of Allis-Chalmers' acquisitions that proved to be profitable for many years to follow.

The Monarch 50 and 75 were improved versions of earlier Monarch crawlers that still used antiquated chain-driven final-drive assemblies and steered with a single steering wheel that activated the steering clutches. By 1931, the Monarch 50 and 75 were replaced by the more modern-designed Model S and L crawlers. These newer models had more speeds available with their five- and six-speed transmissions, and the old chain drive was eliminated. The aging Monarch facilities in Springfield, Illinois, were infused with $350,000 for a new addition in 1936. With the board of directors' vision and the potential of the industrial equipment line, the design and quality of the crawlers were a big priority. Competition was vicious in the crawler industry and constant improvements were initiated to keep the A-C crawlers among the best available.

The novelty of the diesel engine had grown into high regard by the 1930s when its reliability and efficiency offered huge advantages over the gasoline and kerosene engines. Allis-Chalmers engineers worked a diesel-fuel engine into the popular Model K, S, and L crawlers. This Hesselman design was a sort of hybrid between a gasoline engine and a true diesel. Unlike a real diesel that relies on extremely high compression to ignite the fuel when it is injected into the engine cylinders, the Hesselman uses a spark plug to ignite the fuel after injection. Fuel economy was not as favorable with the Hesselman-type engines. Production of the Allis-Chalmers' spark-ignition diesel crawlers was low even though much expense was used to advertise certain benefits. By 1940, Allis-Chalmers turned away from the Hesselman design and began producing three new models of crawlers equipped with General Motors diesel engines. The HD-14, HD-7, and HD-10 sold well against the competition of such firms as Caterpillar, Cletrac, and International Harvester. The two-cycle GM diesel engine was well respected in the industry for being powerful, efficient, and reliable.

The early HD-series led Allis-Chalmers into a position of being an industry leader in the production of some of the finest crawlers built at the time.

continued on page 113

Color Gallery

Banting Manufacturing Company modified Allis-Chalmers' Model E tractors into the impressive "Greyhound Specials," with a canopy and optional exhaust whistle. In the tradition of the threshing crews from the steam era, the whistle was used to signal diligent workers for fuel, water, grain, and especially lunchtime. This Greyhound owned by Craig Detwiler is a rare tractor today. *Craig Detwiler*

This Model 10-18 belongs to Mark and Dave Pfouts of Chagrin Falls, Ohio. With serial number 1273, this is the earliest restored Allis-Chalmers tractor known. Unlike later versions, this tractor was designed to run on gasoline only. *Photo by Dave Pfouts*

The 10-18 usually came with a manifold preheater and a gasoline-starting tank. Once started and warmed up on gasoline, the fuel could be switched over to the more economical kerosene. The operator would switch back to gasoline just before shutting down the machine to be ready for the next start. This early 10-18 had neither an auxiliary fuel tank nor the typical kerosene manifold. *Dave Pfouts*

To restore a machine to this splendor, it takes hours upon hours of skilled and dedicated work. Parts that are missing on such a rare tractor must often be machined or cast. Requests are made to collectors of rare tractors to have a pattern made from a certain part or have accurate blueprints drawn for fabrication of parts. *Dave Pfouts*

The 10-18 (left) and the 6-12 were unsuccessful attempts by Allis-Chalmers to take a lion's share of the tractor market. Technology in tractor design was advancing in leaps and bounds just as Allis-Chalmers tried to enter the market. About the time a new Allis-Chalmers model was introduced, the design was already losing favor with the market. *Dave Pfouts*

Dave Pfouts and John Nelson of Chagrin Falls, Ohio, own this finely restored 1920 Model 6-12 with serial number 10487. Attached below the seat is an Oliver, single-bottom 16-inch plow. Horse farmers could use their existing implements on this model; they could buy a tractor without spending a fortune on special attachments. The theory seemed right, but most farmers tended to favor tractors of conventional four-wheel design like the Fordson and International Harvester tractors that captured most of the sales during this time. *Dave Pfouts*

The United name was no longer used on any Model U tractors after 1930.

Only a little more than 1,500 high-clearance versions of the Model UC were produced. The Thompson Machinery Company of Thibodaux, Louisiana, marketed most of these tractors to cane farmers with a special arrangement with Allis-Chalmers. This exquisite 1936 model belongs to Al Schubert of Republic, Ohio.

French and Hecht–brand rear-spoke wheels were used until serial number 59636 in 1937 and were replaced with disc-type wheels. Robert Lemmert of Cumberland, Maryland, owns this splendid WC. *Robert Lemmert*

The 16-inch disc-style front wheels for tires replaced the 17-inch round spoke-type in 1936 at serial number 23529. The five-lug front wheel shown here replaced the earlier six-lug wheel in 1937 at serial number 59628. Some WCs have been found after this serial number that still have the six-lug wheels. Roger Culbert of Fillmore, New York, owns this impressive restoration.

The Allis-Chalmers name was imprinted in the top radiator tank from 1934 until the WC was streamlined in 1938. Owner Roger Culbert deliberately left the top radiator tank unpainted to show the attractive brass composition.

The WF was a standard tread version of the popular WC row crop. With the same engine and four-speed transmission, the WF was a reliable machine. Only 1,900 nonstreamlined versions were built. This sharp tractor is from the Roger Culbert Collection.

A total of 6,450 streamlined Model WF tractors were built. The value of a restored copy—like this one owned by Roger Culbert—is close to the nonstreamlined version, which is more scarce. Production numbers are not the only factor in determining the value of a collectible tractor.

Notice the "wishbone" front axle found on the regular B. The style of the axle was used throughout the netire production run of this model. *Vern Veldhuizen*

The Model B is one of the most popular tractors among collectors. Parts are easy to obtain and the small size makes this unit fairly easy to transport to shows. This 1950 version belongs to Robert Lemmert Sr. *Robert Lemmert Sr.*

The Model G had an engine in the rear and little more than a tubular frame to support the axle in front. The 141-pound nose weight cost an extra $14 in 1953 and is in high demand by collectors of the Model G today. Roger Culbert of Fillmore, New York, accomplished this impeccable restoration.

At first glance, this CA looks a lot like the older Model C. The Power-Shift rear wheels and the two cast lugs protruding from the lower part of the grille are a couple of features not found on the Model C. This tractor is from the Roger Culbert collection.

Beginning in 1953, Allis-Chalmers replaced the Model WD with this WD-45. Many options were available to satisfy almost any farmer's needs. Sales were abundant. This WD-45 is part of the Roger Culbert collection.

Martin Wilcox of Canajoharie, New York, owns this WD-45 tractor equipped with ARPS tracks. After-market conversions allowed the tractor to pull like a bulldozer in adverse field conditions. This tractor still earns its keep on the farm.

The D-14 was a hit as soon as it hit dealer show rooms. With a modern style and several new features, farmers could work their fields with utter pride as the bright orange tractor drew attention from passersby. This new design came at an opportune time as competitor's tractors were surpassing the style of the Allis-Chalmers line. Harley Veldhuizen of Elburn, Illinois, owns this sharp D-14. *Harley Veldhuizen*

This D-17 belongs to Martin Wilcox of Canajoharie, New York, and is the earliest style of the Series I. The grille is painted orange like the rest of the tractor. Later versions of the Series I have silver grilles with black horizontal bands. Cream-colored grilles were used in the Series II through IV.

The style of the D-17 changed in 1960 with the Series II that featured this cream-colored grille and wheel centers. Notice the small cylindrical muffler on the Series II that was later replaced by a large black oval muffler with the introduction of the Series III and IV. *Martin Wilcox Collection*

This 1964 D-10 Series II tractor has the optional three-point hitch and Power-Shift rear wheels. The three-point hitch adds to the value of the tractor today. Expect a highly restored version like this one to be worth about $1,000 more than the same tractor without the three-point hitch. *Photo by Harley Veldhuizen*

This D-12 is a Series II. Later Series III models were similar but had a big oval muffler painted black, coming through the hood. The Series II has the older-style muffler and four-speed transmission. Only the later Series III offered an optional midmount lift and a two-range transmission that gave a total of eight forward speeds. *Roger Culbert Collection*

The bore on the gasoline and LPG versions of the D-15 Series II was increased for additional horsepower over that of the Series I models. The diesel engine was basically left unchanged throughout the D-15 production. This gasoline version was rated at more than 46 PTO horsepower. *Roger Culbert Collection*

The D-272 is a rare tractor in the United States, and this high-clearance model is even more scarce. This tractor uses larger 36-inch rear tires and an extended spindle drop on the front-axle assembly to achieve its lofty stance. *Maggie Dean*

To bring a D-21 to such a fine state of restoration is an expensive process. More and more the D-series tractors are being pulled out of active duty and being retired with much dignity by avid collectors. This Series II model belongs to and was restored by Vern Veldhuizen of Richmond, Illinois. It has the factory turbocharger not found on the first series. *Harley Veldhuizen*

Roger Culbert of Fillmore, New York, sits at the wheel of a beautifully restored ED-40. Roger has an extensive collection of restored Allis-Chalmers tractors and was not intimidated by the difficulty in restoring this ED-40. Parts are hard to come by in this country, and restoration can be a major frustration.

Listing the Two-Twenty before the Two-Ten in this book appears to be a mistake. Oddly enough, the Two-Twenty was built first. As a replacement for the D-21 Series II, the Two-Twenty had much in common. The short production life and the low numbers of units built combined with the jumbo size and sleek styling make this tractor especially collectible. Often machines of this vintage are too new and modern to catch the collector's eye, but the Two-Twenty is an exception. This nice example with dual rear wheels is owned and restored by Harley Veldhuizen. *Harley Veldhuizen*

Dennis and Paul McNamara of Hastings, Minnesota, own this Two-Ten. With front and rear wheel weights, it can do some big jobs. Collectors are beginning to restore the Two-Tens and remove them from active service. This example has been restored to look as good as new. *Dennis McNamara*

Dual rear wheels were available such as the set shown here with Power-Shift rails. This Two-Twenty is more valuable with such a significant addition. Wheel weights are always a welcomed addition on these bigger tractors. *Dennis McNamara*

The Model K was the first successful crawler for Allis-Chalmers. Its older brothers, the Monarch 50 and 75, were big, expensive, and outdated. The Model K was smaller, less expensive, and modernized. About 8,300 units were sold during the 15 years of production. *Andrew Morland*

The impressive Model L crawler is a big 11-ton machine. The six-speed transmission was a welcomed improvement over the three-speeds of the Monarch 75 that this crawler replaced. *Andrew Morland*

Collectors of Allis-Chalmers Crawlers are attracted to the sleek Model S because of its impressive size and style as well as the low production of 1,225 units. Other than certain rare orchard and diesel fuel engine variations, the Model S is one of the most rare Allis-Chalmers Crawlers today. *Andrew Morland*

During its six years of production, beginning in 1960, the HD-9 underwent very few changes. This will attest to the reliability of this model as Allis-Chalmers was quick to react to any design weakness. Fierce competition in the crawler market left little room for second-rate machines. *Andrew Morland*

continued from page 96.

Collectibility

Rating	Model	Comments
★★★★	Monarch 50 (Stearns engine)	1,399 built
★★★↙	Monarch 50 (A-C engine)	601 built
★★★↙	Monarch 75	1,066 built
★★★	Monarch 35, Model K (3-speed)	4,450 built
★★★	Model K (4-speed)	3,850 built
★★★★	Model KO	Spark-ignition diesel
★★★	Model L (steering wheel)	1,162 built
★★★	Model L (steering levers)	2,195 built
★★★★	Model LO	Spark-ignition diesel
★★★★★	Model LD	10 built with General Motors diesels
★★★	Model M	14,524 built
★★★★	Model M Orchard	High and low seat versions
★★★	Model S	1,225 built
★★★★	Model SO	Spark-ignition diesel, rare
★★	Model HD-14	6,405 built; 6-speed or torque converter
★★	Model HD-7	18,503 built; regular and wide-track
★★	Model HD-10	10,197 built; regular or wide-track

Reliability

Rating	Model
★★★★	Monarch 50 (Stearns engine)
★★★★	Monarch 50 (A-C engine)
★★★↙	Monarch 75
★★★★	Monarch 35, Model K (3-speed)
★★★★	Model K (4-speed)
★★★	Model KO
★★★★	Model L (steering wheel)
★★★★	Model L (steering levers)
★★↙	Model LO
★★★★	Model M
★★★★	Model S
★★★	Model SO
★★★★↙	Model HD-14
★★★★↙	Model HD-7
★★★★↙	Model HD-10

Parts Availability

Rating	Model
★★	Monarch 50 (Stearns engine)
★★	Monarch 50 (A-C engine)
★↙	Monarch 75
★★★	Monarch 35, Model K (3-speed)
★★★★↙	Model K (4-speed)
★★	Model KO
★★★↙	Model L (steering wheel)
★★★↙	Model L (steering levers)
★	Model LO
★★★	Model M
★★★↙	Model M Orchard
★★★↙	Model S
★★	Model SO
★★★	Model HD-14
★★★	Model HD-7
★★★	Model HD-10

The Monarch 50 and 75 were the first crawlers sold by Allis-Chalmers. Sales of these two models were sluggish as competitors' crawlers offered more modern features. The chain-driven final-drives were never used on Allis-Chalmers crawlers after these two models.

113

The feature of Monarch construction which is mainly responsible for unusual performance is *Monarch traction.*

Engine power is valuable on a tractor only in so far as it can be converted into actual traction. This is accomplished on Monarch Tractors by the famous endless tracks which creep over the ground with an irresistible grip that laughs at hills and makes light of loads.
Monarch tracks are made of wear resisting Manganese steel. They are covered by a broad and absolute guarantee that the tracks will not wear out.

Monarch tractors have "inbuilt" power and strength, mechanical excellence in every detail. Most important of all traction. There is a Monarch Tractor for every farm need.

Monarch tractors are made in the following sizes: 16-9 H. P., 20-12 H. P. and 30-18 H. P.

General Tractors Incorporated
629 Old Colony Building   Chicago, Ill.

Monarch Tractors
NEVERSLIP

"Neverslip" was the title of the Monarch crawler line for many years. The label was cast in the top radiator tanks on several models. With the known reputation for strength and durability in its crawlers, the Monarch Tractor Company became a good investment for Allis-Chalmers at a price of $500,000.

Monarch 50 Crawler

Monarch Tractor Company had been building its Model H 6-ton crawler for about a year when Allis-Chalmers bought the firm in 1928. With a few changes, the Model H became the new Monarch 50 and an Allis-Chalmers diamond logo was placed under the Monarch decal on each side of the cowl. Advertising was loaded with Allis-Chalmers' connection to the well-known Monarch name.

The Monarch 50 was first produced with a 536-cubic inch Stearns engine that was replaced by a 562.8-cubic inch Allis-Chalmers-built engine in 1930. The Stearns Motor Manufacturing Company was bought by Allis-Chalmers in the same year. Stearns had been a producer of engines for many years and even sold its own tractor beginning in 1919. Allis-Chalmers evidently dropped the Stearns engine design; it is likely that the company was interested more with the Stearns electric generating equipment line.

The Monarch 50 only had a three-speed transmission, but by changing the 9-tooth final-drive sprockets to ones with 8, 10, or 11 teeth, the speed ranges could be changed to adapt to different conditions. These drive sprockets powered the track sprockets by use of two 44-link Baldwin chains. Early models of the Monarch 50 had semi-enclosed final-drive assemblies. A wool wick in each side saturated each drive with a quart of oil to keep the chain and sprockets lubricated. Dusty conditions caused excessive wear on these parts, so a fully enclosed design was installed beginning with serial number 60601 in late 1928. Now each final-drive held 2 gallons of oil that bathed the chain and sprockets while keeping out invading dust.

Options were abundant to make the Monarch fit many job descriptions. A Hillside model was offered with a wider track gauge as well as a logging version. Without the cab that was standard on other versions, the logger model had extra shielding to protect the engine sides and bottom as well as the grille. A hook on both the front and rear of this version allowed loggers to pull logs in either direction.

Electric lights were optional until 1930 when they became standard equipment beginning with serial number 61697. A PTO rated at 1,000 rpm was available as well as a 12.5-inch-diameter belt pulley. Cab curtains were sold to help shield operators in adverse weather conditions. Special dust-proof transmission covers were offered to seal the shafts and levers from invading dust in special conditions. Grouser styles were offered that were open or smooth as well as the regular type in either manganese or steel composition.

Collecting Notes: Few restored Monarch 50 crawlers exist. Restoration is an extremely expensive and time-consuming process on models in average condition. Parts are difficult

A total of 1,399 Monarch 50 crawlers were built with the Stearns engine before the Allis-Chalmers engine replaced it in 1930. Only 601 units were built with the slightly more powerful Allis-Chalmers engine until production ended in 1931.

to acquire and the problem is compounded by several major changes made during the relatively short production life of this crawler. For the determined souls who struggle to bring into being a wonderfully restored Monarch 50, the big reward is being the caretaker of a rare and valuable piece of history.

For 2-3 and 3-4 Plow Tractors and Motor Trucks

The Baldwin chain was used in each of the final-drives on the Monarch 50 and 75. Each crawler had four speed ranges by replacing the drive sprockets for these chains. The Monarch 50 came standard with a nine-tooth drive sprocket and a 44-link chain; the Monarch 75 used a 48-link chain and also came standard with a nine-tooth sprocket.

The Stearns engine powered the Monarch 50 until 1930. Allis-Chalmers bought Stearns Motor Manufacturing Company in 1930, but used its own engine in this Monarch thereafter.

Monarch 50 Crawler Specifications (no mounted equipment)

	Stearns engine	Allis-Chalmers engine
Years built	1928–1930	1930–1931
Serial numbers	60298–61697	61698–62297
Horsepower (drawbar/belt)	50.55/no belt test	53.28/62.18
Cylinders	4	4
Engine bore and stroke (inches)	5.125x6.5	5.25x6.5
Engine rpm	1,000	1,000
Speeds (standard gearing, forward, mph)	1.81, 2.74, 3.96	1.81, 2.74, 3.96
Speed (standard gearing, reverse, mph)	3.17	2.07
Weight (shipping, pounds)	13,500	15,100
Length (inches)	127.81	127.81
Standard track gauge (inches)	57	57
Height (to top of cab, inches)	85.25 (smooth shoes)	89.81 (integral grousers)
Standard track shoe width (inches)	13	13
Lower track rollers per side	5	5
Belt pulley (inches, dia. x w.)	12.5x9.5 (950 rpm)	12.5x9.5 (950 rpm)
Fuel capacity (gallons)	31	35
Cooling capacity (gallons)	8.5	8
Ignition (battery) injector pump	American Bosch ZR4	American Bosch ZR4 or Eisemann GV4
Carburetor	Zenith 76 or 77	ZenithC6
Suggested new retail price	$3,625 in 1928	$3,540 in 1930

Monarch 50 Crawler Production History
Serial number is found stamped on the front frame and dash plate.

Year	Serial Numbers
1928	60298–60610
1929	60611–61558
1930	61559–62146
1931	62147–62297

Monarch 50 Crawler Progression History

Year	Serial Number	Modification
1928	60298	First Monarch 50 produced
1928	60494	Track support rollers improved
1928	60600	Truck frame modified
1928	60601	Final-drives are fully enclosed
1929	60698	5-inch track equalizer beam replaces 4-inch beam
1929	60898	Optional low-speed reverse discontinued
1929	61059	Stearns engine modified with different block, carburetor, governor, oil pump, etc.
1929	61348	Hollow-tooth track sprockets replace pin type
1930	61698	Stearns engine replaced with Allis-Chalmers engine
1930	61999	Crawler tested at Nebraska (test no. 179)
1931	62171	Double-tooth track sprocket replaces hollow tooth type
1931	62297	Last Monarch 50 produced

Monarch 75 Crawler

The flagship of the new Allis-Chalmers' crawler line in 1928 was the Monarch 75. Contractors and farmers who could afford the hefty $5,350 price would feel quite important sitting atop the seat of this majestic crawler. The huge 929-cubic inch Beaver-LeRoi engine barked out with more than 78 drawbar horsepower. This Monarch was a beautiful and impressive machine. With the angled-vertical bar grille and sleek canopy, this machine had quite a modern look for its day. Any shortcomings of the tractor were hidden beneath the streamlined exterior. Although the Monarch 75 was a solid machine, the drive train had archaic, chain-driven final-drive assemblies, and the crawler had a snail-like top speed of less than 4 miles per hour. To the dismay of the company, the Monarch 75 was not competitive with other major brands and sales were meager.

A 14.5-inch-diameter belt pulley and a PTO were options offered as well as a hydraulic system. For cold climate, a two- or three-man enclosed cab was available. Special pistons could be ordered for high-altitude operations. A special low-speed reverse could be ordered for special situations. The farmer could order a swivel drawbar to replace the rigid type that was standard equipment. Among the most important options were three replacement final-drive sprocket sets. The standard sprockets had 9 teeth, but by changing them with 10-, 11-, or 12-teeth sprockets, the speed of the crawler were increased. These sprockets would turn a massive 48-link Baldwin chain in each of the two final-drive housings that powered the track drive sprockets.

The regular Monarch 75 came with a solid canopy as standard equipment, but a logger version with special shielding and different gearing came without the obstructing cover. This logging version came with a special high seat and a front pull hook.

The Monarch 75 was an improved version of the older Monarch Model F 10-ton. The Nebraska test results were adopted from the Model F. Sales of the Monarch 75 were sluggish and Allis-Chalmers began to design a more modern crawler that came out in 1931, the Model L.

Collecting Notes: The Monarch 75 is a brute and will empty a wallet quickly when restoration begins. Parts are difficult to obtain and the average collector will likely go broke or get discouraged before finishing a righteous restoration on this crawler. The collector who perseveres to a fine restoration will have the privilege of owning a valuable and majestic machine.

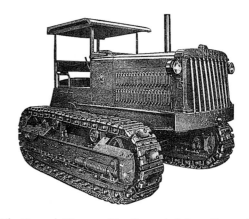

The Monarch 75 came with a Beaver-LeRoi gasoline engine. An experimental 75 had a huge Atlas diesel engine. The Monarch 75 with the gasoline engine would gobble down 8 1/2 gallons of fuel per hour under full load. It is no wonder that diesel engines were a logical solution to fuel economy. Spark-ignition diesel fuel engines were tried from the mid-1930s, but it wasn't until 1939 that Allis-Chalmers finally produced a crawler with a true diesel engine.

Monarch 75 Crawler Specifications (no mounted equipment)

	Early engine	Late engine
Years built	1928–1929	1929–1931
Serial numbers	70001–70266	70267–71066
Horsepower (drawbar)	78.17	78.17 (not retested)
Cylinders	4	4
Engine bore and stroke (inches)	6.50x7.0	6.75x7.0
Engine rpm	850	850
Speeds (standard gearing, forward, mph)	1.55, 2.64, 3.56	1.55, 2.64, 3.56
Speed (standard gearing, reverse, mph)	2.64	2.64
Weight (shipping, pounds)	21,700	21,700
Length (inches)	158.69	158.69
Standard track gauge (inches)	74	74
Height (to top of cab, inches)	104	104
Standard track shoe width (inches)	16	16
Lower track rollers per side	5	5
Belt pulley (optional, inches, dia. x w.)	14.5x11	14.5x11
Belt pulley rpm	420, 713, or 960	420, 713, or 960
PTO speeds (optional)	500, 850, 1,150	500, 850, 1,150
Fuel capacity (gallons)	60	60
Cooling capacity (gallons)	13	13
Ignition (battery)/injector pump	American Bosch ZR4	Eisemann GV4
Carburetor	Zenith 77A	Zenith 76
Suggested new retail price	$5,350 in 1929	$5,350 in 1930

Monarch 75 Crawler Production History

Serial number is found stamped on the front frame below the radiator and on the dash plate.

Year	Serial Numbers
1928	70001–70207
1929	70208–70654
1930	70655–70894
1931	70895–71066

Monarch 75 Crawler Progression History

Year	Serial Number	Modification
1928	70001	First Monarch 75 produced
1929	70217	Full-length truck shields replaced by partial type, radiator with larger lettering introduced, cylinder head and block strengthened, three compression rings instead of the previous two
1929	70232	Battery box moved from engine side to dash
1929	70267	Crankcase and block changed to accommodate changed carburetor, magneto, water pump, and governor; optional 6.75-inch engine bore becomes standard feature
1929	70317	Transmission cover changed to provide simultaneous steering clutch disengagement to operate PTO attachments
1929	70385	Two track support rollers used on each side instead of the previous three
1930	70767	Drawbar redesigned
1931	71066	Last Monarch 75 produced

Monarch 35, Model K, and KO Crawlers

With the big Monarch crawlers, Allis-Chalmers learned all too quickly that the crawler business was highly competitive and that the engineering department would have a lot of work ahead. The Monarch 35 (later renamed the Model K) was introduced in 1929 with modern features including gear-driven final-drive assemblies and a welded track frame. Sales of this model were a big improvement over that of the Model 50 and 75. The engineers at Allis-Chalmers were constantly making improvements to fulfill the needs of contractors and farmers. Any parts that began to show signs of weakness were redesigned to protect the rugged reputation of the Monarch 35. By the time the last Model K was built, most every major assembly was revamped. The early three-speed transmission was upgraded to four speeds and the undercarriage was beefed up. The engine had the crankshaft strengthened and the bore was later increased for added horsepower. The steering wheel was replaced with two levers. Gears and rollers were improved for longer life. Allis-Chalmers worked its way to become an industry leader in the manufacturing of crawlers with its constant attention to quality and alertness to the needs of the customers.

With a 7-foot turning radius, the standard Monarch 35 could operated well in confined areas. An upholstered seat gave operators added comfort over the steel seats found on many other brands of crawlers. By 1939, the crawler was tested at Nebraska with 11,785 pounds maximum pull; not bad for a crawler that weighed in at 13,340 pounds. About 8,300 units were produced before this model was retired in 1943.

Crawlers were used for so many different applications; numerous options were needed to adapt to the assigned task. Allis-Charmers offered options galore, including a wide-track version (WK) and by 1934, a diesel-fuel model (KO). Special engine guards, a front bumper, and a pull hook could be added to fulfill the needs of the logger. A belt pulley and PTO were offered to satisfy the needs of certain farmers. A canopy or winter cab were offered as well as an electric starter to make life a little easier for the operator. Optional track fenders became standard equipment in 1935. The Monarch 35 was renamed the Model K sometime in 1933. Model K crawlers were sold in regions all over the United States.

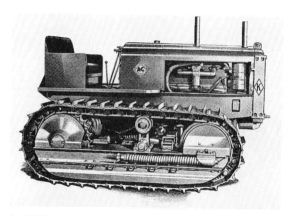

In 1935 beginning with serial number 4451, two steering levers replaced the steering wheel of the Model K. At the same time, the three-speed transmission was updated to a four-speed. A total of 3,850 four-speed models were built before production ended in 1943.

The front-mounted engine air cleaner and the "35" designation give the clues needed to determine that this crawler was made sometime during 1931 through 1933. The "Monarch" name eventually faded from advertising by 1933. Allis-Chalmers used the Monarch name for credibility in the first few years after it purchased the crawler firm. Apparently Allis-Chalmers felt that its own name had built a solid reputation in the crawler industry by 1933.

This Monarch 35 was built in 1930 or 1931. The air cleaner was moved toward the front of the engine early in 1931. The model designation "35" was dropped in favor of "K" in 1933.

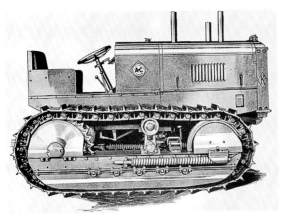

This Model KO was built in 1934 or 1935. Midway into 1935, the steering wheel was replaced by steering levers. The oil-fuel engine of the KO was first offered in 1934. This almost-a-diesel engine used spark plugs for ignition and gained fuel economy over that of the gasoline engine. This expensive engine option cost 30 percent more than the regular gasoline version. Few copies were sold even though much expense was put into advertising this version.

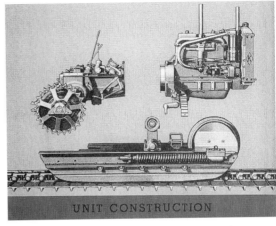

UNIT CONSTRUCTION

The Model K was the first crawler built by Allis-Chalmers to use a gear-driven final-drive assembly. The Monarch 50 and 75 models used huge chains and sprockets. Modern gear-type final-drives offered less maintenance and longer service in most cases. Many patents for the crawler design were inherited by Allis-Chalmers when it bought the Monarch Tractor Company. Other companies were paying licensing fees to use some of these patents.

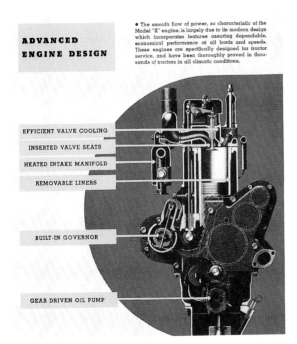

ADVANCED ENGINE DESIGN

● The smooth flow of power, so characteristic of the Model "K" engine, is largely due to its modern design which incorporates features assuring dependable, economical performance at all loads and speeds. These engines are specifically designed for tractor service, and have been thoroughly proved in thousands of tractors in all climatic conditions.

EFFICIENT VALVE COOLING
INSERTED VALVE SEATS
HEATED INTAKE MANIFOLD
REMOVABLE LINERS

BUILT-IN GOVERNOR

GEAR DRIVEN OIL PUMP

The gasoline engine in the Model K was similar to the Model E wheeled tractors. The 4.75x6.5-inch bore and stroke was raised to 5.0x6.5 inches in 1933 beginning with serial number 2669. The rpm was raised from 930 to 1,050. This later engine put out over 62 belt horsepower.

MODEL "KO"

STANDARD AND WIDE TREAD TRACTORS

The Model KO was first offered in 1934. The early versions only displayed the "K" on the sides of the radiator. By about 1936, the "K" had the "O" around the emblem. Allis-Chalmers claimed that its crawlers were the only ones to have both high speed and the ability to burn diesel fuel. It also claimed to have the only diesel-fuel tractors that were properly balanced for weight and power. Its advertising campaign was in vain as only the true diesel crawlers made by other companies were selling well.

The WK (wide-track) model was sometimes referred to as the "Hillside" version. The regular Model K has a 48-inch track gauge, while the Model WK has a 63-inch track gauge. (Track gauge refers to the measurement of width between the center points of each track.) Up to 15-inch-wide track shoes were available for the Model K, but the Model WK shown here could be bought with shoes up to 28 inches wide.

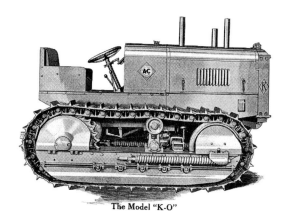

The Model "K-O"

This early version of the Model KO with its steering wheel was either built in 1934 or early in 1935. The engine covers were an option.

Collecting Notes: Restoring the Model K is expensive, but the parts are not extremely difficult to find. Expect more trouble when obtaining parts for models built before 1933. KO versions are seldom found and will be a bigger challenge to restore. The cost of a proper restoration may likely exceed the value of the finished product on common model versions at this time. Collector interest in crawlers has been growing fast in recent years and values are apt to improve in leaps and bounds within 10 years. To restore crawlers as a profitable venture would most likely be a big disappointment at this time, but real crawler lovers will not do the math.

Monarch 35, Model K, and KO Crawler Specifications (no mounted equipment)

	Early Gas Engine	Late Gas Engine	Diesel Fuel Engine (K0)
Years built	1929–1933	1933–1943	1934–1943
Serial numbers	1–2668	2669–9468	KO5200–?
Horsepower (drawbar/belt)	40.99/no belt test	53.60/62.22	49.26/59.06
Cylinders	4	4	4
Engine bore and stroke (inches)	4.75x6.5	5.00x6.5	5.25x6.5
Engine rpm	930	1,050	1,050
Speeds (standard gearing, forward, mph)	2.08, 3.1, 4.5	1.72, 2.59, 3.26, 5.92	1.72, 2.59, 3.26, 5.92
Speed (standard gearing, reverse, mph)	2.39	2.10	2.10
Weight (as tested, pounds)	10,680	13,340 (wide-track)	13,000
Length (inches)	119.56	119.56	119.56
Standard track gauge (inches)	48	48	48
Height (to top of radiator, inches)	64	64	61.5
Standard track shoe width (inches)	13	15	15
Lower track rollers per side	5	5	5
Belt pulley (inches, dia. x w.)	10 or 12x8.75	10 or 12x8.75	10 or 12x8.75
Belt pulley rpm	930	1,050	1,050
Fuel capacity (gallons)	34	39	39
Cooling capacity (gallons)	10	11.5	11.5
Ignition	Eisemann GL4	Bendix or Fairbanks-Morse	Mallory
Carburetor/injector pump	Kingston or Zenith	Zenith	Bosch
Suggested new retail price	$2,450 in 1930	$2,400 in 1934	$3,150 in 1934

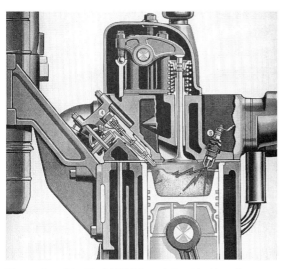

The engine of the Model KO injected diesel fuel into the cylinders and was ignited by spark plugs. A Bosch injection pump was used and the special spark plugs were a Champion W-95D or equivalent. A special priming tank for the Model KO holds gasoline for starting. A couple of pumps on the primer plunger spray gasoline into the intake manifold where it is drawn into the cylinders for an easy engine start.

Notice the track fenders on this Model KO. The four-speed models of the K-series all came with these fenders. The three-speed models built before mid-1935 were fitted with fenders at an extra cost. The Bosch injection pump shown near the center of the engine in this view used a separate plunger pump for each cylinder. A small camshaft in the bottom of the pump forced up each plunger at the precise time.

Monarch 35, Model K, and KO Crawler Production History

Serial number is found stamped on the front frame below the radiator and also on the dash plate.

Year	Model K Serial Numbers	Model KO Serial Numbers
1929	1–48	
1930	49–1372	
1931	1373—2333	
1932	2334–2653	
1933	2654–3045	
1934	3046–3593	KO5200–?
1935	3594–4792	
1936	4793–6335	KO6019–?
1937	6336–7707	
1938	7708–8017	
1939	8018–8522	
1940	8523–8956	
1941	8957–9268	
1942	9269–9393	
1943	9394–9468	

Monarch 35, Model K and KO Crawler Model Progression History

Year	Serial Number	Modification
1929	1	First Monarch 35 produced
1929	?	Nebraska test no. 171
1930	51	3-inch main bearings replace 2-inch, v-belt and pulleys replace flat belt and pulleys, Vortox air cleaner replaces Allis-Chalmers brand
1930	1306	Drawbar improved (second type)
1931	1480	Vortox air cleaner moved from the rear of the engine toward the front
1931	1901	Battery box moved from under seat to side of seat
1933	2669	Engine displacement increased from 460 to 510 cubic inches, undercarriage redesigned for strength, drawbar improved (third type)
1933	2848	Nebraska test no. 215
1935	3701	Drawbar improved (fourth type)
1935	4451	Battery box moved from side of seat to under the seat again
1934	KO5200	Model KO (diesel fuel) introduced
1935	4451	Two levers replace the steering wheel, four-speed transmission replaces the three-speed
1935	4672	Flange-mount magneto replaces base-mount
1936	6269	Pinion and bull gears get improved teeth
1937	6989	Model WKO (wide-track, diesel fuel) Nebraska test no. 285
1939	8276	Nebraska test no. 336
1943	9468	Last Model K crawler built

Model L and LO Crawlers

The Model L was a replacement for the outdated Monarch 75. The Monarch 75 had a three-speed transmission and used chain-driven final-drive assemblies. The new Model L had a six-speed transmission and used gear-driven final-drive assemblies. Sales of the Model L were never outstanding, but the market for huge crawlers was somewhat limited compared to mid-sized machines.

This 11-ton Model L tested at almost 92 PTO horsepower. Two Zenith carburetors supplied fuel from the 75-gallon tank to the six huge 5 1/4-inch pistons in this Allis-Chalmers-built engine. With the standard 16-inch grousers, the Model L had a 9-foot turning radius. When tested at Nebraska, a maximum pull of 15,086 pounds was registered.

Although track gauge options were not offered, options of all sorts were offered to make the Model L a versatile machine in many different industries including farming, construction, and logging. Grouser widths of 20 and 24 inches were offered in several different styles for use in loose dirt, hard roads, soft fields, swampy ground, snow, and ice. Mufflers or spark arresters could be added to the twin exhaust stacks to avoid excess noise or fires. A front bumper and pull hooks could be added for special applications, including logging. An open canopy or even a fully enclosed winter cab could be added to shelter the operator, and an optional padded seat could soften the ride. Engine shields could be added to protect from rupturing the oil pan or damaging engine components when in rough areas. A belt pulley or 2-3/4-inch PTO were offered to power different kinds of equipment.

In 1934 an oil-fuel Model LO was added to the line that used a spark-ignition system to ignite the injected diesel fuel at a 6.5:1 compression ratio. Sales of the LO models were poor because the initial cost of the crawler was much higher and the efficiency was not as good as a true diesel engine that used extremely high compression for fuel ignition. Ten experimental LD models were produced with General Motors two-cycle diesel engines that led toward the introduction of the later HD-series.

Collecting Notes: These big Model L crawlers are impressive but expensive to restore to a high state of condition.

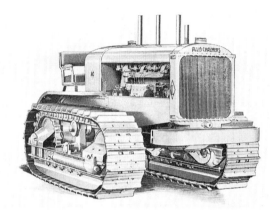

With basically the same engine design as the gasoline version, the engine in this LO crawler uses a bit higher compression and a Bosch injector pump to allow it to run on diesel fuel. Only 3,357 gasoline versions of the Model L were built. The total of LO diesel-fuel crawlers built was only a fraction of this number. Actual production numbers for the LO have yet to be found.

The big Model L crawler put out more than 108 belt horsepower in its later years of production. The engine was basically half-again as big as the four-cylinder Model K engine. This six-cylinder crawler would devour more than 10 1/2 gallons of fuel an hour under full load. A diesel-fuel version offered in 1934 used about 7 1/3 gallons an hour under full load, but produced about 17 less belt horsepower than this gasoline version.

The massive engine in the Model L crawler has an 844-cubic inch displacement. Allis-Chalmers marketed stationary power units that used the same engines as the Model U tractor, Model E tractor, and Model L crawler. Many internal parts of the Model L engine were the same as the Model E wheeled tractor.

These pieces of equipment were some of the numerous items offered as options for the Model L crawler. The PTO had shaft speeds of 288 or 221 rpm. The power pulley is 20 inches in diameter and 15 inches wide with belt speeds of 3,040 and 2,330 feet per minute. With the dual exhaust on the Model L, twin spark arresters were needed in fire hazard areas. These units also served as mufflers for areas where sound was considered a nuisance.

The steering clutches for the Model L crawler were a multiple-disc type with alternating fiber and steel components. These clutches were among the best in the industry and offered a long service life. Unlike differential-type crawlers like the Cletrac, the Allis-Chalmers crawlers did not speed up the track opposite of the one held stationary. The straight drive axle on the A-C crawlers did not swap power between the tracks as did the design of the Cletrac. The Cletrac's differential kept both tracks under power during a turn; other brands slipped power to the inside track to make a turn. Each style had its advantages; operator preferences usually decided a crawler purchase.

Rarely found copies of the LO are in high demand among crawler collectors, but the numbers of collectors are much, much lower than that of wheeled-tractor collectors. Rare crawler values will seldom match that of wheeled tractors with similar production numbers. Restoration for one's own grati-fication would make sense, while restoration for profit may be considered foolhardy in light of expenses that can be outrageous. Anyone who finds one of the 10 rare LD models with a GM engine will own a real treasure.

Model L and LO Crawler Specifications (no mounted equipment)

	Model L (gasoline)	Model LO (diesel fuel)
Years built	1931–1942	1934–1942
Serial numbers	1–3357	LO1547–?
Horsepower (drawbar/belt, after 1939)	91.99/108.84	76.75/91.56
Cylinders	6	6
Engine bore and stroke (inches)	5.25x6.5	5.25x6.5
Engine rpm	1,050	1,050
Speeds (standard gearing, forward, mph)	1.48, 1.94, 2.68, 3.5, 4.9, 6.41	1.48, 1.94, 2.68, 3.5, 4.9, 6.41
Speeds (standard gearing, reverse, mph)	1.72, 2.25	1.72, 2.25
Weight (as tested, pounds)	26,105	24,925
Length (inches)	153.25	153.25
Standard track gauge (inches)	68	68
Height (to top of radiator, inches)	81	81
Standard track shoe width (inches)	16 (20 after June 1937)	20
Lower track rollers per side	5	5
Belt pulley (inches, dia. x w.)	18 or 20x15	18 or 20x15
Belt pulley rpm	444 and 580	444 and 580
Fuel capacity (gallons)	75	75
Cooling capacity (gallons)	19	19
Ignition	Eisemann, Bendix, or Fairbanks-Morse	Mallory MO4
Carburetor/injector pump	Zenith (two used)	Bosch
Suggested new retail price	$5,302 in 1942	$6,600 in 1942

Two Zenith carburetors fed gasoline to the hungry cylinders of the gigantic Model L. Instead of gravity feeding the gasoline to the carburetors, a fuel pump was utilized as the carburetors were positioned higher than the bottom of the fuel tank.

A canopy with added enclosures or a fully enclosed cab were available to protect the operator from adverse weather conditions. This design offered little protection in case of a rollover. Safety was not a concern at the time. In later years, safety glass was used in crawler cabs as well as a built-in rollover protection design.

Model L and LO Crawler Production History

Serial number is found stamped on the shelf at the right side of the rear end of the transmission case.

Year	Serial Numbers
1931	1–34
1932	35–498
1933	499-660
1934	661–887 (LO1547–?)
1935	888–1438
1936	1439–2136
1937	2137–2705
1938	2706–2943
1939	2944–3232
1940	3233–3251
1941	3252–3272
1942	3273–3357

The operator of the Model L crawler sat to the left side. Steering levers disengaged the steering clutches and pedals were brakes for each side. The lever on the far left operated the master clutch. The shifter in the center would give the operator a choice of six forward and two reverse speeds.

Model L and LO Crawler Progression History

Year	Serial Number	Modification
1931	1	First Model L crawler built
1931	26	Water pump improved, transmission gears improved, track rollers and idlers with improved bearings
1932	69	First Model L tested at Nebraska test no. 200
1934	678	2-inch frame rails replace 1 1/2-inch rails
1934	699	Friction-disc throttle lever replaces ratchet type
1934	LO1547	First oil-fuel engine model
1935	1163	Steering levers replace steering wheel
1935	1366	Transmission gears changed
1936	1881	Air filter precleaner used
1937	2360	Cast drawbar replaces flat-steel type
1937	LO2459	LO tested at Nebraska test no. 287
1939	3031	Steering levers beefed up
1939	3133	Model L tested again at Nebraska test no. 338
1940	3273	Steering clutches improved
1942	3357	Last Model L crawler built

Model M Crawler

The Model M crawler used the same engine as the Model U farm tractor. During its 11 years of production, 14,524 units were sold. Considered the "baby" of the crawler line at a bit over 3 tons, the Model M was about one-fourth the size of the giant Model L. A four-speed transmission and a host of add-on accessories made the little M popular for all sorts of different jobs.

The 40-inch track gauge was standard while a 50-inch version (WM) was offered for hillside conditions. This hillside model came with longer tracks. Two versions of an orchard model were offered, one with a top-mounted seat and another with the seat down low and to the rear of the machine. The orchard models used full-length track fenders and a special grille guard. A logging version of the Model M had engine, sprocket, and grille shielding.

Not unlike the bigger crawlers, the Model M could be bought with a canopy or cab, electric starter, and lights. Although most Ms ran on gasoline or kerosene, a limited number had conversion kits installed that allowed the engine to run on alcohol.

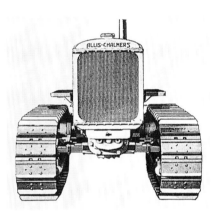

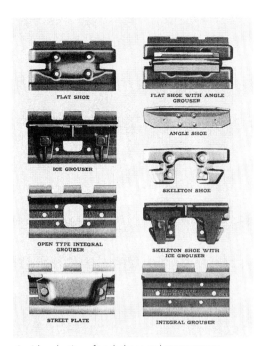

A wide selection of track shoes and grousers were offered on Allis-Chalmers crawlers. With many years of experience, crawler companies learned that without properly designed track shoes, packed snow, ice, mud, and sand could cause treachery for the machine and operator. Snow would pack under the solid shoes of early logging crawlers and throw a track or pop off shoes. Conventional grousers often behaved like skates on ice as the machines would slide sideways quicker than a wink. Standard grousers cut up a road surface like a cookie cutter. The right shoes for the right job would prevent a lot of predicaments.

The wide-track version of the Model M was called the WM. Standard models could accept track shoe widths up to 12 inches wide, but this WM could be fitted with angle shoes that were 22 inches wide. The wide crawlers were popular for hillside farms, and in soggy areas the wider shoes could augment flotation.

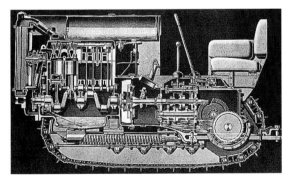

This cutaway shows the well-built and compact design of the Model M. With a four-speed transmission and hand-operated clutch, this little unit had many of the same features as bigger crawlers on the market.

The "baby" of the Allis-Chalmers crawler line was this Model M. By using the same engine as the popular Model U farm tractor, the tooling costs were lessened. In its 11 production years, 14,524 copies of this crawler were built. Weighing only a little over 6 tons, this crawler was ideal for a farmer with smaller acreage to use in wet conditions.

Collecting Notes: The Model M is perhaps the easiest of the early Allis-Chalmers crawlers to get parts for. Because of its small size and fairly good parts availability, the M should be restored at much less cost than its bigger brothers. Storage, trucking, and restoration costs are all in the favor of small crawlers. Orchard versions are seldom found with nice fenders, but a restored model will get much attention at shows.

Model M Crawler Specifications (no mounted equipment)

Years built	1932–1942
Serial numbers	1–14524
Horsepower (drawbar/belt, gasoline)	29.65/35.43
Cylinders	4
Engine bore and stroke (inches)	4.375x5 (4.50x5 after serial no. 2942)
Engine rpm	1,200
Speeds (standard gearing, forward, mph)	1.83, 2.23, 3.20, 4.15
Speed (standard gearing, reverse, mph)	2.55
Weight (as tested, pounds)	6,855
Length (inches)	101.375
Standard track gauge (inches)	40
Height (to top of radiator, inches)	56.19
Standard track shoe width (inches)	12
Lower track rollers per side	4
Belt pulley (inches, dia. x w.)	10 or 12x8.75 (960 rpm)
Fuel capacity (gallons)	24
Cooling capacity (gallons)	6
Ignition	Eisemann, Bendix, or Fairbanks-Morse
Carburetor	Zenith K5
Suggested new retail price	$1,650 in 1934

MANIFOLD SETTING FOR KEROSENE OR DISTILLATE

MANIFOLD SETTING FOR GASOLINE

As with farm tractors of the day, many thrifty people preferred to burn kerosene in their Model M crawler. Kerosene delivered somewhat less horsepower, but was not as expensive as gasoline.

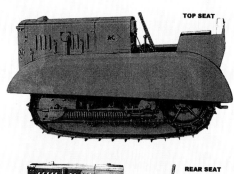

TOP SEAT

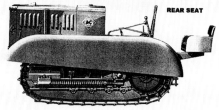

REAR SEAT

Here is a picture from an early advertisement showing a Model M crawler pulling an Allis-Chalmers Rumely No. 2 prairie-type combine harvester. To harvest grain with 20-foot-swath rows is quite impressive for such a little crawler.

The Model M crawler could be purchased as an orchard crawler. The two styles offered are shown here. The rear-seat version was used in orchards with low branches so the operator could duck below the top of the hood if necessary. These machines were an excellent choice for pulling a spray rig between tree rows.

Model M Crawler Production History

Serial number is found stamped on the shelf at the right side of the rear end of the transmission case.

Year	Serial numbers
1932	1–41
1933	42–401
1934	402–841
1935	842–1941
1936	1942–3841
1937	3842–7066
1938	7067–8126
1939	8127–9539
1940	9540–11379
1941	11380–12946
1942	12947–14524

Model M Crawler Progression History

Year	Serial Number	Modification
1932	1	First Model M crawler built (at museum in Vista, California)
1933	255	Model tested on gasoline at Nebraska test No. 216
1935	Not known	Model tested on distillate at Nebraska test No. 239
1936	2942	Engine bore increased from 3.375 inches to 3.50 inches
1938	7742	Starting fuel tank relocated from the front to the rear of the main tank
1939	8196	Steering clutch levers improved
1939	8342	Track rollers and idler have roller bearings to replace bushings
1939	8386	Oil fill moved from rear of transmission to top transmission cover
1942	14524	Last Model M crawler built

Model S and SO Crawlers

The 84-horsepower Model S crawler was introduced to fill a size gap between the 62-horsepower Model K and the 108-horsepower Model L. Sales were sluggish with only 1,225 units built during six years of manufacturing. Caterpillar was having much success with its diesel engines in its big crawlers. The Allis-Chalmers Model S would empty the contents of its 64-gallon tank in less than 8 hours under full load conditions. Caterpillar's much bigger RD-8 was rated at 103 horsepower and used fewer gallons of fuel per hour than the Allis-Chalmers S under full load. The Model SO was offered to compete. The Hesselman design was a sort of hybrid engine that injected the diesel fuel and ignited it with spark plugs. Power dropped to about 75 PTO horsepower and the efficiency went up. Now the horsepower class was comparable to the Caterpillar RD-7. The RD-7 used almost a gallon an hour less than the Model SO under full load. Allis-Chalmers learned in short order that a true diesel was needed to stand up to the market.

The operator sits atop the upholstered seat of the Model S and brings it to life with the 12-volt starter that was a standard feature. Shifting was smooth with the five-speed constant-mesh transmission. He could pull seven- or eight-bottom 14-inch plows in most soil conditions. The Model S was a handsome and powerful machine.

A wide-track version with a 74-inch track gauge was offered that was 12 inches wider than the standard version. Several styles of grousers were offered from 16 to 24 inches wide for all different working conditions. A PTO or power pulley could be added to power special accessories. To protect the engine, louvered covers were offered. Special pistons were available for high-altitude conditions.

The poor sales of the Model S helped lead to the introduction of a whole new line of crawlers that Allis-Chalmers brought out about 1940. The HD-series would show better performance and efficiency for which the design of the Model S was a huge steppingstone.

Collecting Notes: Model S crawlers are rather scarce while certain parts can be a challenge to find. The SO is an extremely rare machine that would be cherished by many collectors. The downside would be the great expense of a high-class restoration. Many collectors do not have the resources to complete a righteous restoration on a battered Model S or SO. Collectors who have the money and dedication needed to restore one of these crawlers can own a true treasure.

The gasoline-fuel Model S and this diesel-fuel SO were built to fill the size gap between Models K and L. Sales of both S models were poor—only 1,225 units were produced in six years of production. Collectors seldom find a Model SO, only a small number of the total were built with this less popular engine version.

Model S and SO Crawler Specifications (no mounted equipment)

	Model S (gasoline)	Model SO (diesel fuel)
Years built	1937–1942	1937–1942
Serial numbers	3–1227	?
Horsepower rating (drawbar/belt)	68.86/84.34	62.39/74.82
Cylinders	4	4
Engine bore and stroke (inches)	5.75x6.50	5.75x6.50
Engine rpm	1,050	1,050
Speeds (standard gearing, forward, mph)	1.52, 2.32, 3.25, 4.55, 6.37	1.52, 2.32, 3.25, 4.55, 6.37
Speed (standard gearing, reverse, mph)	1.76	1.76
Weight (as tested, pounds)	20,330	20,100
Length (inches)	146	146
Standard track gauge (inches)	62	62
Height (inches)	74	74
Standard track shoe width (inches)	18	18
Lower track rollers per side	5	5
Belt pulley (inches, dia. x w.)	13.375x10 (770 rpm)	13.375x10 (770 rpm)
Fuel capacity (gallons)	64	64
Cooling capacity (gallons)	12.5	12.5
Ignition	Delco-Remy	Mallory MO4
Carburetor/injector pump	Zenith 62AJ-12	Deco
Suggested new retail price	$4,095 in 1942	

Model S Crawler Production History

Serial number is found stamped on the upper right side of the rear end of the transmission case and dash.

Year	Serial Numbers
1937	3–412
1938	413–584
1939	585–1084
1940	1085–1127
1941	1128–1211
1942	1212–1227

Model S and SO Crawler Progression History

Year	Serial number	Modification
1937	3	First production Model S crawler built
1937	7	Michiana oil filter assembly replaces Purolator
1937	52	Purolator oil filter assembly used again
1937	SO218	Model SO (diesel fuel) tested at Nebraska test no. 286
1939	628	Track roller bearings and seals improved
1939	703	Front idler bearings and seals improved.
1939	901	Gasoline model tested at Nebraska test no. 337 (wide-track)
1939	1069	36-inch exhaust stack replaces extension type with angled top
1941	1199	Release bearing assembly in master clutch improved
1942	1227	Last Model S crawler built

Model HD-14 and HD-14C Crawlers

In 1939, Allis-Chalmers introduced a really impressive and revolutionary crawler, the HD-14. Weighing in at over 14 tons, this six-speed giant was powered by a true diesel engine. General Motors made this powerful engine that put out 145 PTO horsepower. These GM engines had developed a reputation for being reliable, powerful, and consistent. By making engines with many common parts, GM offered different sizes by changing the number of pistons. Allis-Chalmers eventually used GM engines in other crawlers in two, three, four, and six cylinders. The HD-14 was a six-cylinder version.

In 1946, Allis-Chalmers introduced the first torque converter crawler, the HD-14C. What a profound idea to have infinite speed control among three different speed ranges! To this day, the torque converter is one of the most popular transmissions found in modern crawlers.

Electric starting was a standard feature on the HD-14 as well as all its other GM-powered crawlers that followed. A front

bumper and upholstered seat were no longer options, but standard features. This huge crawler came right out of the factory with the capability of more than 28,000 pounds of pull.

An open canopy and a fully enclosed cab were available as well as a power pulley and a 935-rpm PTO. Optional grouser styles were offered to adapt to special conditions. The HD-14 put Allis-Chalmers back in the big crawler market, and the torque converter model gave it a new edge.

An engine heater was mounted in the air intake box to assist in cold starting. This unit used fuel oil pumped by hand at the cowl to a nozzle in the heater box; a spark plug ignited the diesel fuel mist to heat the incoming air to the engine. An optional preheater was available for colder conditions. This preheater was a steel container mounted at the air intake box with a nozzle and a small reservoir for diesel fuel. The operator would pump by hand a small plunger on the unit until 120 pounds of pressure was reached. A wire was hooked to the hot starter terminal to run an internal fan on the preheater. The

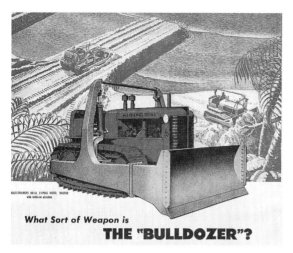

ALLIS-CHALMERS HD-14, 2-CYCLE DIESEL, TRACTOR
with bulldozer attached.

What Sort of Weapon is

THE "BULLDOZER"?

The HD-14 became a handy machine with the bulldozer attachment. Early crawlers were designed mainly for agricultural purposes, but by the time World War II came about, the value of bulldozers was confirmed. This Baker blade was massive and the whole unit attached to the undercarriage. Allis-Chalmers bought out the Baker Manufacturing Company in 1955.

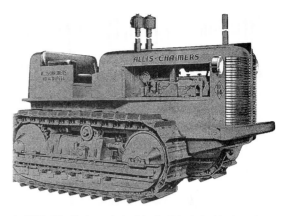

In 1939, Allis-Chalmers lacked the facilities to build a line of its own diesel engines. Conversions of gasoline engines to burn diesel fuel proved a poor compromise—competitors made true diesel engines that produced a much greater fuel economy. General Motors made a time-tested line of two-cycle diesels that were both snappy and efficient. The HD-14 was the first production crawler made by Allis-Chalmers to use a true diesel GM engine.

unit separated to expose the nozzle, then a needle valve was opened to start a good mist. The operator ignited this mist with a match or other means and the unit was slid back in place for 7 to 30 minutes, depending on how cold it was. The engine cylinders would be warmed for starting. The starters on all the Allis-Chalmers crawlers with GM engines were electric. Other crawler brands commonly used pony motors to warm

and turn over the engines. In all cases, starting diesels in extremely cold weather has always been a challenge.

Collecting Notes: The HD-14 collector value rivals the practical value. Only in the last few years has this crawler even been considered to be collectible. Restoration can be expensive, but most parts are readily available. One may expect collector interest to increase slowly over the next several years.

Model HD-14 and HD-14C Crawler Specifications (no mounted equipment)

	Model HD-14	Model HD-14C
Years built	1939–1947	1946–1947
Serial numbers	18–6422	5455 (approx.)–6422
Horsepower rating (drawbar/PTO)	57.29/68.68	not tested
Engine manufacturer	General Motors	General Motors
Cylinders	6	6
Engine bore and stroke (inches)	4.25x5.0	4.25x5.0
Engine rpm	1,500	1,650
Speeds (standard gearing, forward, mph)	1.72, 2.18, 2.76, 3.5, 4.36, 7.0	0–3.1, 0–3.8, 0–7.2
Speeds (standard gearing, reverse, mph)	2.0, 3.2	0–3.5
Weight (pounds)	28,750	29,330
Length (inches)	165	165
Standard track gauge (inches)	68	68
Height (inches)	108.75	108.75
Standard track shoe width (inches)	22	22
Lower track rollers per side	5	5
Belt pulley (inches, dia. x w.)	20x15	20x15
Belt pulley rpm	405 or 650	585
Fuel capacity (gallons)	68	68
Cooling capacity (gallons)	12	12
Injector	GM unit injectors	GM unit injectors
Suggested new retail price	$9,250 in 1947	

Model HD-14 and HD-14C Crawler Production History

Serial number is found stamped on the top flange of the right rear side of the transmission case.

Year	Serial Numbers
1939	18–25
1940	26–548
1941	549–1165
1942	1166–2112
1943	2113–3137
1944	3138–4258
1945	4259–5454
1946	5455–5814
1947	5815–6422

Model HD-14 and HD-14C Crawler Model Progression History

Year	Serial Number	Modification
1939	18	First production Model HD-14 built
1940	265	Crawler tested at Nebraska (test no. 362)
1940	759	Transmission improved; better gears, shafts, and bearings
1942	2079	Steering clutches improved with better ventilation and adjustment
1946	not found	Model HD-14C (torque converter) introduced
1947	6422	Last HD-14 crawler built

Model HD-7 Crawlers

Introduced in 1940 as the smallest of the three diesels in Allis-Chalmers' new crawler line, the HD-7 became its best-selling model. More than 18,000 units were built during its 11 production years. The demand for reliable and efficient crawlers became stronger every day.

The truck frame on agricultural models came with a spring-mounted front support, while construction versions had a rigid-beam support. Wide-track gauge (HD-7W) and long-track versions were offered. The wide-track model has a 63-inch track gauge compared to the 52-inch gauge of the regular model. Constant improvements were made throughout the HD-7 production life.

Due to the HD-7's strength and reliability, the U.S. military adopted about 5,000 wide-track versions for use during World War II. These crawlers were powerful and reliable. Referred to as the Medium Tractor M1, these HD-7W crawlers were used to build airstrips, roads, and to do numerous other heavy-duty jobs. Several of these crawlers were fitted with Baker bulldozer blades. The Baker bulldozer model came with an arched frame that was hydraulically dropped and raised by two rams that stood vertically at both sides of the operator. A Baker Gradebuilder model was similar, but with a manual angle adjustment. A Buckeye bulldozer with a cable-lift system was sometimes found on the civilian versions of the HD-7. The Buckeye had no provision for down-pressure other than gravity. Although originally intended for agricultural purposes, crawlers had developed into a more important role as earthmovers and road builders.

Options were abundant as with other Allis-Chalmers' crawlers. Long-track versions offered contractors more ground contact and stability. Special hooks and shielding for loggers, PTO and power pulley for farmers, and all sorts of track grouser styles for contractors were offered. A three-man cab was even available with a windshield that opened. In

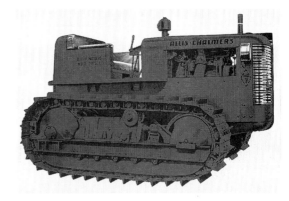

The HD-7 used a three-cylinder GM diesel engine and was a perfect size for many farmers and contractors. The model was a hit with more than 18,000 copies built.

extremely warm conditions, a four-core radiator was offered in place of the standard three-core type. Special provisions were offered for dusty conditions as well as conditions that had loose debris or leaves floating around. With an extended air-filter stack and a radiator screen guard, problems with dust and debris were minimized.

The success of the early HD-series carried Allis-Chalmers into more models with a larger range of sizes. The HD-7 was a fine midsized crawler, but competition and demand called for crawlers that were a bit larger or smaller. Allis-Chalmers had an alert and talented engineering department that seemed to be able to build machines to suit the need of the day. Its cutting-edge developments kept competitors on their toes. Allis-Chalmers was not a follower, but an industry leader that often was years ahead of other companies in its technology. It took a brave company board of directors to allow new ideas that were considered somewhat absurd at the time to go into production. The constant upgrades and new innovations gave Allis-Chalmers a powerfully solid reputation for quality that made them some honest profits for many years.

Collecting Notes: Collector values for restored Model HD-7 crawlers are not high. The usefulness of a healthy machine tends to dictate the values as collector interest is limited at this time. The General Motors diesel engines are relatively easy to service and obtain parts for when compared to many other crawlers of this era. The undercarriage is always a huge consideration for restoration. A trained eye will find welded sprockets, cracked idler wheel brackets, and worn track pins and bushings. Much expense can be invested in renewing the undercarriage. A nice running machine with a poor undercarriage is worth only a fraction of the value of a similar crawler with a fresh undercarriage.

Model HD-7 Crawler Specifications (no mounted equipment)

Years built	1940–1950
Serial numbers	3–18505
Horsepower rating (drawbar/PTO)	57.29/68.68
Engine bore and stroke (inches)	4.25x5.0 (three-cylinder General Motors)
Engine rpm	1,500
Speeds (standard gearing, forward, mph)	1.59, 2.19, 2.97, 5.0
Speed (standard gearing, reverse, mph)	1.89
Weight (pounds)	13,835
Length (inches)	128
Standard track gauge (inches)	63
Height (inches)	86
Standard track shoe width (inches)	16
Lower track rollers per side	5 (standard-track model)
Belt pulley (inches, dia. x w.)	10 or 12x8.75 (1,031 rpm)
Fuel capacity (gallons)	31
Cooling capacity (gallons)	5.75
Injector	GM unit injectors
Suggested new retail price	$6,900 in 1950

Model HD-7 and HD-7W Crawler Progression History

Year	Serial Number	Modification
1940	3	First production Model HD-7 built
1940	176	Tractor tested at Nebraska (test no. 360, wide-track)
1940	303	Fuel system improved with better sump and filter
1940	323	Radiator gets seven fins per inch instead of six
1940	403	Stack-mounted air precleaner replaces underhood type
1940	482	2.5-inch-thick radiator fan replaces 2.0-inch fan
1941	approx. 788	Air precleaner improved and replaces glass-jar type
1941	1102	36- and 38-link long-track models introduced; seals in track rollers improved
1945	11497	27.5-inch front track idler replaces 23.5-inch on long-track models
1946	12858	Final-drive gears improved
1947	13453	3.0-inch-thick radiator fan replaces 2.5-inch fan
1948	16697	Ether dispenser replaces oil-fired preheater as standard starting aid
1950	18505	Last HD-7 crawler built

Model HD-7 and HD-7W Crawler Production History

Serial number is found stamped on the upper right corner on the rear of the transmission case. The serial numbers for the Model HD-7 and HD-7W are interspersed with one another.

Year	HD-7 Beginning Serial Numbers	HD-7W Beginning Serial Numbers
1940	3	3
1941	503	503
1942	1137	1137
1943	5403	2977
1944	none	5285
1945	none	7998
1946	12382	12091
1947	13236	13078
1948	15117	15156
1949	16769	16752
1950	18094	18086
Ending serial number	18505	18505

Model HD-10 Crawler

The HD-10 was the midsized crawler in the first trio of HD-series crawlers. Like the earlier Model S, this crawler was made to fill a size gap. The demand for a true diesel led to the demise of the older Model SO and the introduction of the efficient HD-10. The four-cylinder General Motors diesel gave this crawler more than 98 PTO horsepower. Sales of the HD-10 were fairly good with more than 10,000 units built during its 11 years of production.

As many as 1,760 Model HD-10W (wide-track) were used by the military during World War II. These crawlers were referred to as the Heavy Tractor M1. These reliable government crawlers had performed admirably during their hitch, which by reputation, helped the sales of Allis-Chalmers crawlers for many years to follow.

With an electric starter and lights as standard equipment, even people of small size could start the crawler and the machine could work through the night. Each standard track had 32 links and five rollers until 1945, when the 34-link track and six rollers became the norm. Special long-track versions were available with 35 links and the shorter 32-link tracks were still available after 1945 on special order. A 33-link track was also offered. The 62-inch track gauge was popular for farming, but the military and contractors preferred the HD-10W with its 74-inch gauge.

For logging, the bumper was already a standard feature and for extra cost, guards were offered for the engine and tracks. Farmers could pay extra to get a belt pulley or PTO assembly if needed. Contractors could add bulldozer blades that were sold through Allis-Chalmers dealers, but at the time made by other firms.

As the best-selling of the three new HD-series crawlers, the HD-10 became a strong precedent for many improved models to follow. The strength of the Allis-Chalmers dealerships and factories was only through the determination of its engineers and effective support from the company leaders.

Collecting Notes: The value of the HD-10 for collectors is limited. At this time, the fairly high production numbers and the somewhat generic appearance of this machine makes it perhaps more valuable as a useful machine. Parts are not often a huge job to obtain, but to restore a 10-ton crawler to its full glory would be outrageously expensive. A collector's own fascination and appreciation of this crawler may be the only way one will be restored to a high state because economics are not in its favor.

The HD-10 sold more than 10,000 copies. Its value during World War II was proven over and over. The reputation of this HD-series put Allis-Chalmers high into the ranks of crawler manufacturers. Heads were turning at Caterpillar and Cleveland Tractor Company (Cletrac) as the popularity of A-C crawlers climbed.

This ad from November 24, 1945, announces the track improvements recently made to the HD-10. At serial number 5574, the 32 shoes on each track were increased to 34 and an extra bottom track roller was added to give 10 percent more ground contact.

Model HD-10 Crawler Specifications (no mounted equipment)

Years built	1940–1950
Serial numbers	2–10198
Horsepower rating (drawbar/PTO)	82.19/98.47
Engine bore and stroke (inches)	4.25x5.0 (four-cylinder General Motors)
Engine rpm	1,600
Speeds (standard gearing, forward, mph)	1.49, 2.39, 3.37, 3.91, 5.38, 8.81
Speeds (standard gearing, reverse, mph)	1.65, 3.71
Weight (pounds)	20,960
Length (inches)	150
Standard track gauge (inches)	62
Height (inches)	100
Standard track shoe width (inches)	18
Lower track rollers per side	5 (6 after 1945)
Belt pulley (inches, dia. x w.)	13.375x10 (413 or 930 rpm)
Fuel capacity (gallons)	44
Cooling capacity (gallons)	9.75
Injector	GM unit injectors
Suggested new retail price	$9,250 in 1950

Model HD-10 and HD-10W Crawler Production History

Serial number is found stamped on the upper right corner on the rear of the transmission case.

The serial numbers for the Model HD-10 and HD-10W are interspersed with each other.

Year	HD-10 Beginning Serial Numbers	HD-10W Beginning Serial Numbers
1940	2	2
1941	642	642
1942	none	1446
1943	none	2082
1944	3652	2339
1945	none	4095
1946	6103	5964
1947	6576	6463
1948	7799	7602
1949	8710	8676
1950	9634	9631
Ending serial number	10198	10198

Model HD-10 Crawler Progression History

Year	Serial Number	Modification
1940	2	First production Model HD-10 built
1940	201	Crawler tested at Nebraska (test no. 361)
1940	515	Stack-mounted air precleaner replaces underhood type
1941	approx. 1146	Air precleaner improved and replaces glass-jar type
1942	1785	Several transmission gears changed
1945	5574	34-link track chain replaces 32-link chain as standard equipment; 32-link still available as special order
1950	10198	Last HD-10 crawler built

Chapter 9

The Postwar Allis-Chalmers Crawlers

World War II had thwarted the introduction of new crawler models. Some practical improvements to components were allowed, but government war rules were aimed for the one goal of keeping supplies flowing. The HD-7, HD-10, and HD-14 were applauded war machines that had proven themselves over and over. With the war over, new models and innovations could be freely initiated by Allis-Chalmers.

The demand for a smaller diesel crawler was strong, and the HD-5 was the logical answer. The HD-7 was powered by a General Motors three-cylinder diesel, while the HD-10 and HD-14 used four- and six-cylinder diesels, respectively. The new HD-5 used a two-cylinder version of the same design. Sales of this model were excellent, and Allis-Chalmers continued to move forward. In 1953, Allis-Chalmers purchased the engine builder, Buda Manufacturing Company. In 1955, a newer HD-6 with an Allis-Chalmers diesel replaced the GM-powered HD-5. The company went on to sell more than 25,000 copies of the HD-6 in its 20 years of production.

An improved version of the aging HD-14C labeled the HD-19 was introduced in 1947. This huge crawler weighed 6 tons more than its predecessor and, with a higher rpm, produced more power with basically the same engine. Further refinements brought on the replacement HD-20 in 1951. With an Allis-Chalmers engine to replace the GM engine in 1954, the HD-21 evolved from the HD-20 with increased horsepower at each model change.

The HD-9 was brought out in 1950 to replace the time-tested HD-7. With a boost in rated rpm and one extra cylinder, the four-cylinder HD-9 had added horsepower. A bigger brother with a six-cylinder GM diesel called the HD-15 filled a gap in size between the huge HD-19 and the midsized HD-9. When Allis-Chalmers brought out its own diesel engine in 1954, the new HD-11 replaced the HD-9 and the HD-16 replaced the HD-15.

To fill the needs of a small crawler in the 25-drawbar horsepower class, the H-3 (gasoline) and HD-3 (diesel) were introduced in 1960. Tooling costs were minimal on these models because they were basically the same as the popular D-15 wheeled tractors with the addition of steering clutches and tracks; otherwise most major assemblies were the same.

Allis-Chalmers crawlers continued to improve and new models were introduced, but competition was growing strong. In 1974, the Allis-Chalmers construction line became the Fiat-Allis line. Fiat bought 65 percent of the operations as crawler production continued until 1985, when all U.S. production ended.

Model HD-5 Crawler

What is there for the guy who needs a smaller diesel crawler? In 1946, the HD-5 was introduced by Allis-Chalmers as a little brother to the HD-14, HD-10, and HD-7. The war was over and restrictions lifted, which allowed companies to pursue new models. The HD-5 was fitted with a two-cylinder version of the General Motors diesel that was almost identical to the engines in the bigger models. Each cylinder of these GM diesels was 71 cubic inches, and by offering engines with different numbers of cylinders, several sizes were available using many of the same engine parts. The HD-5 was the best-selling single model crawler that Allis-Chalmers built. A big factor in its high sales was the good reputation of the GM diesels.

The General Motors diesels were different from most other brands in that they were a two-cycle design. The pistons in the two-cycle engines fired at every stroke unlike the four-stroke engines that used every other stroke to push out exhaust. These GM engine sounds as if it is revving higher than conventional diesel engines. Unlike conventional diesels that used an injection pump to feed fuel through nozzles in the cylinder head, however, the GM engines used unit injectors. These unit injectors were plunger-type injectors that were in the head at each cylinder. Just as a camshaft and rocker arms opened valves, the plungers were pressed by rocker arms through a camshaft on the GM engines to spray fuel in the cylinder with precision timing. The size of the injector and a precise gap measurement was critical to the

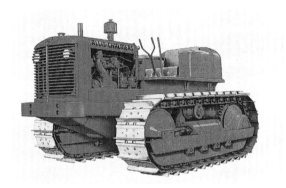

The HD-5 was the best-selling Allis-Chalmers crawler with 29,255 units built. Sales figures reflected the huge demand for a 6-ton crawler, and private contractors or farmers who did not need or could not afford a big crawler now had an option.

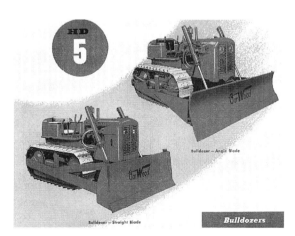

Gar Wood bulldozer attachments, as well as rippers, scrapers, and other equipment, were sold through Allis-Chalmers dealers. The HD-5 equipped with a Gar Wood blade was a big seller.

Collectibility

Rating	Model	Comments
★★★	HD-5	29,255 built
★★	HD-19	2,650 built
★★	HD-9	5,850 built
★★	HD-15	3,909 built
★★	HD-20	3,100 built
★★	HD-21 Series A	8,207 built
★★	HD-16 Series A	9,519 built
★★	HD-11 Series A	15,000 built
★★★	HD-6	25,171 built
★★★	H-3 and HD-3	8,243 built

Reliability

Rating	Model
★★★★	HD-5
★★★★	HD-19
★★★	HD-9
★★★	HD-15
★★★★	HD-20
★★★★	HD-21 Series A
★★★★	HD-16 Series A
★★★★	HD-11 Series A
★★★★✦	HD-6
★★★✦	H-3 and HD-3

Parts Availability

Rating	Model
★★★✦	HD-5
★★★	HD-19
★★★✦	HD-9
★★★✦	HD-15
★★★	HD-20
★★★	HD-21 Series A
★★★	HD-16 Series A
★★★✦	HD-11 Series A
★★★★	HD-6
★★★✦	H-3 and HD-3

amount of fuel forced into the cylinders. The HD-5 crawlers built in 1948 came with an air heater for cold-weather starting. Afterwards, an ether-dispenser starting aid replaced the air heater unless the buyer paid extra. The ether dispenser was a cowl-mounted unit in which the operator placed either a 7- or 17-cc ether capsule inside. The dispenser was sealed and a plunger pierced the gelatin casing of the capsule. The ether would then be pumped by hand with the primer plunger to the engine as it was being turned over by the starter.

The five-speed transmission was standard on all the HD-5 versions except for the HD-5G (loader), which came with four speeds forward and two speeds reverse after 1954. This transmission basically traded the fourth gear of the standard model for an extra reverse gear that was twice as fast as the regular reverse. This modification was pleasing to loader operators who were constantly backing from stockpiles to load trucks. The reverse was 4.1 mph in high and 2.0 mph in low.

The HD-5 came with a standard 33-link track or with a longer track of 37 links. The front track support was mounted on a seven-leaf spring assembly except on the construction versions HD-5F and HD-5G, which were long-track models that had a rigid-beam support in the front. The "G" designation was for HD-models with a mounted front loader. Spring-mounted front supports were excellent for agricultural purposes, but with mounted bulldozer blades and loaders, the flexing springs were detrimental to grading and lifting.

Just like the other HD-series crawlers, the HD-5 was offered with a big list of options for loggers, farmers, contractors, and military operators. A canopy, full cab, track guards, engine guards, radiator guard, rear seat guard, and grousers from 7 to 20 inches wide were available. A regular 663-rpm PTO was offered as well as a reversible-reduction type that turned 539 rpm. A belt pulley was available in either 10- or 12-inch diameter. For the demanding contractor, a heavy-duty radiator core was offered as well as a heavy-duty radiator guard and heavy-duty oil and fuel filters. Smaller options such as a rain cap, pull hook, pusher-type fan, rear floodlight, rear taillight, hour meter, and air precleaner extension were some of the other items offered to buyers.

Collecting Notes: The HD-5 is one of the easier A-C crawlers to get parts for. Be careful when changing track shoes—two different bolt patterns were used. With a production of more than 29,000 units and with the GM engine, few parts should be hard to find. The size of the crawler makes it handy for many jobs on the farm or on small construction projects. Don't expect collectors to value the HD-5 extremely high, because it is not at all rare nor extremely old.

Model HD-5 Crawler Variations

HD-5A	Agricultural, 44-inch track gauge, spring-mounted front track support, 33-link track
HD-5B	Agricultural, 60-inch track gauge, spring-mounted front track support, 33-link track
HD-5E	Agricultural/construction, 60-inch track gauge, spring-mounted front track support, 37-link track
HD-5F	Construction, 60-inch track gauge, rigid front track support, 37-link track
HD-5G	Construction, 60-inch track gauge, rigid front track support, 37-link track, front-mounted 1-yard loader (0.75- and 1.5-yard optional)

Model HD-5 Crawler Specifications (no mounted equipment)

Years built	1946–1955
Serial numbers	1–29255
Horsepower rating (drawbar/PTO)	38.24/47.85
Engine bore and stroke (inches)	4.25x5.0 (two-cylinder General Motors)
Engine rpm	1,800
Speeds (standard gearing, forward, mph)	1.46, 2.44, 3.3, 3.96, 5.47
Speed (standard gearing, reverse, mph)	1.99
Weight (pounds)	11,815
Length (inches)	124.875
Standard track gauge (inches)	44
Height (inches)	60.375
Standard track shoe width (inches)	13
Lower track rollers per side	4 (5 on long-track versions)
Belt pulley (inches, dia. x w.)	10 or 12x 8.75 (963 rpm)
Fuel capacity (gallons)	37
Cooling capacity (gallons)	3.75
Injector	GM unit injectors
Suggested new retail price	$6,585 in 1955 (HD-5A)

Model HD-5 Crawler Production History
Serial number is found stamped on the right side of the steering clutch housing at the upper right corner.

Year	Serial Numbers
1946	1–6
1947	7–1357
1948	1358–4315
1949	4316–7498
1950	7499–11070
1951	11071–14289
1952	14290–17557
1953	17558–21836
1954	21837–25563
1955	25564–29255

Model HD-5 Crawler Progression History

Year	Serial Number	Modification
1946	1	First production Model HD-5 built
1947	1053	Track shoes use 7.5-inch spacing instead of the previous 9.5 inches
1948	2104	HD-5 tested at Nebraska (test no. 396)
1948	4208	Ether-starting aid dispenser becomes standard equipment
1955	29255	Last HD-5 crawler built

Model HD-19 Crawler

The giant HD-19 was advertised to be the world's largest and most powerful crawler. With a 6-ton advantage over the HD-14C that it replaced, this crawler was tested to pull up to 37,536 pounds. Imagine the pride of the operator sitting high on the wide upholstered seat as this enormous machine devoured almost 12 gallons of fuel every hour under full load. Allis-Chalmers was proud of this achievement of building the biggest crawler. In four years, 2,650 HD-19 models were sold. This number may seem low, but as with other extra-large crawlers of the day, it was a healthy number. With the $16,500 price tag in 1950, the single model profits for Allis-Chalmers and its dealers were many times higher than for a small crawler. The success of this model carried into the improved HD-20 and later the HD-21.

The transmission of the HD-19 had two speed ranges with a torque converter made by Twin Disc Inc. By running in diesel oil from the fuel tank, the torque converter transmitted power in an infinite number of speeds in each range. The operator spent less time shifting. With hydraulic-assisted steering, this big machine could be turned by even the smallest operators. The HD-19 came with a front

As "King of the Hill" for a time, the HD-19 was a real giant. The rank of the Allis-Chalmers HD-19 as the biggest and most powerful crawler was advertised without humility.

bumper, crankcase guard, and a pull hook as standard equipment. The radiator guard was hinged for easy access. The HD-19H has a 37-link track and a spring-mounted front track equalizer, making this machine well suited for farming. The HD-19F has a longer 40-link track and a solid front-track equalizer, making it best adapted for construction work. A 4-yard capacity Tractomotive-brand loader was on the HD-19G, which otherwise was much the same as the HD-19F.

The HD-19 option list included a front pusher plate that replaced the bumper. A canopy and fully enclosed cab were offered as well as engine and track shielding for certain conditions. Track shoes in several styles were offered from 22 to 30 inches wide. Although electric starting and headlights were standard items, a rear taillight or floodlight was an extra cost.

Collecting Notes: The HD-19 is both gigantic and impressive. Collectors tend to be attracted to the biggest models of tractors and crawlers. The restoration of a run-down machine will be a significant job and may likely be priced into five digits. One might be prudent to shop around to find a well-maintained HD-19 instead of going with a poor unit. To restore a HD-19 only for its collector appeal would be better suited to collectors with fat wallets.

Model HD-19 Crawler Specifications (no mounted equipment)

Years built	1947–1950
Serial numbers	4–2653
Horsepower rating (drawbar/PTO)	110.64/129.08
Engine bore and stroke (inches)	4.25x5.0 (six-cylinder General Motors)
Engine rpm	1,750
Speeds (standard gearing, forward, mph)	0–3, 0–7 (torque converter)
Speeds (standard gearing, reverse, mph)	0–5.5
Weight (pounds)	40,395
Length (inches)	190.75
Standard track gauge (inches)	84
Height (inches)	87.8125
Standard track shoe width (inches)	24
Lower track rollers per side	6
Belt pulley (inches, dia. x w.)	20x15
Fuel capacity (gallons)	99 (120 after serial no. 1122)
Cooling capacity (gallons)	11 (13 after serial no.1801)
Injector	GM unit injectors
Suggested new retail price	$16,500 in 1950 (HD-19H)

Model HD-19 Crawler Production History

Serial number is found stamped on the rear face of the steering-clutch housing near the upper right corner.

Year	Serial Numbers
1947	4–120
1948	121–1195
1949	1196–2001
1950	2002–2653

Model HD-19 Crawler Progression History

Year	Serial Number	Modification
1947	4	First production Model HD-19 built
1948	452	HD-19 tested at Nebraska (test no. 397)
1948	1166	Ether-starting aid dispenser becomes standard equipment
1949	1352	Compound brake rods replace single rod, air cleaner attachment improved
1949	1802	30-inch fan replaced by 36-inch fan, hood, grille, and radiator widened, serial nos. 1776 and 1777 also have the improvements
1950	2653	Last HD-19 crawler built

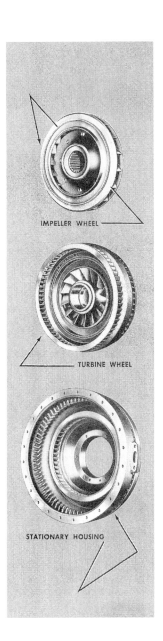

IMPELLER WHEEL

TURBINE WHEEL

STATIONARY HOUSING

This torque converter was made by Twin Disc and was offered on the HD-19 and other A-C crawlers. The assembly was immersed in diesel oil from the fuel tank. The engine drove the impeller wheel and oil was hurled toward the turbine wheel. The turbine wheel would spin like a child's pinwheel and powered the transmission. The design of the stationary housing efficiently guided the oil back to the impeller to avoid cavitation. A pump starved at its suction side can cause such low pressure around the fluid it can create low-temperature boiling. The vapor bubbles drawn into the impeller will damage the fins. This condition is called cavitation. The clever Twin Disc design was built to avoid this condition.

Model HD-9 Crawler

In 1950, Allis-Chalmers introduced the HD-9 crawler. With six forward speeds and a four-cylinder GM diesel engine, this 10-ton machine could almost pull its own weight. Like other models, the HD-9 was offered in agricultural and construction versions. For farming, the HD-9 came with 38-link tracks and a spring-mounted front track support with six leafs. The construction version, HD-9F came with longer 41-link tracks and a rigid front track support. By adding a Tractomotive-brand front loader with a 2-yard capacity to the construction model, the HD-9G was introduced. Tractomotive supplied front loaders for most Allis-Chalmers crawlers. Side booms made by Tractomotive used massive counterweights that could be lowered to keep the crawler from tipping when setting heavy pipe and such. In 1959, Allis-Chalmers bought out Tractomotive and produced the mounted equipment under its name.

The HD-9 came standard with a full-width crankcase guard and a hinged radiator guard. A Delco-Remy starter and Guide-brand lights also came with the deal as well as a muffler. The extra shielding of the tracks, engine, and seat were only available at extra cost. The optional cab came with safety glass. A rear taillight and floodlight could be added for night work and the heavy-duty fuel and oil filters could be added for dusty conditions. The PTO and belt pulley were available if the farmer chose to pay more. Track shoes in widths of 16 to 22 inches in several styles were offered.

Sales of the HD-9 were not great, but they sold slightly better than its big brother, the HD-15. The biggest difference between the tractors was that the HD-15 had a bigger engine. To fill the needs of farmers and contractors, Allis-Chalmers was diversifying its crawlers and tractors, which caused some competition within its crawler line. With only 5,850 units built in six years of production, the HD-9 was not setting the world on fire.

Collecting Notes: The HD-9 is a good, solid machine that probably won't excite most Allis-Chalmers collectors. The mediocre production numbers do not make it a rare machine. Parts for restoration are not difficult to acquire in most cases. Restoration costs are high in relation to the collector appeal. Seldom will one perform a righteous restoration on such a crawler with profit as a motive.

This 10-ton Model HD-9 was just over 6 feet tall at the hood. The results of the Nebraska test showed a maximum pull of 19,035 pounds: it could almost draw its own weight. A constant-mesh gearbox was the only transmission available on this model. It offered six forward and three reverse gears.

With a modern-styled Carco bulldozer assembly and the added accessories of the canopy and grille guard, this HD-9 was a sleek-looking machine. Baker, Gar Wood, and Carco were three brands of bulldozers sold by Allis-Chalmers equipment dealers for its crawler line. This medium-duty Carco bulldozer was hydraulically operated. Carco also offered cable-lift blades as did Baker and Gar Wood. Cable-lift blades were offered for high-production leveling jobs and were offered on all but the smaller HD-5, H-3, and HD-3 crawlers.

Model HD-9 Crawler Specifications (no mounted equipment)

Years built	1950–1955
Serial numbers	1–5850
Horsepower (drawbar/PTO)	67.39/79.10
Engine bore and stroke (inches)	4.25x5.0 (four-cylinder General Motors)
Engine rpm	1,600
Speeds (standard gearing, forward, mph)	1.4, 2.1, 2.9, 3.8, 4.4, 5.7
Speeds (standard gearing, reverse, mph)	1.6, 3.5, 4.4
Weight (pounds)	19,995
Length (inches)	150
Standard track gauge (inches)	74
Height (without stacks, inches)	73.125
Standard track shoe width (inches)	16
Lower track rollers per side	6 (7 on long-track models)
Belt pulley (inches, dia. x w.)	13.375x10 (929 rpm)
Fuel capacity (gallons)	55
Cooling capacity (gallons)	7.25
Injector	GM unit injectors
Suggested new retail price	$10,720 in 1955 (HD-9B agricultural)

Model HD-9 Crawler Production History

Serial number is found stamped on the right side of the steering-clutch housing at the upper right corner.

Year	Serial Numbers
1950	1
1951	2–737
1952	738–1882
1953	1883–3590
1954	3591–5208
1955	5209–5850

Model HD-9 Crawler Progression History

Year	Serial Number	Modification
1950	1	First production Model HD-9 built
1951	196	HD-9 crawler tested at Nebraska (test no. 463)
1952	1038	Shifting lock plunger and boot changed
1955	5850	Last HD-9 crawler built

Model HD-15 Crawler

The HD-15 was similar to the HD-9, but it had a bigger engine. By putting the six-cylinder GM diesel in the chassis, the 27,500-pound HD-15 could pull more than its own weight. For making turns, hydraulic steering controls with self-energizing mechanical brakes were an advantage over the HD-9. Even a boy could turn this crawler in a 106-inch radius.

Two types of transmissions were offered. The six-speed was a smooth constant-mesh design that included three reverse speeds. The other version (HD-15C) used a Twin Disc torque converter and three speed ranges forward to deliver infinite speeds up to 7 miles per hour. The HD-15C has two reverse speeds that made it a dandy for loader work.

The optional PTO came as a straight type or as a reversible-reduction type. A big, 18-inch power pulley was offered for big-time belt jobs. The safety-glass cab and special shielding for the engine, tracks, and seat were options for jobs in adverse conditions. Heavy-duty fenders could be added for abusive conditions (recommended with a cab). Just like the HD-9, the HD-15 came standard with headlights and a Delco-Remy starter, a taillight or floodlight were options.

Only 3,909 HD-15 crawlers were built during its six production years. The size was a tight fit below the HD-19 that had a 6-drawbar horsepower advantage and a loose fit to the smaller HD-9 that had 37 less drawbar horsepower. The cost differences were small between the HD-15 and HD-19, but the HD-15 cost about 40 percent more than the smaller HD-9. By using an engine from the big HD-19 and tuning it down a bit then placing it in the chassis and transmission much like that of the HD-9, the HD-15 was probably built with minimal retooling costs at Allis-Chalmers. Rarely did this type of parts swapping result in abundant sales. Allis-Chalmers engineers were creative with existing stock and often filled the needs of some smaller markets without creating huge retooling costs.

The Baker bulldozer was a popular choice for the HD-15. Baker, Carco, and Gar Wood were all well-built bulldozer assemblies offered for the HD-15. Tractomotive was a builder of front-mounted loaders and was another player in this Allied Equipment grouping. In 1955, the last year that the HD-15 was built, Allis-Chalmers bought Baker Manufacturing Company. Four years later, Tractomotive was acquired.

Collecting Notes: The HD-15 is big and powerful, making it more attractive to collectors than medium-sized models. Many parts are common with other models and therefore are generally available without a helpless search. Restoration costs are steep and a model with a poor undercarriage is often scrapped because the rebuild may not be cost effective. Admirable restorations are usually the product of passion, not profit.

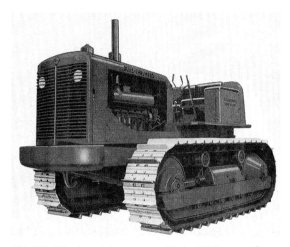

This HD-15 had much in common with the HD-9 except for the engine. The six-cylinder General Motors diesel in the HD-15 put out over 38 more PTO horsepower than the four-cylinder HD-9. At 117.68 PTO horsepower, the HD-15 could pull over half-again as much as its little brother.

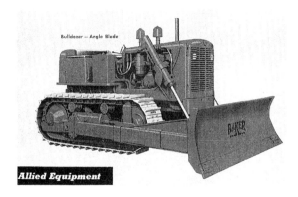

141

Model HD-15 Crawler Variations

HD-15A	Agricultural, spring-mounted front track support, 38-link track
HD-15B	Agricultural, spring-mounted front track support, 38-link track
HD-15C	Torque converter, agricultural/construction, spring-mounted front track support, 37-link track
HD-15F	Construction, rigid front track support, 41-link track
HD-15G	Construction, rigid front track support, 41-link track, front-mounted 3-yard loader

Model HD-15 Crawler Specifications (no mounted equipment)

Years built	1950–1955
Serial numbers	1–3909
Horsepower rating (drawbar/PTO)	104.37/117.68
Engine bore and stroke (inches)	4.25x5.0 (six-cylinder General Motors)
Engine rpm	1,600
Speeds (standard gearing, forward, mph)	1.39, 2.09, 2.97, 3.87, 4.46, 5.8
Speeds (torque converter, forward, mph)	0–2.5, 0–4.3, 0–7.0
Speeds (standard gearing, reverse, mph)	1.54, 3.47, 4.51
Speeds (torque converter, reverse, mph)	0–3.2, 0–5.5
Weight (shipping, pounds)	27,500
Length (inches)	172.75
Standard track gauge (inches)	74
Height (without stacks, inches)	84
Standard track shoe width (inches)	20
Lower track rollers per side	6 (7 on long-track models)
Belt pulley (inches, dia. x w.)	18x15 (693 rpm)
Fuel capacity (gallons)	91.5 (100 for HD-15C)
Cooling capacity (gallons)	11.75
Injector	GM unit injectors
Suggested new retail price	$15,165 in 1955 (HD-15A)

Model HD-15 Crawler Production History

Serial number is found stamped on the right side of the steering-clutch housing at the upper right corner and on the cowl.

Year	Serial Numbers
1950	1
1951	2–810
1952	811–1857
1953	1858–2855
1954	2856–3684
1955	3685–3909

Model HD-15 Crawler Progression History

Year	Serial Number	Modification
1950	1	First production Model HD-15 built
1951	90	HD-15 crawler tested at Nebraska (test no. 464)
1955	3909	Last HD-15 crawler built

Model HD-20 Crawler

As a replacement for the huge HD-19, this HD-20 had about 6 extra drawbar horsepower and weighed a ton more. As the new flagship of the crawler line in 1921, the new HD-20 could pull 41,321 pounds. By raising the engine speed 100 rpm over the 1,600-rpm engine speed of the HD-19 and increasing the compression ratio, the GM engine in the HD-20 put out a little more horsepower. Otherwise these two models were very similar.

Three basic versions were built: one for farming, one for construction, and one with a front-mounted loader. The HD-20H, built for agricultural jobs has a 37-link track chain and a big double seat. The HD-20F was a long-track version with 40-link tracks and a single seat, built for construction jobs. The HD-20G has a huge 4-yard bucket for a Tracto-motive-brand loader on a crawler that is otherwise basically the same as the HD-20F. These models were built until the HD-21 replaced them in 1954.

The only transmission offered in the HD-20 was a torque-converter type with two speed ranges forward and one range in reverse. It was the third model in the line of Allis-Chalmers' biggest crawlers to use the Twin Disc torque converter. As a centrifugal pump rotating in oil, the torque converter is driven by the energy of the discharged oil turning the blades of a matching turbine. The stator redirects the

oil back to the impeller. The short version is that the torque converter is a gearless transmission with variable speeds. Twin Disc had refined the turbocharger and even used it in railroad locomotives. With a history for quality dating back to 1918, Twin Disc was an industry leader in clutches, power reduction and reverse gearboxes for marine use, and of course, torque converters.

With the 24-volt electric starting plus lights as standard features and a massive front bumper, the HD-20 was built for big jobs and easy operating. Shielding for the engine and tracks were optional as on other models, and a steel safety cab with safety glass could be purchased to protect the operator from the elements. A large 20-inch power pulley could be added for some large belt jobs. Several track shoe styles were offered in widths from 22 to 28 inches. For cold-weather starting, an optional engine preheater that was fired by diesel fuel could have been added as an improvement over the standard ether dispenser.

Collecting Notes: Big crawlers are impressive. Collectors of big crawlers usually need big fat wallets to bring them back to good condition. The average collector does not own a rig large enough to haul a HD-20; therefore, the cost of transportation is a major consideration. To the person who completes a restoration of a HD-20, my hat is off to you—it is an enormous task.

This enormous 41,000-pound crawler, the HD-20 stands almost 16 feet tall to the top of the stacks. Built as a rugged and powerful machine, engineers did not forget the men who had to service this crawler. The torque converter, gearbox, steering clutches, truck frame, and final-drive gears could all be removed without disturbing other major adjoining assemblies. Positive-seal bearings gave a long service life with almost no maintenance to the track rollers and idlers. No grease fittings were used underneath this crawler.

"Finger-tip" steering was a heavily advertised feature of the HD-20. With hydraulically activated steering, the operator of the largest crawler in the world (for a time) only needed less than 5 pounds of pressure on each lever to disengage the steering clutches. Self-energizing brakes made quick turns without the operator standing with all his weight on each pedal. The torque converter operated with only two forward ranges so shifting was infrequent compared to manual-type transmissions. Less effort was needed to operate this 20-ton crawler than other crawlers that were one-fourth its size.

Model HD-20 Crawler Specifications (no mounted equipment)

Years built	1951–1954
Serial numbers	3001–6100
Horsepower (drawbar/PTO)	116.69/no PTO test
Engine bore and stroke (inches)	5x5.6 (six-cylinder General Motors)
Engine rpm	1,700
Speeds (torque converter, forward, mph)	0–3.0, 0–7.0
Speeds (reverse, mph)	0–5.5
Weight (pounds)	42,625
Length (inches)	190.75
Standard track gauge (inches)	84
Height (without stacks, inches)	94.25
Standard track shoe width (inches)	24
Lower track rollers per side	6
Belt pulley (inches, dia. x w.)	20x15 (400 rpm)
Fuel capacity (gallons)	120
Cooling capacity (gallons)	15
Injector	GM unit injectors
Suggested new retail price	$21,260 in 1954 (HD-20H agricultural)

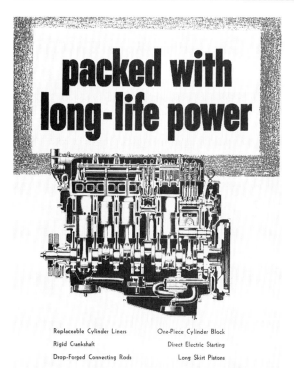

Replaceable Cylinder Liners   One-Piece Cylinder Block

Rigid Crankshaft   Direct Electric Starting

Drop-Forged Connecting Rods   Long Skirt Pistons

This 6-110 General Motors diesel powered the HD-20 crawler. Rated at 175 brake horsepower, this engine produced 116.69 drawbar horsepower for the crawler at the Nebraska testing facility. The HD-20 was tested for a maximum pull of 29,400 pounds, only 1,304 less pounds than the machine's own weight.

Model HD-20 Crawler Production History

Serial number is found stamped on the right side of the steering-clutch housing at the upper right corner.

Year	Serial Numbers
1951	3001–3827
1952	3828–492
1953	4923–5736
1954	5737–6100

Model HD-21 Series A Crawler

Buda was an engine builder well known for its quality diesel engines. Allis-Chalmers bought Buda near the end of 1953. The following year, Allis-Chalmers announced its new HD-21 with an engine built in its newly purchased facilities. With the same basic build as the HD-20, the new HD-21 was introduced with a supercharger on the Allis-Chalmers engine that gave it 135.12 horsepower, 18 drawbar horsepower more than the HD-20's General Motors diesel engine produced. By the time the HD-21 was introduced in 1954, Allis-Chalmers had been making road graders, wheeled loaders, motor scrapers, and even forklifts. The purchase of Buda gave Allis-Chalmers the diesel engines it needed.

The HD-21AC was the regular crawler version with the 37-shoe tracks. A longer 40-shoe track version was offered called the HD-21P. This version used a Power-Shift transmission instead of the torque converter that was used on the regular HD-21AC. An even longer 42-shoe track version was offered with the torque converter transmission and a 4-yard capacity loader; it was referred to as the HD-21GC. The loader version with a Power-Shift transmission replaced the HD-21GC in 1968; it was called the HD-21G. The HD-21 crawlers came standard with power steering and superchargers

In 1960, the new, oval-model designation transfer was introduced. This HD-21 has a Farr-brand dry-type air filter that replaced the Donaldson oil-type air cleaner in 1963. The HD-21 was the first diesel crawler using a true Allis-Chalmers diesel engine.

on the engines of early models. A turbocharger replaced the supercharger in 1956. Both units accomplished the same task of pumping air into the engine cylinders. The turbocharger was powered by exiting engine exhaust while the supercharger robbed some power from the crawler engine that powered it.

The HD-21AC was a version well suited for farming. A 1,800-rpm PTO came as standard equipment, and a 20-inch-diameter power pulley was added for an extra cost. A

cab was offered as on all the Allis-Chalmers' crawler line during the 1950s. For special jobs, a low-speed option offered speed ranges of 0 to 2.5 and 0 to 6.0 miles per hour forward and 0 to 3.5 miles per hour in reverse. Lumberjacks could buy a logging version of the HD-21 with a heavy-duty grille guard and guards for the engine and tracks. A front bumper and hook came on both the farm and logging versions.

The HD-21 was the first A-C crawler to use the Buda-designed diesels. By 1955, the whole A-C crawler line was fitted with Buda engines, all with new model names. The reliable General Motors diesels served Allis-Chalmers well for 16 years, but the crawler industry was not standing still. New technology allowed more horsepower and efficiency in engines and conveniences for the crawler operators. Allis-Chalmers was quick at the draw to use the torque converter and the turbocharger. Most other companies had to be convinced of the advantages of these two inventions by watching Allis-Chalmers crawlers perform for many months. To be a pioneer in anything involves courage and vision, two qualities Allis-Chalmers was blessed with.

Collecting Notes: The value of a nice-operating HD-21 as a useful workhorse is high. To restore one for a static collector piece would be a rare case. The interest in crawlers as collectibles is growing, but has not yet developed to the level of wheeled tractors. The huge expenses incurred from restoring large crawlers are a detriment to the growth of crawler collecting as a hobby. Affluent contractors and equipment operators are commonly big-time crawler collectors. This author's opinion is that the value of collectible crawlers will grow at a faster rate than that of the average wheeled tractors over the next several years.

Model HD-21 Series A Crawler Specifications (no mounted equipment)

Years built	1954–1969
Serial numbers	7001–15207
Horsepower (drawbar only)	135.12 (147.18 in 1958)
Engine bore and stroke (inches)	5.25x6.25 (six-cylinder Allis-Chalmers)
Engine rpm (regular model)	1,800 (1,825 after serial no. 9001)
Speeds (serial nos. 7001–9000, mph)	0–3.0, 0–7.5 (0–5.5 reverse)
Speeds (serial nos. 9001–year 1961, forward, mph)	0–3.1, 0–8.0 (0–6.0 reverse)
Speeds (year 1961 and up, forward, mph)	0–3.3, 0–6.3 (0–6.3 reverse, 0–4.5 optional)
Speeds (Power-Shift models, mph)	0–4.1, 0–7.8 (0–3.7, 0–7.1 reverse)
Weight (pounds)	44,725
Length (inches)	194.75
Standard track gauge (inches)	84
Height (without stacks, inches)	98.875
Standard track shoe width (inches)	24
Lower track rollers per side	6 (7 after serial no. 9001, 8 on HD-21G)
Belt pulley (inches, dia. x w.)	20x15 (400 rpm)
Fuel capacity (gallons)	130
Cooling capacity (gallons)	20 (21 on Power-Shift models)
Injector pump	Bosch
Suggested new retail price	$56,885 in 1969

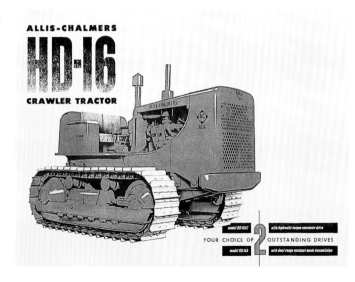

As a replacement for the General Motors–powered HD-15, this newer HD-16 used the Buda diesel that now was under the ownership of Allis-Chalmers. Like its predecessor, the HD-16 came with either a constant-mesh standard transmission or with the torque converter drive.

Model HD-16 Series A Crawler

With the new Buda-designed Allis-Chalmers six-cylinder engine placed in the chassis of the older HD-15, the new HD-16 was introduced. Transmission speeds in both the HD-15 and HD-16 are practically identical in both the standard and torque converter models. The later HD-16 was offered with a third type of transmission called the Power-Shift. The older General Motors diesel from the earlier HD-15 and the newer Buda diesel in the HD-16 both ran at 1,600 rpm on the standard transmission versions. The engines were much, much different with the GM engine running as a two-cycle and the Buda-type running as a four-cycle. The latter produced more horsepower as the HD-16 was tested at almost 134 PTO horsepower compared to the just-under 118-horsepower rating of the HD-15. Like General Motors, Buda engines had a long and well-respected reputation among the construction industry. With the replacement of the GM engine with the equally respected Buda engine, Allis-Chalmers kept crawler sales from dropping. Without having to rely on buying engines from a competitor in the construction industry, Allis-Chalmers could gain more profits without being at the mercy of General Motors.

Improvements to the engine design in 1958 made the engine more efficient and made starting easier. The early type used energy cells in the engine head, which were installed directly across from the injectors. The direct-injection heads injected the fuel downward and directly into the engine cylinders for a more complete combustion and smoother operation. Continued improvement by Allis-Chalmers kept it a hearty contender in the construction equipment manufacturing business.

Power steering and brakes made the HD-16 a nice machine to operate. An operator running this machine for an 8- or 10-hour day would not want to revert to an older machine without these luxuries. The increases in horsepower over time in various crawler models gave the HD-16 more horsepower than the older and bigger HD-19 that weighed an additional 4 tons. Improvement in the final-drive units such as the straddle-mount and double-reduction gears gave the HD-16 added reliability over older models. The combination of more power, better reliability, and easier operation were big factors that helped A-C crawlers sell well. Problems occurred and Allis-Chalmers addressed them, a sign of great management.

Options for the HD-16 were about the same as other A-C models including a wide array of track shoes to pick from, guards to protect both operator and engine, and added features to adapt the crawler to most any industry. An enclosed cab and lighting equipment were offered to keep the crawler going in all weather day and night. Two different PTO assemblies were offered, one at 430 rpm forward only and the other with the same speed forward and the ability to reverse at 355 rpm. The power pulley was still offered for this model as well.

Collecting Notes: The HD-16 is a wonderful crawler to operate, and a working example is valuable for its practical applications. Collectors have recently been viewing this crawler as collectible, but not in a big way. As with other big crawlers, restoration costs will likely be high. Collector interest seems to be growing but at a slower rate than smaller machines. Economic gain would probably be the wrong reason to restore this crawler. Parts are out there and the biggest challenge in acquiring them would be the cost. Only a dedicated collector with great vision of the end result will bring one of the HD-16s to a like-new condition.

Model HD-16 Series A Crawler Variations

HD-16A   38-link track, constant-mesh six-speed transmission
HD-16AC   38-link track, torque converter transmission (three-range forward, two-range reverse)
HD-16D   41-link track, constant-mesh six-speed transmission
HD-16DC   41-link track, torque converter transmission (three-range forward, two-range reverse)
HD-16DP   41-link track, Power-Shift transmission (two-range forward, two-range reverse)
HD-16GC   Front-mounted 3-yard loader, 43-link track, torque converter transmission (three-range forward, three-range reverse)

Model HD-16 Series A Crawler Specifications (no mounted equipment)

Years built	1955–1970
Serial numbers	101–9619
Horsepower (drawbar/PTO, six-speed)	118.69/133.83
Engine bore and stroke (inches)	5.25x6.5 (six-cylinder Allis-Chalmers)
Engine rpm	1,800 (1,600 on six-speed model)
Speeds (torque converter, mph)	0–2.5, 0–4.3, 0–7.2 (0–3.2, 0–5.5 reverse)
Speeds (six-speed, mph)	1.39, 2.09, 2.97, 3.87, 4.46, 5.8 (1.54, 3.47, 4.51 reverse)
Speeds (Power-Shift, mph)	0–3.5, 0–7.5 (0–3.0, 0–6.5 reverse)
Weight (pounds)	32,375
Length (inches)	178
Standard track gauge (inches)	74
Height (overall, inches)	89.8125
Standard track shoe width (inches)	20
Lower track rollers per side	6 or 7 (8 on HD-16GC)
Belt pulley (inches, dia. x w.)	18x15 (693 rpm)
Fuel capacity (gallons)	100
Cooling capacity (gallons)	17
Injector pump	Bosch
Suggested new retail price	$23,500 in 1960 (HD-16A)

Model HD-16 series A Crawler Production History

Serial number is found stamped on the rear of the right final-drive housing.

Year	Serial Numbers
1955	101–1008
1956	1009–2462
1957	2463–2756
1958	2757–4143
1959	4144–4725
1960	4726–5097
1961	5098–5447
1962	5448–5731
1963	5732–6269
1964	6270–6964
1965	6965–7467
1966	7468–8075
1967	8076–8424
1968	8425–8793
1969	8794–9564
1970	9565–9619

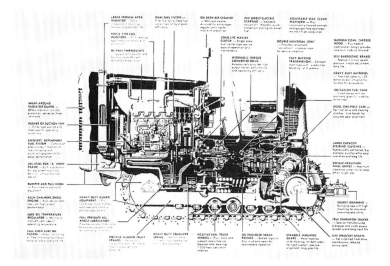

The features that made Allis-Chalmers crawlers among the finest in the industry came from years of constant improvements. The drive pinions of older models were mounted at the end of a shaft. The "straddle-mounted" gears that drove the newer double-reduction final-drives had bearings at both ends of the gears for added strength and extended service life. Competition in the industry from such firms as Caterpillar kept Allis-Chalmers designers constantly on their toes. Reliability was the name of the game. A downed machine could cost a farmer or contractor a loss in work accomplished, plus repair costs associated with crawlers were expensive.

Model HD-11 Series A Crawler

Following the variations of the midsized Model HD-11 is confusing, to say the least. This crawler was offered in regular, long, and extra-long track assemblies. To make things more confusing, three different transmissions were used, six-speed standard, torque converter, and Power-Shift. Loader-mounted versions used a G-suffix and the frosting on the cake is that the HD-11 was made in two series. The wide assortments of HD-11 models were produced to satisfy the needs of different industries. Farmers didn't need the added expense of a heavy-duty grille and track shields; bulldozer operators would have trouble leveling roads with short tracks; loader operators would have problems with stability and load capabilities without extra-long tracks; and loggers needed hooks and extra engine and operator guards to keep them satisfied. Allis-Chalmers knew what the potential customers needed and made sure that it could meet those needs.

About 15,000 of the HD-11 crawlers were built in the Series A. The popular size and the ability to tailor-fit a crawler to each customer gave Allis-Chalmers abundant sales. Weighing about 11 tons, this crawler pulled more than 10 tons in the Nebraska test. The Buda-designed A-C engine had six cylinders and produced almost 90 PTO horsepower. Power steering and double-wrap band and drum brakes made operating this crawler anything but an awful chore. With a 90-gallon fuel tank, the HD-11 could work at full capacity for about 13 hours before needing a refill. The improved gears in the final-drive assemblies gave fewer letdowns than older models.

The list of options for the HD-11 was long. Besides all sorts of guards for the engine, tracks, and operator, reinforced track fenders were offered as well as a heavy-duty grille screen. Special radiators were offered that had either in-line cores to help prevent plugging or armored rear tubes to prevent punctures. Hydraulic track adjusters were offered that eliminated the need of a huge wrench and tedious yanking

to do the job. A power pulley or PTO could be added to power outside accessories. Heavy-duty oil and fuel filters were available for dusty working conditions and an oil-type air cleaner instead of a dry-element filter was standard equipment. The ether dispenser was the standard cold-weather starting aid, but a diesel-fuel air heater was available for starting in colder climates. Headlights, taillights, or a rear floodlight were offered for the nighttime worker.

The reputation of this model was excellent. Allis-Chalmers had listened to its customers and dealers and was quick to make improvements or offer new accessories if it meant augmenting sales. With competitors like Caterpillar and International Harvester constantly improving their crawlers, Allis-Chalmers worked hard to keep its customers. By producing a model that proved to be a "lemon" or even by standing still, these crawler companies would begin to lose sales quickly—reliability and efficiency were the name of the game. With constant testing and careful engineering, Allis-Chalmers produced crawlers throughout its lifetime without ever putting a lemon into production. Some models were perhaps better than others, but the esteemed reputation Allis-Chalmers developed in the industry was only won by hard work and great expense.

Collecting Notes: As with other crawlers from this era, collectors are just beginning to look at the HD-11. As the hobby of crawler collecting advances over the next several years, the value of the HD-11 will undoubtedly increase. The great expenses that are often incurred in bringing such a machine to a like-new condition will discourage the greater share of collectors. The others not scared away are growing in number. Parts are generally not a problem to locate and the collector's value of a restored machine is in line with the functional field value. Be careful to get the right parts for the right machine, the differences between versions of the Series A and Series B are many. Spending a large sum of money for the wrong part can cause even the most patient person to rant.

Model HD-11 Series A Crawler Variations

HD-11S	38-link track, constant-mesh six-speed transmission, agricultural
HD-11ES	41-link track, constant-mesh six-speed transmission, agricultural
HD-11ST	38-link track, torque converter transmission (three-range forward, two-range reverse) agricultural
HD-11AG	Replacement for the HD-11ST
HD-11B	38-link track, constant-mesh six-speed transmission
HD-11E	41-link track, constant-mesh six-speed transmission
HD-11EC	40- or 41-link track, torque converter transmission (three-range forward, two-range reverse)
HD-11F	44-link track, torque converter transmission (three-range forward, two-range reverse)
HD-11EP	40-link track, Power-Shift transmission (two-range forward, two-range reverse)
HD-11G	2.25-yard front loader, 44-link track, constant-mesh six-speed transmission
HD-11GC	2.25-yard front loader, 44-link track, torque converter transmission (three-range forward, two-range reverse)

Model HD-11 Series A Crawler Specifications (no mounted equipment)

Years built	1955–1970
Serial numbers	101–not found
Horsepower (drawbar/PTO)	73.80/89.75
Engine bore and stroke (inches)	4.4375x5.5625 (six-cylinder Allis-Chalmers)
Engine rpm	2,050 (1,800 on six-speed model)
Speeds (torque converter, mph)	0–2.3, 0–4.0, 0–6.9 (0–2.9, 0–5.1 reverse)
Speeds (six-speed, mph)	1.39, 2.10, 2.93, 3.77, 4.41, 5.68 (1.56, 3.45, 4.43 reverse)
Speeds (Power-Shift prior to year 1967, mph)	0–3.3, 0–6.3 (0–2.9, 0–5.5 reverse)
Speeds (Power-Shift year 1967 and up, mph)	0–2.79, 0–5.38 (0–3.19, 0–6.15 reverse)
Weight (pounds)	22,375 (HD-11B)
Length (inches)	154
Standard track gauge (inches)	74
Height (overall, inches)	84
Standard track shoe width (inches)	13
Lower track rollers per side	6 (7 on HD-11ES, 8 on HD-11G, GC, F)
Belt pulley (inches, dia. x w.)	13.375x10 (1,045 rpm)
Fuel capacity (gallons)	90
Cooling capacity (gallons)	11
Injector pump	Bosch (Roosa-Master at serial no. 12201 and up)
Suggested new retail price	$18,795 in 1967 (HD-11B)

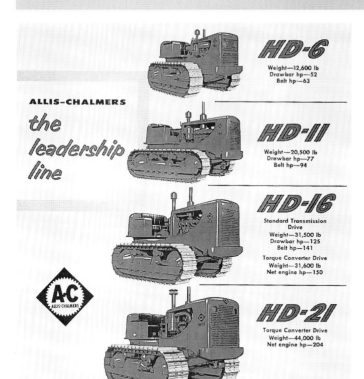

The four crawlers using the new Allis-Chalmers diesel engines are shown here. Grilles with small round holes replaced the bar-type grilles of earlier years These new crawlers were blessed with many internal improvements.

Model HD-11 Series A Crawler Production History

Serial number is found stamped on the rear of the right final-drive housing.

Year	Serial Numbers
1955	101–1057
1956	1058–3254
1957	3255–4114
1958	4115–4767
1959	4768–5801
1960	5802–6447
1961	6448–6994
1962	6995–7869
1963	7870–8605
1964	8606–10532
1965	10533–11450
1966	11451–12250
1967	12251–13130
1968	13131–13656
1969	13657–14680
1970	14681–?

Model HD-11S and HD-11ES Crawler Production History

Serial number is found stamped on the rear of the right final-drive housing.

Year	Beginning Serial Number
1967	1
1968	344
1969	514
1970	660
1971	1044

Model HD-6 Crawler

The HD-6 became the best-selling model in the Allis-Chalmers line of Buda-powered crawlers. This model stayed in production for 20 years. A popular size for small contractors, Midwest farmers, and many loggers, this HD-6 sold more than 25,000 copies. Only its predecessor, the HD-5 sold more with 29,000 built. In fact, the HD-6 was pretty much the same machine except the four-cylinder Buda-designed engine replaced the two-cylinder General Motors engine of the HD-5. The HD-6 had about 25 percent more horsepower with less than a ton weight advantage over the HD-5.

The sliding-gear five-speed transmission was offered as well as a torque converter model with two ranges in both forward and reverse. With either a 44- or 60-inch track gauge, the HD-6 came in a variety of different versions for many different industries. The improved direct-injection engine replaced the energy-cell design in 1963, and the HD-6EP replaced the HD-6PS. These Power-Shift models were popular with contractors, whereas the HD-6A and B were more adapted for farming. Farm versions were usually painted in the orange color and the models sold through construction dealers were most often yellow.

With 972 square inches of total friction area on each steering clutch, the HD-6 could go for years without having a clutch replacement. The HD-6E came with power steering and with 1,166-square inches of total friction area on each clutch for even more durability. This Model HD-6E with longer tracks had only 6.4 pounds of ground-pressure per square inch compared to 7.2 pounds on the HD-6B. The HD-6E also had a heavy-duty master clutch that consisted of four plates running in a constant spray of oil for a longer life and few adjustments. Without grease fittings below the tracks, maintenance time was greatly reduced. The "hunting tooth" track sprockets have an odd number of teeth so that each tooth engages the track pins on every other revolution. This system saved on sprocket wear and was used on all A-C crawlers of this time. The cushioned seat with big, wide armrests was placed ahead of the sprocket drive shaft for a more comfortable ride.

With all sorts of track shoe styles and widths up to 28 inches on wide-track models, the HD-6 could work in almost any terrain. PTO assemblies came either as a regular 963-rpm unit, or another type that turned 539 rpm in reverse, as well as 963 rpm forward. Both were offered to meet the needs of farmers and certain contractors. A power

The HD-6 was a big seller with more than 25,000 copies produced. Three different transmission types were available, sliding-gear, torque converter, and Power-Shift. Only large-scale farmers and contractors could afford to own a giant crawler, but one could purchase five HD-6 crawlers for the price of a single HD-21. The HD-6 also sold more than three times as many copies as the huge HD-21.

Massive bearing assemblies in the HD-6 supported the double-reduction final-drive gears at both ends. Crawler owners could spend a fortune on repairing worn or broken gears in the final-drives. Any edge Allis-Chalmers could use to fortify the design would be favorable in sales over brands with a lesser reputation.

The grille assembly on the regular HD-6 was designed for easy access to the radiator. A heavy-duty grille, hinged on the side, was offered on construction models. With mounted equipment obstructing entry, this grille style would not be an advantage. Cleaning the radiator was essential in preventing overheating. Crawlers with loaders often used a reverse-flow radiator fan to help prevent debris from sucking into the radiator fins.

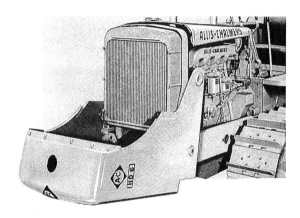

pulley was also offered. Heavy-duty oil and fuel filters and a radiator with armored rear cores could be installed for rough conditions. Guards for the fuel tank, radiator, engine sides, crankcase, and tracks were available for logging and working around large rocks and trees. The HD-6 was a popular machine for good reasons; it was durable and handy.

Collecting Notes: Most parts for the HD-6 are not hard to find. It is a handy-sized unit to own. A collector who has a restored HD-6 can accomplish heavy-duty jobs while owning a piece of history. Expect to pay dearly for major engine work and undercarriage parts as with any crawler. Col-lectors are most often ahead of the game by buying a machine with a good undercarriage and healthy engine. Restoring a rough HD-6 may prove to be a real money pit. Collector values of the HD-6 may never get too high; it is not that rare.

Model HD-6 Crawler Variations

HD-6A (prior to serial no. 5100)	44-inch track gauge, 33-link tracks, five-speed transmission
HD-6A (serial no. 5100 and up)	44-inch track gauge, 34-link tracks, five-speed transmission
HD-6B (prior to serial no. 5100)	60-inch track gauge, 33-link tracks, five-speed transmission
HD-6B (serial no. 5100 and up)	60-inch track gauge, 34-link tracks, five-speed transmission
HD-6E	60-inch track gauge, 37-link tracks, five-speed transmission
HD-6F	60-inch track gauge, 39-link tracks, five-speed transmission
HD-6PS	60-inch track gauge, 37-link tracks, torque converter/Power-Shift, energy-cell engine
HD-6EP	60-inch track gauge, 37-link tracks, torque converter/ Power-Shift, direct-injection engine
HD-6F	1.5-yard front-mounted loader, 60-inch track gauge, 39-link tracks, four-speed transmission (two reverse gears)

Model HD-6 Crawler Specifications (no mounted equipment)

Years built	1955–1974
Serial numbers	101–25271
Horsepower rating (drawbar/PTO)	49.95/60.51
Engine bore and stroke (inches)	4.4375x5.5625 (four-cylinder Allis-Chalmers)
Engine rpm	1,800
Speeds (five-speed, mph)	1.46, 2.44, 3.30, 3.96, 5.47 (2.0 reverse)
Speeds (HD-6E five-speed, mph)	1.39, 2.10, 2.93, 3.77, 4.41, 5.68 (1.56, 3.45, 4.43 reverse)
Speeds (torque converter, mph)	0–3.0, 0–5.9 (0–2.6, 0–4.2 reverse)
Weight (pounds)	13,580 (HD-6B)
Length (inches)	127 (HD-6B)
Standard track gauge (inches)	60
Height (overall, inches)	68.625
Standard track shoe width (inches)	13
Lower track rollers per side	4 (5 on HD-6E, EP and PS; 6 on HD-6F, G)
Belt pulley (inches, dia. x w.)	10 or 12x8.75 (963 rpm)
Fuel capacity (gallons)	40
Cooling capacity (gallons)	6.5
Injector pump	General Motors
Suggested new retail price	$11,050 in 1967 (HD-6A)

Model HD-6 Crawler Production History

Serial number is found stamped on the rear of the right steering-clutch housing and on the dash.

Year	Serial Numbers
1955	101–1146
1956	1147–6465
1957	6466–7947
1958	7948–10053
1959	10054–12505
1960	12506–13776
1961	13777–14897
1962	14898–16041
1963	16042–17104
1964	17105–18188
1965	18189–19400
1966	19401–20200
1967	20201–20808
1968	20809–21431
1969	21432–22271
1970	22272–23354
1971	23355–24011
1972	24012–24671
1973	24672–25011
1974	25012–25271

Model H-3 and HD-3 Crawlers

The H-3 and HD-3 are gasoline- and diesel-powered crawlers, respectively. The popular D-15 farm tractor was the basis for these two crawlers. The need for a little crawler was met without the tremendous tooling costs of building a model from scratch. John Deere began its venture into crawlers this way. A clever John Deere dealer in the state of Washington named Jesse Lindeman converted a John Deere Model D tractor into a crawler as an experiment. Later, Model B Orchard tractors were converted and sold. The John Deere Company bought out Lindeman and began converting some of its Dubuque-built models into crawlers. Sales were excellent and many parts were shared with their rubber-tired brothers. This concept was not foreign to Allis-Chalmers. During its association with the United venture in the late 1920s, several A-C Model U tractors were converted into crawlers by the Trackson Company. This company had been successful in selling track kits to convert the Fordson tractors before the Model U conversions. Converting farm tractors into crawlers generally worked fine on small units, but big tractors often lacked the durability needed for big crawler applications.

The H-3 and HD-3 had many of the same features found in bigger A-C crawlers. The "hunting tooth" drive sprockets cut down on tooth wear and the multiple-disc steering clutch packs and brakes can be removed without disassembling the tracks or final-drive housings. Connecting the heavy-duty links that drive the overlapping track shoes are 1 1/4 -inch track pins. The tracks were available in either a four- or five-roller version. Twelve different types of track shoes were available with 10-inch grousers as standard.

A swinging drawbar came as standard equipment, but could be substituted for a rugged three-point hitch. A standard-sized 1 3/8-inch PTO was also a factory installed option that was rated at 540 rpm. The shuttle clutch was a device that reversed the direction of the crawler in any gear. This most popular transmission accessory had the Power-Director as the alternative. The Power-Director gave each of the four forward and single reverse speeds two different ranges. Farm versions of these two crawlers were painted Persian Orange No. 2 and had cream-colored grilles. The more common industrial versions were all yellow with a heavy-duty grille guard.

The Model M crawler was the smallest crawler Allis-Chalmers built, with the H-3 and HD-3 slightly heavier. The Model M ended production in 1942 and it wasn't until 18 years later in the fall of 1960 that these two newer crawlers would fill the space at the bottom of the A-C crawler line. These little crawlers sold moderately well with 8,243 units produced in less than nine years. The demand was limited, but Allis-Chalmers didn't spend a fortune in producing the two crawlers. Sales were not a big disappointment as a slightly larger H-4 and HD-4 were launched in 1965. By this time, an Allis-Chalmers crawler for any size job was available. By 1970 Allis-Chalmers was producing a 50-ton monster, the biggest crawler ever built up to that time and for several years afterwards. This HD-41 weighed almost 14 times as much as a HD-3 and filled a space in the crawler line at the top. No A-C collector should ever forget the marvels this company produced. Each A-C tractor and each A-C crawler is a precious part of the company's history that should be treasured by its owners.

Collecting Notes: The H-3 and HD-3 are a good choice for a crawler collector to restore. Parts availability is good and the smaller size makes the restoration costs more manageable than bigger machines. An orange farm version, when fully restored, is a handsome machine with its own identity. Other than size, many of the other A-C crawlers looked similar; the orange H-3 and HD-3 are an exception. The D-series of A-C farm tractors has been generating huge interest among collectors; the H-3 and HD-3 models are getting added attention too. As crawler collecting increases over the next few years, the value of these machines should grow greatly. This author expects the values to increase faster than any of the bigger A-C crawlers built during the era.

Model H-3 and HD-3 Crawler Specifications (no mounted equipment

	H-3	HD-3 (diesel)
Years built	1960–1967	1960–1968
Serial numbers	1001–9700	1001–9949
Horsepower (drawbar/PTO)	25.48/32.11	26.17/32.53
Engine bore and stroke	3.5x3.875 (3.625 bore at serial no. 6001)	3.562x4.375
Engine rpm	1,650 (1,800 at serial no. 8698)	1,650 (1,800 at serial no. 8694)
Speeds (forward, mph)	1.3, 2.0, 2.0, 4.9	1.3, 2.0, 2.0, 4.9
Speeds (reverse, mph)	1.3, 2.0, 2.0, 4.9 (shuttle clutch)	1.3, 2.0, 2.0, 4.9 (shuttle clutch)
Weight (pounds)	7,395	7,645
Length (inches)	108.75	108.75
Standard track gauge (inches)	48	48
Height (overall, inches)	71.6875	71.6875
Track shoe width (inches)	10	10
Lower track rollers per side	4	4
Belt pulley (inches, dia. x w.)	10x6 (950 rpm)	10x6 (950 rpm)
Fuel capacity (gallons)	14	14
Cooling capacity (quarts)	9	9
Carburetor or injector pump	Marvel-Schebler TSX	Roosa-Master
Suggested new retail price	$6,269 in 1967	$6,914 in 1967

Model H-3 and HD-3 Crawler Production History

Serial number is found stamped on the left front side of the torque housing.

Year	Serial Numbers
1960	1001–1195
1961	1250–3198
1962	3199–4294
1963	6001–6944
1964	6945–7889
1965	7890–8855
1966	8856–9482
1967	9483–9699
1968	9700–9949

Put a pair of tracks under a D-15 farm tractor and you will end up with an H-3 (gasoline) or HD-3 (diesel) crawler. This crawler, built at the West Allis factory used tracks that were built in the Springfield plant, where all the other A-C crawlers were built. Early farm models were Persian Orange No. 2 with cream-colored grilles. Collectors are more apt to find the more popular yellow-painted industrial models.

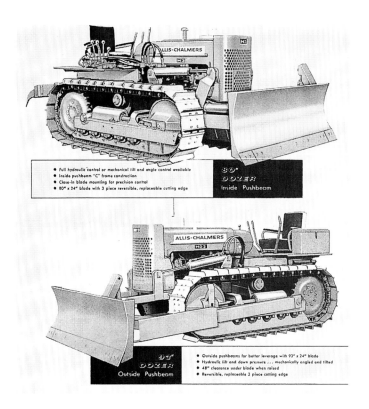

Today's Values

The following values will give you an idea of what you may expect an Allis-Chalmers tractor to sell for. These values are a sample from *The Antique American Tractor and Crawler Value Guide* by Terry Dean and Larry Swenson, with pictures by Randy Leffingwell. You can refer to this source for values of more than 180 Allis-Chalmers model variations as well as most every U.S. antique tractor. Please note that some tractors are restored to a condition that is so exquisite they will exceed the bounds of this rating system.

The rating system includes five states of condition based on the overall condition of the tractor: "one" is poor condition, "five" is like-new condition. Broken castings, missing parts, lost serial number tags, mends, and tire wear are just a few of many different factors that may downgrade the condition of a tractor. The following is a brief explanation of each rating:

Five (5) is impeccable condition, the highest rating. A tractor must be next to new in this exquisite state of restored condition. The overall condition will draw special attention at shows and will get nods of approval from the most hard-to-please critics. Few restored tractors are a grade five.

Four (4) is excellent condition. These tractors are restored to a high state. The overall condition should impress the average passerby at a show, and the trained eye will find only trivial flaws.

Three (3) is very good condition. These tractors are in sound mechanical condition and perhaps need only minor work to run like new. The overall condition should appear presentable, although probably not impressive. Restoration to the next higher grade should not be a huge undertaking.

Two (2) is good condition. The overall condition should appear complete with all parts there, but not necessarily attractive.

One (1) is restorable condition. These machines may be borderline to being "parts tractors," but are complete enough to be eligible for restoration. The overall condition may appear poor, but the tractor has most of its mechanical integrity intact.

Model 10-18 (1914–1923)

| (1) $12,750 | (2) $16,500 | (3) $21,750 | (4) $27,500 | (5) $33,750 |

Model 6-12 (1919–1926)

| (1) $5,250 | (2) $8,000 | (3) $11,500 | (4) $15,250 | (5) $18,750 |

Model E 15-30 (rerated 18-30) (1918–1921)

| (1) $1,850 | (2) $4,000 | (3) $6,600 | (4) $8,000 | (5) $12,500 |

Model E 20-35 (long fenders) (1923–1926)

| (1) $1,500 | (2) $3,000 | (3) $5,500 | (4) $7,000 | (5) $11,000 |

Model E 20-35 (short fenders, steel wheels) (1927–1930)

| (1) $750 | (2) $2,050 | (3) $3,200 | (4) $5,500 | (5) $7,200 |

Model E 25-40 (rubber tires, standard bore, 1930–1936)

| (1) $2,500 | (2) $4,000 | (3) $5,000 | (4) $7,500 | (5) $10,000 |

Model L 12-20 (1920–1921)

(1) $2,850 (2) $5,500 (3) $7,000
(4) $8,500 (5) $13,000

Model L 15-25 (1922–1927)

(1) $1,850 (2) $2,500 (3) $4,000
(4) $5,000 (5) $9,000

Model U (Continental engine, steel wheels, 1929–1932)

(1) $965 (2) $1,425 (3) $2,175
(4) $3,500 (5) $4,400

Model U (Allis-Chalmers engine, rubber tires, 1932–1952)

(1) $300 (2) $775 (3) $1,400
(4) $2,600 (5) $3,475

Model UC (Continental engine, steel wheels, 1930–1933)

(1) $2,250 (2) $3,850 (3) $5,500
(4) $7,500 (5) $8,850

Model UC (Allis-Chalmers engine, rubber tires, 1933–1953)

(1) $500 (2) $1,000 (3) $2,500
(4) $4,500 (5) $6,000

Model WC Nonstreamlined (Waukesha engine, steel wheels, 1933)

(1) $7,000 (2) $10,000 (3) $15,000
(4) $22,000 (5) $28,500

Model WC Nonstreamlined (rubber tires, dual-narrow-front, 1934–1938)

(1) $225 (2) $675 (3) $1,500
(4) $2,275 (5) $3,200

Model WC Streamlined (rubber tires, dual-narrow-front, 1938–1948)

(1) $250 (2) $575 (3) $1,025
(4) $2,275 (5) $2,775

Model WF Nonstreamlined (rubber tires, 1937–1940)

(1) $975 (2) $1,550 (3) $2,525
(4) $4,075 (5) $5,275

Model WF Streamlined (rubber tires, 1940–1951)

(1) $1,000 (2) $1,775 (3) $2,475
(4) $3,925 (5) $5,275

Model TW Speed Ace (1935–1937)

(1) $2,000 (2) $2,800 (3) $4,000
(4) $8,000 (5) $11,500

Model A (rubber tires, 1936–1938, prior to serial no. 26526)

(1) $1,000 (2) $4,000 (3) $5,500
(4) $8,000 (5) $12,000

Model A (rubber tires, 1938–1942, serial no. 26526 and up)

(1) $2,000 (2) $5,000 (3) $6,500
(4) $9,000 (5) $13,000

Model B (Waukesha engine, 1937, prior to serial no. 100)

(1) $2,000 (2) $3,000 (3) $4,250
(4) $5,500 (5) $7,500

Model B (rubber tires, 1938–1957)

(1) $225 (2) $1,025 (3) $1,650
(4) $2,500 (5) $3,250

Model IB (rubber tires, 1939–1958)

(1) $600 (2) $1,700 (3) $2,475
(4) $3,500 (5) $4,800

Model RC (rubber tires, 1939-1941)

(1) $350 (2) $1,100 (3) $1,825
(4) $3,325 (5) $4,925

Model C (rubber tires, dual-narrow-front, 1940–1950)

(1) $225 (2) $525 (3) $1,250
(4) $2,050 (5) $2,600

Model G (hydraulic lift, 1948–1955)

(1) $1,200 (2) $2,000 (3) $3,000
(4) $3,300 (5) $4,000

Model WD (dual-narrow-front, 1948–1953)

(1) $425 (2) $800 (3) $1,400
(4) $2,250 (5) $3,500

Model CA (dual-narrow-front, 1950–1958)

(1) $475 (2) $1,300 (3) $1,825
(4) $3,300 (5) $4,825

Model WD-45 (gasoline, dual-narrow-front, 1953–1957)

(1) $625 (2) $1,500 (3) $2,000
(4) $3,925 (5) $5,000

Model WD-45 (diesel, dual-narrow-front, 1954–1957)

(1) $900 (2) $2,450 (3) $4,250
(4) $5,500 (5) $6,825

Model D-14 (gasoline, dual-narrow-front, 1957–1960)

(1) $700 (2) $1,750 (3) $2,250
(4) $3,000 (5) $3,800

Model D-17 gasoline (Series I, II, and III, dual-narrow-front, 1957–1964)

(1) $1,025 (2) $2,000 (3) $2,900
(4) $3,900 (5) $5,150

Model D-17 gasoline (Series IV, wide-front, Snap-Coupler, 1964–1967)

(1) $2,050 (2) $3,150 (3) $4,150
(4) $5,250 (5) $6,000

Model D-10 Series I and Series II (1960–1965)

(1) $1,750 (2) $3,050 (3) $4,550
(4) $5,300 (5) $6,000

Model D-10 Series III (four-speed, 1965–1968)

(1) $2,000 (2) $3,650 (3) $5,250
(4) $5,950 (5) $6,700

Model D-12 Series I and Series II (1960–1965)

(1) $1,750 (2) $3,050 (3) $4,550
(4) $5,300 (5) $6,000

Model D-12 Series III (eight-speed, 1965–1968)

(1) $2,250 (2) $3,900 (3) $5,500
(4) $6,200 (5) $6,950

Model I-40 (without mounted equipment, 1964–1966)

(1) $2,000 (2) $3,500 (3) $4,500
(4) $5,500 (5) $6,400

Model I-400 (without mounted equipment, three point hitch, 1966–1968)

(1) $2,000	(2) $3,600	(3) $4,800
(4) $6,000	(5) $6,800	

Model D-15 Series I (gasoline, wide-front, 1960–1962)

(1) $1,600	(2) $2,650	(3) $3,450
(4) $4,400	(5) $5,350	

Model D-15 Series I (diesel, wide-front, 1960–1962)

(1) $1,750	(2) $3,000	(3) $4,450
(4) $4,950	(5) $5,700	

Model D-15 Series II (gasoline, wide-front, 1963–1968)

(1) $1,850	(2) $3,650	(3) $4,750
(4) $5,500	(5) $6,250	

Model D-15 Series II (diesel, wide-front, 1963–1968)

(1) $1,750	(2) $3,650	(3) $4,750
(4) $5,500	(5) $6,250	

Model I-60 Industrial (without mounted equipment, 1965–1966)

(1) $2,100	(2) $2,950	(3) $4,400
(4) $5,100	(5) $5,700	

Model I-600 Industrial (without mounted equipment, 1966–1968)

(1) $1,700	(2) $2,750	(3) $3,650
(4) $4,450	(5) $5,400	

Model D-19 (gasoline, wide-front, 1961–1964)

(1) $1,500	(2) $2,500	(3) $3,600
(4) $4,450	(5) $5,250	

Model D-19 (diesel, wide-front, 1961–1964)

(1) $1,350	(2) $2,900	(3) $4,100
(4) $5,000	(5) $5,900	

Model D-19 (diesel, wide front, three-point hitch, 1961–1964)

(1) $2,350	(2) $4,400	(3) $5,600
(4) $6,500	(5) $7,400	

Model D-21 Series I (three-point hitch 1963–1965)

(1) $2,150	(2) $3,200	(3) $6,000
(4) $6,900	(5) $8,400	

Model ED-40 (British, 1960–1968)

(1) $1,400	(2) $2,350	(3) $3,500
(4) $4,100	(5) $5,200	

Model D-272 (British 1957–1963)

(1) $1,500	(2) $2,500	(3) $3,500
(4) $5,000	(5) $7,000	

Model Two-Twenty (three-point hitch 1969–1972)

(1) $2,000	(2) $4,500	(3) $6,500
(4) $8,000	(5) $10,500	

Model Two-Twenty (front-wheel assist, three-point hitch ca. 1970)

(1) $4,000	(2) $6,500	(3) $9,500
(4) $11,500	(5) $14,000	

Model Two-Ten (1970–1972)

(1) $2,500	(2) $5,500	(3) $8,500
(4) $10,500	(5) $12,500	

Monarch 50 crawler (1928–1931)

(1) $8,000	(2) $12,000	(3) $15,000
(4) $18,000	(5) $20,000	

Monarch 75 crawler (1928–1931)

(1) $8,000	(2) $12,000	(3) $16,000
(4) $20,000	(5) $27,000	

Monarch 35 crawler (1928–1933)

(1) $1,500	(2) $2,400	(3) $4,800
(4) $7,000	(5) $12,000	

Model K crawler (steering levers, 1935–1943)

(1) $800	(2) $2,500	(3) $5,500
(4) $7,000	(5) $9,000	

Model L crawler (1931–1942)

(1) $750	(2) $3,000	(3) $7,000
(4) $11,000	(5) $15,000	

Model LO crawler (diesel fuel 1934–1942)

(1) $2,250	(2) $7,000	(3) $9,000
(4) $14,000	(5) $22,000	

Model LD (General Motors diesel, 1939)

(1) $6,500	(2) $12,000	(3) $19,000
(4) $27,000	(5) $35,000	

Model M crawler (1932–1942)

(1) $500	(2) $1,850	(3) $3,000
(4) $6,000	(5) $8,500	

Model S (1937–1942)

(1) $2,500	(2) $5,000	(3) $7,000
(4) $10,000	(5) $15,000	

Model HD-7 (General Motors diesel, 1940–1950)

(1) $1,500	(2) $3,500	(3) $4,055
(4) $5,000	(5) $7,750	

Model HD-10 (General Motors diesel, 1940–1950)

(1) $1,700	(2) $4,000	(3) $5,000
(4) $6,250	(5) $8,500	

Model HD-14 (General Motors diesel, 1939–1947)

(1) $2,400	(2) $4,500	(3) $5,750
(4) $7,500	(5) $9,750	

Model HD-5 (General Motors diesel, 1946–1955)

(1) $1,600	(2) $3,000	(3) $4,800
(4) $6,000	(5) $8,250	

Model HD-19 (General Motors diesel, 1947–1950)

(1) $2,700	(2) $4,700	(3) $6,250
(4) $8,000	(5) $10,500	

Model HD-9 (General Motors diesel, 1950–1955)

(1) $1,800	(2) $4,250	(3) $5,500
(4) $6,500	(5) $9,000	

Model HD-15 (General Motors diesel, 1950–1955)

(1) $1,950	(2) $4,400	(3) $5,750
(4) $6,800	(5) $9,450	

Model HD-20 (General Motors diesel, 1951–1954)

(1) $2,900	(2) $4,900	(3) $6,750
(4) $8,500	(5) $11,000	

Model HD-21 Series A (diesel, 1954–1969)

(1) $3,000	(2) $5,100	(3) $7,000
(4) $9,250	(5) $13,000	

Model HD-16 Series A (diesel, 1955–1970)

(1) $2,200	(2) $4,600	(3) $5,950
(4) $7,000	(5) $10,000	

Model HD-11 Series A (diesel, 1955–1970)

(1) $2,200	(2) $4,400	(3) $5,650
(4) $6,750	(5) $9,750	

Model HD-6 (diesel, 1955–1974)

(1) $1,650	(2) $3,200	(3) $5,000
(4) $6,200	(5) $8,450	

Model H-3 (gasoline 1960–1967)

(1) $1,400	(2) $2,700	(3) $4,250
(4) $5,500	(5) $7,250	

Appendix B: Paint Suggestions

*To the best of this author's knowledge, the following paint formulas are close to original colors. Any recommendations in this book are made without any guarantee on the part of the author or publisher. You should compare to paint company samples before committing to a color.

Allis Dark Green (1914–1928)		
	Martin-Senour	99L-11511
	TISCO	TP380
Allis Red (for wheels 1914–1929)		
	Martin-Senour	99N-4359
Persian Orange (1929–1960)		
	PPG	DAR 60080
	Martin-Senour	90R-3723
	TISCO	TP280
Persian Orange No. 2 (1960–1977)		
	DuPont	29047
	PPG	DAR 60396
Allis Cream (1960–1977)		
	DuPont	29049
	TISCO	TP270
Allis Yellow (ca. 1950 and up)		
	DuPont	Dulux 421
Rumely Green (prior to 1926)		
	Martin-Senour	99L-2599
	DuPont	Dulux 24166
Rumely Blue (1926–1932)		
	DuPont	Dulux 71939

Appendix C: Decimal Equivalents (fractions to decimals)

1/64	0.015625
1/32	0.03125
1/16	0.0625
1/8	0.125
3/16	0.1875
1/4	0.25
5/16	0.3125
1/3	0.333
3/8	0.375
7/16	0.4375
1/2	0.50
9/16	0.5625
5/8	0.625
2/3	0.667
11/16	0.6875
3/4	0.75
13/16	0.8125
7/8	0.875
15/16	0.9375

Appendix D: Resources for Learning More About A-C Tractors

Recommended Books

Fay, Guy, and Andy Kraushaar. *Original Allis-Chalmers 1933–1957*. Osceola, Wisconsin: MBI Publishing Company, 2000.

Gray, R. B. *Agricultural Tractor 1855–1950*. St. Joseph, Michigan: American Society of Agricultural Engineers, 1980.

Grooms, Lynn K., and Chester Peterson Jr. Vintage *Allis-Chalmers Tractors*. Stillwater, Minnesota: Voyageur Press, 2000.

Huxley, Bill. *Allis-Chalmers Agricultural Machinery*. London: Osprey Publishing, 1988.

King, Alan C. *Allis-Chalmers: An Informal History 1918–1960*. Delaware, Ohio: Independent Print Shop Company, 1989.

Mills, Robert. *Implement & Tractor Reflections on 100 Years of Farm Equipment*. Overland Park, Kansas: Intertec Publishing Corporation, 1986.

Morland, Andrew, and Peter Henshaw. *Allis-Chalmers Tractors*. Osceola, Wisconsin: MBI Publishing Company, 1997.

Swinford, Norm. *Allis-Chalmers Construction Machinery & Industrial Equipment*. Osceola, Wisconsin: MBI Publishing Company, 1998.

Swinford, Norm. *Allis-Chalmers Farm Equipment*. St. Joseph, Michigan: American Society of Agricultural Engineers, 1994.

Swinford, Norm. *Guide to Allis-Chalmers Farm Tractors*. St. Joseph, Michigan: American Society of Agricultural Engineers, 1996.

Wendel, C. H. (Photography by Andrew Morland.) *Allis-Chalmers Tractors*. Osceola, Wisconsin: MBI Publishing Company, 1992.

Wendel, C. H. *Allis-Chalmers Story*. Osceola, Wisconsin: MBI Publishing Company, 1988.

Wendel, C. H. *Nebraska Tractor Tests Since 1920*. Osceola, Wisconsin: MBI Publishing Company, 1993.

Recommended Magazines

Antique Power
Circulation Dept.
P.O. Box 500
Missouri City, TX 77459
(800) 310-7047

Belt Pulley
P.O. Box 83
Nokomis, IL 62075
(217) 563-2612

Engineers and Engines
2240 Oak Leaf St.
P.O. Box 2757
Joliet, IL 60434-2757
(815) 741-2240

Gas Engine
P.O. Box 328
Lancaster, PA 17608
(717) 392-0733

Old Allis News
10925 Love Rd.
Bellevue, MI 49021
(616) 763-9770

Recommended Internet Sites

http://allischalmers.com/index.html
      Unofficial Allis-Chalmers site
http://www.agcocorp.com/
      AGCO Corporation
http://www.geocities.com/Heartland/Shores/2378/
      Granddads Allis-Chalmers Rest Home
http://www.atis.net/ Antique Tractor Internet Services
http://www.ytmag.com/cgi-bin/ntracz.pl?m=ac
      Yesterday's Tractors (Allis-Chalmers section)
http://www.oldengine.org/members/harrold/#Allis
      Harrolds' Antique Tractor and Engine Links

Index